Earth Awakens:
Prophecy 2012 - 2030

Sal Rachele
With his spirit guides, the Founders

Earth Awakens: Prophecy 2012 - 2030

Nonfiction – Spirituality, Self-Help, Prophecy

Earth Awakens:
Prophecy 2012 - 2030

Published by: Living Awareness Productions
P.O. Box 39, Wentworth, NH 03282 USA

First Edition: September 2011

Author's website: www.salrachele.com

Printed in the United States of America by BooksJustBooks.com
51 East 42nd Street, Suite 1202, New York, NY 10017

Cover photograph "Andromeda and Earth," courtesy of NASA infrared telescopy and photography

ISBN: 978-0-578-09157-0
Library of Congress Catalog Number Pending

TABLE OF CONTENTS

Table of Contents

Table of Contents

Table of Contents

List of Tables

FOREWORD

I know some of you are not used to reading the foreword to a book. If you are one of those people, I urge you to break with tradition and take the time to read this, as it contains important information to help you get the most out of the material.

This book is my third, and the second written in conjunction with my spirit guides, the Founders. The prior books (*"Life On the Cutting Edge,"* and *"Earth Changes and 2012: Messages From the Founders"*), are referenced several times in this book, not because I desire to sell more copies of my previous books, but because there is a lot of relevant information to digest at this time, and to overly repeat the ideas given previously in order to bring you up to date would result in a book too large for the average reader.

Nevertheless, this work is designed to stand on its own, with a lot of valuable information for those who have not read the two previous books. If this is your first exposure to my work and that of my spirit guides, the Founders, then I suggest you read this book first and then go back and purchase the other ones in order to get the necessary background information.

The book you are now holding in your hands (or viewing on your computer screen) is quite comprehensive in its scope. It covers the most important subject facing all of us on planet Earth: the future of our evolution as a species.

The prophecies and predictions given herein are explored from virtually every major angle possible, including spiritual, metaphysical, scientific, philosophical, psychological, biological, economical, political, geophysical, and more. Think of us as the blind men and women touching the elephant and trying to get an accurate picture of what the elephant looks like. Science could be the tail, biology the trunk, and spirituality the feet, etc. All disciplines have some value, and all have limitations. We hope the big picture presented here will help you fit the pieces of the cosmic jigsaw together.

A Comment on the Method of Delivery

The information in this book comes through in a manner that is a bit difficult to explain. Some would call it "conscious channeling," while those who are *somewhat* skeptical might call it "inspired writing." Those *completely* skeptical (if they manage to get through the first few pages without throwing it down in disgust) would likely dismiss it as the work of a madman or seriously deluded airy-fairy "new ager."

I call the method of delivery, "telepathic transmission," and include as a description, "This is a collaboration between the higher self of the author and a group consciousness originating in the higher dimensions."

In this case, "higher self" and "higher dimensions" are subjective terms, but refer to actual aspects of our Being and the Creation. In my previous books, I go into the meaning of these terms at great length. In this material, my guides and I will occasionally revisit these concepts to refresh your memory and accommodate those who are new to the work.

So what exactly is "telepathic transmission" and how does it work? Is it something anyone can do with enough practice and the right methods? The answer to the second question is "Yes." If you peruse my website (www.salrachele.com), you will note that there are various meditation CDs and mp3s designed to help you awaken your own "higher" abilities. Also, I encourage you to check out the work of other teachers to find the approach that works best for you.

In my case, the energy, consciousness and wisdom of a group of souls, whom I call the Founders, share their perspective of reality with me, or more specifically, with my higher aspects of Being. Those higher aspects deposit the information in my superconscious mind, much like the process of downloading a file into a personal computer from the Internet. The higher mind (likened to the operating system of the computer) then organizes the information in a way that the conscious mind (similar to the computer screen) can interpret and use in a practical way.

In the higher realms, time is very different than it is on Earth. In this case, you can think of the information received from my spirit guides as coming through in both batch mode and real time. While it is difficult to explain this in technical terms, think of it this way. Information comes through and is placed in my higher mind for later retrieval (batch mode). Then, when it is retrieved, I enter into a state of Oneness with the source of that information and it is transmitted in real time through me, as if the source had already arranged that time in advance and is fully present with me during the transmission. The data can be visualized as "intelligent energy packets" and is recorded using either the computer keyboard (spirit types through me), or an audiovisual format such as the telephone, video, Skype, or in person (using various recording devices).

Because of this simultaneous time aspect, my spirit guides are almost always available at a moment's notice, to work with individuals, groups, or just me.

Basically, I tune into the energy of my spirit guides and merge a part of my consciousness with theirs. I am just as important to them as they are to me, and they learn a lot from me, even though they come from a level of reality that is much more rarified than Earth. In other words, they are vibrating at a considerably higher frequency than human beings.

As you probably know, Earth is a free will planet. Because of the non-interference policy inherent within free will planets, beings from higher dimensions are not allowed to forcefully intervene in our affairs (except in a few extraordinary cases, such as preventing nuclear holocaust or other major cataclysms). There are, however, malevolent spirit guides that intentionally attempt to violate the free will of humans. There are also beings from slightly higher realms than Earth that are ignorant of the non-interference doctrine, and these groups have presented quite a challenge to evolving humanity over the long history of Earth.

The most enlightened spirit guides see us as equals. Most of them admire us for having the courage to incarnate into such a difficult environment.

There is a misunderstanding about spirit guides that needs to be clarified. Just because they are from another level or dimension of reality does not automatically mean that they know more than we do here on Earth. In fact, they might, in some cases, be learning more from us than we are learning from them.

It is quite dangerous to assume that information from spirits is accurate just because the beings claim to be from some lofty level.

This brings us to the issue of discernment, one that you will find repeated often in all my books, teachings and events. I urge you to ask some basic questions about the nature and quality of messages received through channels. Some of the questions include:

"Does this spirit entity encourage us to think for ourselves and investigate the nature of reality and truth, or does the being demand reliance upon him/her, the channel, or a particular teaching? Is the spirit respectful or patronizing? Does the information coming from this entity promote self-empowerment and well-being, or self-sacrifice and obedience? How does the message feel?"

Tune into your own body. You will find that the body almost never lies. If you do not feel good about a particular energy, even if the message is couched in lovely language, then that energy (and spirit being or beings presenting it) is probably not right for you.

That said, it is important to focus on the content and value of the message, and not so much on the form it comes in. You have probably heard the expression, "If you do not like the news, do not kill the messenger." In this case, it is not really all that important what level the Founders come from (level 12 in my model system), or what they look like (large blue-white stars in my perception), or even what star system they are from (originally Lyra/Vega). What is important is the quality of the message.

When reading this book, ask yourselves the following questions:

"Is this information useful in my everyday life? How can I apply it effectively? Can I use the ideas to help others? Does the teaching assist me on my soul path? Do I feel self-empowered when applying the tools and techniques given herein? Does the material stimulate my own creativity?"

I would humbly suggest that in addition to this work, you read and explore other paths that adequately address these questions, since our time on Earth is valuable and we all want to spend it in the best way possible. If you find another book or class that works better for you, go for it.

A Look into the Future

This brings us to the subject matter of the book, Earth changes in the years following 2012. By the time this book goes to print, it will be little more than a year before the first of the portal shifts, involving the period around December 21, 2012 (known as the "precessional alignment").

Throughout most of the text, we (I and the Founders) make the assumption that the future begins around that date and carries forward through the second portal (the close passage of a comet in 2017), past the third portal (the appearance of Nibiru in early 2030) and on into the completion of the Galactic Shift (around 2100). See *"Earth Changes and 2012"* for a detailed description of the three portals and the Galactic Shift. The majority of the information given herein applies to the time period 2012 to 2030.

I have been told that my accuracy rating is approximately 80 to 90 percent on predictions. This means there is a considerable margin of error possible. No psychic, seer, visionary, prophet or mystic can ever be 100% accurate because Earth is a free will planet. This is especially true on the individual level. Any one of you can prove me wrong on a prediction simply by changing your mind and choosing differently than what you seem predisposed to do. That is why I would use the following statement of clarification along with the above disclaimer: "If you continue on your present course without changing your consciousness, then the scenarios, events and changes depicted in this book represent the most likely outcome during the aforementioned time period." In some cases, I might be able to anticipate changes you will make in your consciousness, but you are the sovereign entities occupying your individual bodies and you have the final word.

All any of us can do is look into the possible and probable timelines of the future and extrapolate and intuit, based on many factors. The criterion used to assess the future includes the realization that the quality of consciousness of an individual determines that person's experience of reality. If a large percentage of humanity is operating at a certain level of consciousness, such as fear, it is sensible to assume that those souls will create fearful scenarios until they learn how to change their consciousness and move in a different direction.

My guides and I can see and feel energy. We observe the patterns of energy emanating from souls on Earth and see the possible and probable timelines being projected outward from the consciousness of those souls. In these transmissions, we go into detail on three of the probable timelines being created. In other words, the vast majority of humanity is in the process of creating three dominant realities, or simultaneous scenarios. This will be explained further in the following chapters.

You, dear reader, have an integral part to play in the drama unfolding on Earth. Never believe, for one moment, that you are powerless to change what is occurring. The illusion of separation is precisely the reason souls feel powerless in the first place. If you have not already discovered that you are intricately and intimately connected to the entire Universe, then very soon you will have this realization. In fact, it has already been proven in quantum physics (through the non-locality principle). Although the effect you have on your world may seem small, especially on things outside your immediate environment, every thought you think, every feeling you have, and every action you perform, affects everything in the Universe in some way.

We are all powerful beyond belief. That is a play on words. You could say we are powerful when we go beyond belief.

The purpose of this book is to help empower you by giving you not only a vision of the future of humanity, but by giving you tools, techniques and practical advice on how to meet the challenges you will likely face in the years to come. Unlike many channeled works that stay in a light, fluffy and overly general space, the Founders and I go into some specific paths for achieving harmony and balance on the planet.

Most of the topics discussed herein can be researched on your own. We encourage you to find other sources of wisdom for each discipline or practice, in order to give you greater depth and technicality. The practical advice given in this book is not designed to make you an expert in any given field. It is merely there to point you in a certain direction where you can do your own research. An example would be the advice to install alternative energy devices on your land (such as wind, hydro or solar power generators). We do not give you schematics and step-by-step instructions on how to hook up inverters, run wires from batteries, etc., because that information can be found in other places.

A few of the topics discussed can only be found in this book. At the very least, such topics are not explored to this much depth and detail elsewhere.

This is a "big picture" book, designed to give you an overview of what is happening. It is about fitting the pieces of the cosmic jigsaw puzzle together and forming a beautiful picture from which you can derive great joy as well as an impetus for practical application.

While some of the information could be construed as negative, or at least sobering, the topics are presented from an enlightened perspective. As you will see by perusing the introduction, there is a lot of very good news awaiting those who are ready for a radical change in the direction of higher truth. If you are tired of the status quo and weary of business as usual, please read on.

At first, you might have the impression that it is wishful thinking that there could ever be a Golden Age on Earth, but I assure you it is knocking on our doorstep and we have included many of the details to prove it.

Humanity is a varied race. We have people from all walks of life, at all levels of consciousness, from the depths of darkness to the heights of enlightenment. In the following pages, we have addressed this wide range of perspectives. We have not left anyone or anything out. (At least we have covered the major bases.) If you find you somehow do not fit into one of the scenarios given here, then let us know by contacting the author. In the meantime, we think you will find this a fascinating read at the very least.

Welcome to the future that all of us are creating right now.

--Sal Rachele, August 2011

INTRODUCTION
The New Dawn

Humanity is poised at the beginning of a wondrous experience. We are graduating to a new way of life. We are awakening to our vast creative potential.

While there is a promise of a new Golden Age, getting there will be a bit rocky. We are in the midst of the Earth changes, and they will continue to intensify and accelerate. Not everyone is going to make it through intact. In fact, a lot of souls will be leaving the Earth over the next 20 to 30 years. Although this might look like a tragedy from a third density perspective, from the higher realms it is a perfect unfolding of the Divine Plan. Every soul ultimately manifests its true desires. Young souls often feel the desire to experience war, poverty, pain and suffering, and may choose to leave the Earth through debilitating illness, starvation, or natural or man-made disaster.

It is important not to judge the decisions of young souls. The soul does not consider things to be "good" or "bad." It wants to experience everything there is in the lower planes. As the soul evolves, he or she will eventually become weary of experiencing the more "negative" things and will seek out lifetimes of peace, prosperity, joy, love and compassion.

Many older souls come to Earth to help the younger souls grow and evolve. In order to do this, the older souls must re-familiarize themselves with things learned in past lifetimes in order to relate to the younger souls. Put another way, it is difficult to communicate with someone about grief if you have not recently experienced it yourself. The goal, therefore, of many of the more advanced souls is to immerse themselves just enough to be one with suffering humanity, but not so much as to become enmeshed in the drama and forget who they are.

The Graduation

The entire Earth is graduating. She is shifting from a predominantly third-dimensional to a fourth-dimensional planet. Consequently, humanity is graduating from a third-density to a fourth-density vibration. All life forms living upon and within the Earth must make this shift in order to remain here.

Note: The words "density" and "dimension" are sometimes used interchangeably. However, strictly speaking, "density" refers to a specific level of vibration of a life form, while "dimension" refers to a plane of existence, which may or may not be the same as the life forms vibrating within it. A complete description of "density" and "dimension" is given in this author's first book, "*Life On the Cutting Edge*."

In order for human beings to grow and evolve into higher states, a lot of purging and purification is necessary. This is what we are seeing today in the world. It is stated in many religious texts that there will be a time of judgment, or sorting the wheat from the chaff. This is not really a judgment by some supreme being, but rather, a process of deciding whether or not one is ready to move forward into the New Earth.

In order to move ahead and become part of the new Golden Age, you must let go of all that is no longer serving you, including false and limiting belief systems, emotional pain, subconscious and unconscious attitudes and conditioning, prejudices, habits, and ways of thinking and feeling that are holding you back from awakening to your higher nature.

If your soul wants you to grow and evolve, and you are not listening and have become distracted by the myriad of detours offered everywhere you turn, then your soul will gently nudge you through experiences designed to get your attention. If you still refuse to acknowledge the desires of your soul, it will knock a bit louder, perhaps creating an illness, job loss, relationship dispute, or mid-life crisis that cannot be easily ignored. This is what you are witnessing in many souls at this time on the planet.

It is important to have compassion for those who are going through tough times. Concurrently, it is vital not to identify with the drama and trauma taking place in the lives of many. You cannot help people out of the quicksand if you jump in to commiserate with them. All you can really do is throw them a rope and instruct them in how to pull themselves out. You cannot do it for them. Jumping in through sympathy and codependence is just as ineffective as walking away and pretending there is nobody drowning, plus when you jump in, you now have two people drowning instead of one.

Most souls that are reading this will be called at some point during the shift to offer assistance, rescue or remedy for the calamities befalling others. If you follow the spiritual principles outlined in this book and ask for inner guidance daily, you will only be given as much as you can handle. For some of you, this will be quite a stretch. You will need to get out of your comfort zone and take more risks. For others, it will be an opportunity to finally stop trying so hard and relax. The philosophy of "Let it Be" may be just what you need. Then there are those of you who are in-between these polarities. In some ways you will be called to act and perhaps intervene in the lives of those who have lost their way, and in other situations, you will be asked to release those you wish to help and simply know that they will make choices based on their own free will and it is not up to you to intervene.

Knowing when to act and when to go within is based on your level of self-knowledge. If you listen carefully to your inner wisdom daily, it will get louder, clearer and easier to follow. You will be asked to clear out any negative beliefs, past emotional issues, judgments and self-criticisms. You will be expected to come completely out of denial about what is really taking place both within and without. You will be asked to open your eyes to both the Light and dark.

Darkness is the state of those places that have not yet opened to receive the Light. You cannot dispel darkness by avoiding it. You must shine a high-powered floodlight of wisdom and compassion into the darkest places of this world and within yourself. You must be willing to face your fears and other so-called demons.

There is no separation between the inner and outer. What you see in the world is a mirror of what is in you. If you react emotionally to what you see, then you are still identified with it. In other words, the world still has you in its grip.

In this book, the author and his spirit guides the Founders hope to prove that it is possible to be in the world, but not of the world. We are not going to try and convince you to give up your pleasures and comforts, or sacrifice things that are dear to you. It is okay to make use of the things of this world, including money and material things, especially when you are using them to assist in becoming more effective at awakening humanity. After all, they are just tools, unless you ascribe greater importance to them.

A Journey Into the Future

Chapter 1 will give you a snapshot of what is to come, based on the prophecy of this channel and his spirit guides. It is written in retrospective, as if the changes have already happened, for in nonlinear time they have. Time is a curious thing. From a human perspective, it unfolds along a linear timeline, from past to present to future. But from a higher point of view, all of it happens at once in this eternal now moment. Therefore, you can go anywhere in the whole of time (and space) and perceive what is taking place there.

Creation is not static. The past and future are evolving just as much as the present. This is a difficult concept for the human mind to comprehend. Although the Akashic medium stores all soul experience and allows us to recall a linear past, the past is not set in stone. There are an infinite number of timelines and an infinite number of possibilities. Every time you change your consciousness in the past, present or future, you create a new timeline.

The prophecy given herein is based on the collective creations of humanity and the various beings assisting, as well as hindering, the evolving souls on Earth. Because Earth is a free will planet, none of the predictions given herein can possibly be 100% accurate. However, according to the "Akashic composite," or average probability factor, the level of accuracy is most likely between 80% and 90%.

You make a difference in the fulfillment or denial of the prophecy. Your healing process is critical to the success or failure of the human race (according to the way you typically use those terms). From the perspective of the Founders, there is no success or failure, just a variety of soul experience. Nevertheless, the advanced souls of Earth fervently desire peace, prosperity and the full manifestation of the Golden Age that has been long prophesied. This book is an integral part of the fulfillment of that vision.

We will now introduce you to the Founders, who will open this book with some background information in preparation for our exciting journey ahead.

Greetings, dear Creators, we are the Founders. It is our pleasure to communicate these ideas, concepts and perceptions to you, the enlightened human beings of planet Earth. If you have read our previous dissertation done in collaboration with this channel, entitled, *"Earth Changes and 2012: Messages from the Founders,"* then you are already somewhat familiar with the material being presented in the earlier chapters of this book. If this is your first experience with our messages or this channel's work, then we welcome you and assure you that we will do everything possible within the constraints of this written format to bring you up to date on what is and will be happening on your planet and in the Universe in the years ahead.

In the Foreword and Introduction, we were introduced, and to assist us in getting everyone on the same page, we urge you to read the preparatory material in the front of this book before continuing with us.

So let us begin. You, dear humans, are embarking upon the most exciting adventure possible. You are alive at exactly the right time, in exactly the right place in the Infinite Creation. It is okay if you do not believe this, for within a few short years, almost everything given within these pages will likely manifest itself to some degree within the tangible reality of your lives.

That said, the prophecy given herein is not to be taken as gospel truth, or even as undisputed fact. You live on a free will planet and it is not possible for you, us, or anyone to be accurate 100% of the time with predictions. After all, we could prophesy that you will take a right turn at the next fork in the road and you could, given your free will, decide to turn left instead. We may be quite good in predicting your likely choice, but it is *your* choice, not ours.

Your Earth is awakening. In this book, we will explain precisely what this means for you and humanity. It is a wonderful thing, from your point of view. From our point of view, it is an inevitable part of your soul's journey. Your ability to open and receive the wisdom contained in this book, and more importantly, the wisdom contained within your own hearts, minds and spirit, will determine the quality of your experience in the years ahead. The fundamental principle of life on Earth can be summed up as follows:

The quality of your consciousness determines your experience of reality.

It is not entirely accurate to say that your thoughts create your reality, since your reality can overlap and encompass many other realities that have little to do with your own creative process. If you broaden the definition of thought to include everything within the Mind of God, including the thoughts of all other souls in Creation, than we would say the idea that thoughts create reality would be a bit more accurate. But you are not there yet. You are currently vibrating at what this channel calls "fourth density." At some point in the future of linear time, you will evolve your consciousness to the 12th density, and then you, like us, will be able to create entire universes.

Today, that is not your concern. Even if we could, we are not going to offer you a shortcut to the 12th density. We are not going to erase millions of years of soul experience by bestowing upon you the full manifestation of your potential as Creator Gods before you are even slightly qualified. Yet, paradoxically, we will also remind you that you are already Creator Gods yourselves, with all the potential to become aware of your 12 selves right now.

Our concern at the moment is to give you a road map to help you navigate your way through the multitude of Earth changes. We are here to help you understand the mechanics and dynamics of the transformation of your species.

Did you mistakenly think that *homo sapiens* were the final product of evolution? Your journey through physicality is but one chapter in a long and magnificent story. It is the story of how God comes to know Itself, *through* you, *as* you.

You live in a paradox, what some have called the interplay between linear and nonlinear time. From one vantage point, that of linear time, you are souls experiencing the fourth density world of time and space as enlightened humans, while evolving into fifth, sixth and seventh densities, ever expanding your awareness and raising your vibration to higher and more refined states of Light.

From another vantage point, that of nonlinear time, you are already whole, complete and perfect beings, operating on 12 levels of vibration simultaneously, with past, parallel and future selves all existing at once in their respective dimensions. From this perspective, your creative process is about uncovering the truth of your One Being. To do this, you must remove layer upon layer of illusions, false beliefs, and unawareness that have been placed over your true essence.

This book will go into the nature of both levels of perception, that of linear and nonlinear time. Within the linear perspective, we will paint you a picture of what is likely to occur on Earth over the next 20 to 30 years or so. To those willing to grow and evolve, it is not only a lovely picture, but a truly amazing one. You are waking up. Planet Earth is waking up. Many years from now, the experiences you have had will seem like a fading dream, mostly a nightmare, wherein you imagined you lived in a world of limitation, disease, poverty, misery, suffering and death. As you dispel these illusions and look upon the world beyond them, it will become harder and harder to even recall the reasons you believed them in the first place. They will seem utterly ridiculous, something reserved for the realm of the stark raving mad.

As you awaken from the dream of duality – light and dark, good and bad, right and wrong, us versus them, etc. – you will begin to wonder how anyone could have ever believed in those things at all. You will look around you and see two basic conditions: awake and asleep. You will not judge those who are still asleep, but you will feel immense love and compassion for them, for they know not what they seem to do. In their dreams of despair, all manner of misfortune appears to hurl itself at them throughout every moment, at every turn in the road. Their lives appear to consist of constantly putting out fires, solving one problem, only to be faced with a dozen more.

Your physicist, Albert Einstein, stated that you cannot solve problems at the level upon which they were created. As you rise above the muck and mire of the realms of duality and pierce the veils of illusion, you will see obvious solutions to the problems of humanity. United in this higher vision, the answers to world problems will be readily apparent and straightforward. Implementation of solutions will be quickly forthcoming.

Within these pages, some of the methods of implementing solutions will be discussed. We will take a practical approach to life on Earth in this book, but at the same time, the presentation will differ substantially from our previous work in that it will be a bit more nonlinear, a bit more "right-brained." There will be more emphasis on direct experience and less on the acquisition of knowledge. At one point in your process it may have been important to know about the history of your planet, but now it is time to turn your attention to the present and future and to discover the vast, creative, spiritual beings that you are and how to express that creativity in the new world that lies before you.

This book goes into detail on what to expect as you awaken. We promise not to take the fun out of surprises, for even if we could foretell the entire story, there would still be unexpected twists and turns. That is the nature of free will.

Just as a road map typically does not tell you everything you could potentially see along your journey, this book cannot and will not do that. It will, however, be of great reassurance as it describes some of the things you are already experiencing, but for which you have little or no reference points.

The most critical stage of your awakening involves the need to psychologically detach yourselves from the illusory world that is crumbling around you. We will offer a hands-on approach to coping with the drama and trauma of souls in your environment, especially family members and close friends. We will guide you through realms of consciousness that wax and wane, as you confront the many different levels of reality, some simultaneously imposed upon you by those who falsely believe they are in control of your world. Their little games are coming to an end. As you and your beloved Earth awaken, they have a choice. They either awaken or leave the Earth plane. This is not some sort of ultimatum given them by a judgmental Creator, but rather, an outplaying of natural law.

In one of your teachings, you have a statement that goes something like this:

Every moment you are choosing between the resurrection and the crucifixion.

Those of you who are attracted to this book have reached a level of consciousness whereby you no longer need to learn any more about crucifixion. To quote a popular phrase on your world, "You've been there, done that." Therefore, the advice in this book will steer you in the direction of the resurrection. To resurrect means to make all things new again. It means to breathe new life into old energy patterns. You see this in the natural world every springtime when new blossoms and leaves burst forth from dormant plants. This is the springtime of your souls, dear Creators, and we, the Founders, are privileged to be a part of your blossoming.

A Glimpse of the Three Parallel Earths

From a linear perspective, it might seem as though certain areas on the Earth will be host to three very different scenarios, but from a nonlinear perspective, there are three parallel Earths all existing simultaneously. Depending upon which perspective is taken, each of you will choose a specific version of Earth upon which to continue your embodiment. For you, the descriptions given in Chapter 1 will ultimately have the personal meaning you ascribe to them based on your level of understanding.

In a later chapter, we will explore in more detail the qualities and lifestyles inherent to the three parallel Earths. For now, we are simply introducing the topic and are weaving it into the story to follow.

Personal and Collective Co-Creation

Your personal viewpoint on life is added to the collective viewpoint of humanity because you are all One Being, manifesting itself as individual human beings.

The publishing of this material and your subsequent reading of it reflects one of the "creative urges" of your individual Being that is influencing the collective Being of humanity. Reading this material will affect the outcome of some of the free will events now taking place. The visions given herein are declarations of creative intent, and the willingness of the reader to "come on board" and participate in those creations will determine to some extent the ultimate success and level of manifestation of many of your personal and collective visions. Some descriptions given herein are beyond free will and they will happen no matter what you think, feel or do. Others are largely dependent upon your state of consciousness and resulting actions.

As you read the scenarios presented in Chapter 1, we not only urge you to keep an open mind, but to consider the possibility that as you embrace these scenarios, you add your personal creative energy to the collective vision of humanity and therefore strengthen the dominant timeline that is bringing these scenarios into manifestation on the Earth. Once again, we repeat, these are the most likely scenarios based on what is being created at this time. For the most part, they are not set in stone, even though the celestial events themselves are beyond human free will at the present time.

Passing Through the 2012 Portal

In our previous book, *"Earth Changes and 2012"*, we gave our perception of the precessional shift of December 21, 2012, from various vantage points. We will not duplicate efforts, but in this material we will seek to impart to you our understanding of what this experience will be like for those of you reading this before that date. This will be our starting point: The portal or "stargate" of December 21, 2012. Although this is being written before the actual date, we will move just far enough into the future to present the information in Chapter 1 as if the event had already transpired. For those of you reading this book after December 21, 2012, the following account should make perfect sense, especially if you are connected to and networking with Lightworkers around the planet and are aware of the many activities taking place to help humanity awaken.

For those of you on the path of ascension, moving through the portal might feel a little like having someone in a position of authority tell you that you have made the grade. You could think of a college professor who holds the key to your graduation in his hands as he holds up the final examination for the course you just completed. Your heart beats a little faster as he comes to your desk with paper in hand.

"Congratulations," he says, as he places the exam face up on your desk. "You needed 95% to be admitted to the School of Ascension. You got 97%."

A warm glow moves over you and a deep sense of peace, the kind of peace that comes with knowing you have fulfilled your mission.

For those of you who are part of the new enlightened humanity on Earth but who are not yet ready for ascension, moving through the portal will involve a certainty, a knowing without a shadow of a doubt, that things will never be the same again in your life. Your hard work has paid off. You have tipped the balance. The truth that you are a Divine Being of loving Light is now the dominant thought in your consciousness. There is no longer any doubt that you are on your right path.

You will help rebuild the Earth, along with your fellow travelers, who join in great merriment with you, dancing and rejoicing, as you wipe away the tears of sorrow that still stain your faces from yesterday's drama and trauma.

With the help of your teachers, those members of humanity who are going on into ascension, you, the pioneers of the New Earth, will set about to tackle the great tasks in front of you. You have been entrusted with the responsibility of creating a new society based on principles of higher truth. You are the loving outer expressions of the fourth dimensional Earth. Your task is to come together in communities of Light, utilizing alternative energy sources to power your homes and common areas.

Before we begin our story, we know some of you need further clarification on the meaning of portals and stargates. You have, perhaps, been given some examples in your science fiction books, movies and television shows. The concept of "wormhole" used often in both science and science fiction, is a good place to start our explanation. Let us add to that the idea of a quantum jump, or sudden shift from one level of perception to another. A simple example of this would be coming out of a cloud bank in a jet aircraft that is ascending in altitude. At the moment the plane breaks the top of the cloud deck, the world changes radically from one of dark gray and almost no visibility, to one of bright blue skies with nearly infinite visibility.

The words "portal" and "stargate" are used interchangeably here, but in previous material they were differentiated slightly. A portal is a wormhole, or tunnel, between two relatively localized levels of reality, while a stargate is a similar construct occurring more on a macro scale. The black hole at the center of many galaxies is a type of stargate because it tunnels into a corresponding white hole that resides at the center of a parallel mirror galaxy in a parallel mirror universe.

(As mentioned in previous writings, the phenomenon of black holes is one of the hardest ideas for your modern scientists to grapple with because such objects appear to violate the law of conservation of energy, one of the most basic laws in the Universe. When you consider that the black holes at the center of your galaxies tunnel through into white holes at the center of "sister" galaxies in a "sister" universe that exactly mirrors your own but with opposite polarities not only electromagnetically but gravitationally and with respect to time and space, then all of a sudden things become clear. The law of conservation is restored and, with a little advanced mathematics, a theory of everything, linking all the basic forces together, can be derived. In a later chapter, we have given a partial explanation of how all the basic forces of physics are related.)

Portals and stargates can be considered to be doorways between levels, planes, dimensions, worlds, or regions of the Universe. If a further explanation is needed when discussing a specific realm, we will give the necessary details at that time. Keep in mind that we are aware that most of you are not physicists and will not understand rigorous mathematics, so we will do our best to explain our ideas in lay terms.

Now, let us venture forth and glimpse the New World.

CHAPTER 1
A Future Timeline Overview

Your food is organic. Your water is pure, sweet and clear. Your medicine is a combination of the best that technology has to offer, tempered with common sense and a return to natural, herbal remedies. All are freely provided by loving supportive souls.

The era of haves and have-nots has ended. You are all prosperous beyond your wildest imagination because you have been given the keys to the Kingdom. With the help of your ascended master friends and spirit guides, you have been shown how to turn this Earth into a paradise, a new Garden of Eden.

You know that this time the peace is real. It will not fade and wither with the return of winter. You see the old world crumbling before your eyes, but this is the last time you will be a part of the rise and fall of civilizations. You will no longer see humanity rise to great heights only to fall once again. This New Earth that you can feel within your bones is here to stay.

You are on the other side of the 2012 portal. You feel the energies of the Galactic Shift increasing, even as the precessional energies of the 2012 alignment begin to subside.

You know that more great changes are coming and more of the old Earth is crumbling. Layer upon layer of vested interests, lobbies, self-serving leaders, broken medical models, old economic paradigms, and outdated legal systems keep crashing down around you, leaving a little pile of rubble where once great institutions seemed to sit. You do not mourn the loss of these buildings built on sand.

You feel compassion for those that worshipped in these halls of mirrors, believing their salvation rested on their 401(k) retirement plan, or stock portfolio. Yet you knew these "securities" were anything but secure.

In your fourth density world, you are now living in an extended family setting, or intentional community. Here, the things of real value are grown in five-acre plots, or come streaming into 120-watt solar panels atop a roof. Today, a young inventor comes to your community, demonstrating his zero-point energy device. Up until the portal of 2012, he was having difficulty getting his device to function consistently. Now, on the other side of the portal, it seems to work just fine, as if it had been doing so all along.

The negativity that once counteracted the quantum force is no longer present. Acceptance for the unlimited abundance of Creation has come to this community and now the tangible, physical proof of the immutable law of infinite Love has come as well.

The 2012 Portal Experience

It wasn't always this easy. In fact, when this was first written, the channel was on the other side of the precessional doorway. Although the portal was looming in front of him, the dominant reality on Earth still seemed to involve broken political promises, dire poverty, rampant radiation from leaking power plants, polluted oceans from fossil fuel spills, erratic weather, and monstrous uncontrollable economic debt. So to see through the illusions of the crumbing world to the shining vision of the future, he began, with our help and the help of thousands of Lightworkers, to formulate a plan for maximizing the opportunity afforded by the portal.

The first step in preparing for passage through the portal of December 21, 2012, was to gather the Lightworkers of the world in sacred spots in every continent. In some places, just a few souls were able to be present physically, while in others, several hundred, or even a few thousand, came to pray, meditate, sing, dance, and share stories. Rituals were set up to prepare individuals as the day grew closer.

During the three days from December 20th to 22nd, 2012, light pure food and pristine water were brought into the ceremonial sites, along with portable toilets and, if necessary, electrical generators, depending on the level of need. Transport vehicles were left behind and for three days, souls simply stayed within the relative confines of their sacred sites, camping and resting as needed. Knowing they would likely be unable to use their various electronic devices, they were content to turn them off and simply be with each other, often in silence, sometimes in laughter or tears.

In some locations, great circles or labyrinths were constructed and various sacred rituals were enacted within the circles. Costumes were donned, the talking stick was passed, drums were beat, and heartfelt expression poured forth.

Very few knew what to expect. Some posited that nothing much would change: The days would come and go; they would have fun praying and dancing together; they would go home, back to their families, jobs, and responsibilities. From a third density perspective, this is indeed what happened for many. But even in those hard skeptics and pragmatic realists, something had shifted profoundly.

During the three days, time seemed to move very slowly at first, and then stop. For an undetermined amount of time, the souls who came together felt a deep embrace of something they could not define. It was as if they had always been together, here on the mountain top, or desert, or sacred gathering place. The campfire, labyrinth, medicine wheel, tents, and musical instruments were part of a cosmic dance that went on forever.

Then it was over – or was it? As the souls slowly packed up their gear and returned to their vehicles to begin the journey back to their old lives, there was a distinct feeling that nothing would ever be the same again. A door had opened; they had walked through it; it had closed behind them, never to be revisited in the same way. These souls who had taken part in the three days of celebration were just plain *different*.

The world of wars, disaster, control, manipulation, propaganda, consumerism, and endless mindless entertainment, no longer seemed real at all. These souls no longer had anything in common with that world. It did not even matter whether it existed or not. It was of little or no consequence. The world they had experienced in the sacred circle, high on the mountain top, during those three days, was more real than anything they had experienced up to that point in their lives.

Some souls had been to numerous personal growth workshops and intensive events over the years and knew about the temporary high that happens when like-minded souls come together. They knew all about how it wears off a few days later as they once again become absorbed back into the all-too-familiar world of the rat race. But this time was truly different. They simply could not integrate back into the old ways. Those lives were now meaningless. There was no energy or will left to pursue the old patterns of conquest and dominion. Eagerly, these transformed souls looked forward to the next meeting on the mountain, or journey to the desert, with their new-found friends.

The most difficult lesson for the newly-expanded souls involved how to relate to family and friends who had not participated in the ceremonies and rituals. Some of those who had stayed behind were just fine. Perhaps they had stopped to meditate wherever they were; in the cities, at the office, while walking in the shopping mall. In a few cases, those who did not escape the "daily grind" were already integrated within their souls and were able to detach from the confusion and chaos that seemed to be increasing in the masses of humanity.

But for a great many returning from ceremony that were visiting or living with friends and family, communication became difficult because there was a profound shift of values and perceptions in the enlightened ones. A family member or loved one may have approached a transformed soul and berated him for not taking care of certain "Earthly responsibilities" while on "vacation." To the enlightened soul, such accusations were baseless, pointless and irrelevant.

Of course, love and compassion were still there in the newly transformed souls, probably more so than ever before, but the emotional attachment to living according to a certain set of belief systems had been severed. The awakened souls were *in* the world, but no longer *of* the world.

It became evident to many of the newly awakened souls that some of their friends and family members would not be making the journey into higher planes with them, and so the process of letting go, forgiving and releasing of loved ones began. Much grief was expressed and integrated. The enlightened ones knew that these beloved friends and family had chosen another path and that that path must be honored and respected. All the transformed ones could do was become an example of a new way of life. It was up to each family member to come on board or not.

Physical Changes in Fourth Density Souls

Before the opening of the portal, many souls had heard of physical immortality, longevity, miraculous healing, and spontaneous regeneration, but such ideas sounded like the work of those with an over-active imagination, or perhaps the delusions of those who refused to face their mortality.

"Those things happen to a few saints and yogis who meditate several hours a day, but they would never happen to me."

That was a common reprise in those days. But now something exciting was happening. Blemishes on the skin were disappearing that had been there for years. More energy was moving up and down the spine, even during times of "low" energy. So-called "idle" thoughts seemed to take on a life of their own, and the phrase, "Be careful what you ask for, you just might get it," became the newly recognized law of the land. There were so many synchronicities occurring that the enlightened souls simply could not discount them. Things were happening that no amount of imagination could conjure up.

It was not a case of things being "too good to be true." There was no sense that the shoe would drop and the negative karma would come barreling back in, crushing everything in its path. No, reality *had* changed. The force that seemed to stamp out the hopeful, happy thoughts in times past simply failed to materialize any longer. It was as if a huge segment of the population of Earth, those with the most negativity, had suddenly disappeared. They no longer existed in this new reality, at least not energetically.

The people experiencing this disconnect from the old world were reminded of a movie they saw once, where those with real souls appeared in living color, and everyone else appeared in black and white. While they knew that all creatures had souls, they began to wonder if the souls of many around the world had departed, leaving empty shells for bodies.

It was as though there were now two separate worlds, one with sovereign souls, alive and vital, and one with empty shells simply going through the motions of life without really living.

The fourth density souls were still human. They had feelings other than pure joy and ecstasy. But they were just feelings. These souls were no longer identifying with the feelings. Those sensations and impressions simply came and went like the wind.

The third density humans still had souls, but they were caught up in the drama of daily life and were less and less available for interaction with the enlightened souls.

In actuality, there were now three worlds. For those on the path of ascension into fifth density were starting to see things they had never seen before. The woods were alive with creatures of all shapes and colors. You could literally hear the consciousness of the wind as it whispered in the trees. Everything vibrated and shimmered, not just with light, but with consciousness. A profound sense of Oneness permeated everything. Although the newly ascended could still see and hear those in the fourth density New Earth, it was evident that those in fourth density could not see or experience a lot of these new fifth density realities.

As the days moved along and the precessional alignment began to move out of position, people realized the changes were permanent. The enlightened ones simply could not go back to their old ways of living. Everything in their lives was being orchestrated from on high. They were being moved into their new positions of responsibility. If they attempted to make choices that went against their highest soul path, there would be no energy available to continue along the lines of any of those choices if such actions or ideas were based on ego or old ways of thinking. In some cases, the mind simply stopped working altogether – at least the logical, rational, analytical mind that was used to controlling everything.

Conversely, whenever a soul decided to act on a higher impulse, one in alignment with that soul's true purpose, rushes of seemingly endless energy would be available. The right people would show up. The right situations would present themselves. It became incredibly easy to make wise choices because those decisions coming from the limited perception of ego would be even less than unappealing. They would feel simply awful and disgusting.

Old habits dropped away easily from that point forward in the fourth density souls. All of sudden, smokers had no desire to light another cigarette. Bottles of liquor lost their charm. A batch of prescription medicine lay untouched. Aside from ceremonial or sacramental purposes, drugs held no interest. Dense, processed foods offered no solace. The newly awakened souls were drawn to foods and activities that had aliveness and vitality that promoted their growth and well-being.

Whenever souls on the fourth density path encountered those in third density, they would have nothing in common. For all intents and purposes, third density souls existed in black and white, not in color. Their lives were completely meaningless to those who had gone through the portal.

The enlightened humans had a lot of compassion for those who did not make the journey with them, but try as they might, they simply could not empathize or sympathize anymore. These two groups of souls now seemed to live in separate realities.

The fifth density souls were still able to relate to fourth density. In fact, they became the teachers of the New Earth, having sufficiently integrated their negativity to the point where they could clearly see the dynamics of relationship and energetic interaction within their fourth density students.

The fourth density souls were grateful for the presence of the ascended ones in fifth density. They felt nurtured, loved and cared for deeply and knew the journey into ascension would be much easier now that some had crossed the barrier into true immortality.

The fifth density souls did not disappear into the Light in an instant, like the Christian rapture. They still appeared humanoid and could interact in a somewhat normal way with the fourth density souls, but their bodies were rapidly becoming more radiant and eventually started to glow. As time went along, they became impervious to changes in the environment, able to stay awake for long periods and withstand great differences of temperature. Eventually, they no longer required food or shelter.

The View From Below

To those stuck in third density including souls who willingly refused to be a part of the New Earth, it seemed as if the enlightened ones had stepped off the deep end of the swimming pool, or had fallen off a cliff. They appeared to babble nonsense and behave in lunatic ways.

For a time, the people of the old world felt a sense of loss over the perception that their loved ones had flipped out or joined some crazy environmental movement or spiritual community, but when the unenlightened souls realized there was nothing they could do to bring back their "lost" brothers and sisters, they resigned to go back to business as usual. Although the institutions they had come to rely on were decaying and dying, the ignorant ones hardly noticed.

Chapter 1 – A Future Timeline Overview

Every time a new austerity measure would be introduced, or stricter regulation was placed on consumption of a precious resource, they merely went along with this, rationalizing that it was probably best for all. Their lives had become analogous to frogs in a gradually boiling pot of water. Little by little, their freedoms eroded, but they did not notice.

Many of the unenlightened souls had unexplainable ailments. Their bodies did not seem to work as well as before. The doctors could find nothing wrong, or in some cases, they found everything wrong, and illness became so commonplace that it was considered the norm.

When rationing of goods and supplies began, at first it was weakly protested, but soon the herd mentality took over and people decided that a few basic necessities were better than none at all, and so they decided to put up with the hardships.

The Fourth Density Souls Leave Their Third Density Families Behind

As we mentioned a while ago, one of the hardest aspects of this transition was the divergence that cut across family ties. Many of the enlightened souls were misunderstood by their blood families and in some cases had even been "disowned." Occasionally the awakened ones were mocked outright, with siblings shaking their heads in disbelief. Other family members merely concluded that the enlightened ones were psychologically escaping the many problems facing humanity and had opted for a utopian fairy-tale version of life offering no semblance of reality. Often, spouses and close family members would offer token outer support, such as loaning them money to fulfill their "extravagant and unworldly" dreams, while in other cases they were cut out of the will, or pressured to sell their share of the family fortune.

Of course, the biggest challenges were emotional. Family bonds can run quite deep and it quickly became evident for many that this was a permanent and complete separation, at least for this lifetime. Tears flowed on both sides of the issue, and while those stuck in third density would likely hold resentment and regret for years to come, the Lightworkers quickly forgave and, with the help of their new spiritual family and friends, processed the grief and sorrow that arose from the departure.

As soon as the Lightworkers left their third density families, life began to improve dramatically for most fourth density souls. Suddenly the cloud was lifted and the bright sunshine of their new life illuminated their minds and hearts. For the first time in this embodiment, they felt free and unburdened. Although there were a multitude of challenges facing them as they embarked upon their new lives, there was an enthusiasm they had rarely felt before. Part idealism, part realism and part inspiration, they rejoiced at the opportunities in front of them to finally build a society that truly served the needs of every participating soul.

They came together in twos, threes, fours, sixes, tens, twenties and more. They all had one thing in common. They were here to build a New Earth, in some cases largely from scratch, and in other cases with the help of advanced technologies and experts in various fields of study.

The Period of 2012 to 2013

As 2012 drew to a close and 2013 began to unfold, the three worlds diverged even more. Those in the fourth and fifth densities structured their lives in such a way that they rarely, if ever, needed to go into the places where the third density humans were struggling to live.

A few higher souls were given assignments in the third density world. Perhaps they were working off karma from past lifetimes, or still felt so much empathy and sympathy that they could not completely abandon the world of strife and discord. Or perhaps they had skills that their spirit guides felt were important to offer to those in third density.

Being solidly part of fourth density, however, these enlightened souls were able to venture forth with minimal discomfort and offer assistance to those still stuck in the old ways. Their efforts were sometimes rewarded. These few cases of successful rescue allowed a small number of third density souls to crawl out of their holes of negative belief and enter into the grace of the higher realms.

As the worlds continued their divergence, fewer and fewer higher density beings were able to render assistance to those trapped in third density. Every day, the enlightened ones would pray for those left behind, but it was becoming apparent that souls were reaping the benefits of that which they had sown, over many lifetimes in most cases.

To those building the cities of Light in the fourth density, the daily and ever-escalating crises of the third density world seemed remote and unreal. Even when a disaster was only a few miles away, they did not notice. Eventually, such turbulence completely stopped affecting the enlightened souls.

The cities of Light were not isolated. Fourth density souls did not build barricades against the third density would-be intruders. The enlightened ones did not worry about bands of roving gangs raping and pillaging everything in their path in their desperate search for food and fresh water. Because the vibration of the fourth density souls was so unlike the intruders, a violent gang could walk right past an enlightened community and not even see it. This is psychological invisibility. Having so little in common with others, the law of attraction was not applicable. Actually, it did apply, but in the form of non-attraction. The souls in the New Earth no longer had any negative karma to work out that would attract disaster into their midst and so they were protected.

The enlightened ones developed new technologies that were built to resist the electromagnetic fluctuations hitting the Earth daily. They were able to communicate with other groups around the planet using aspects of telecommunications that were still operational from the old grid system, while slowly replacing those systems with new technologies. While many of the satellites that the old world had come to depend on were being neutralized by solar flares and electromagnetic anomalies, the enlightened ones were able to install new devices in the outer atmosphere that had the same protection around them that was afforded to their communities of Light.

The awakened souls traded and bartered for what they needed. They began to refine and perfect zero-point energy devices, which meant there would be ways of quickly traveling around the world without depleting the Earth's dwindling resources. Using new agricultural methods, they began devising ways of feeding everyone more easily. Although there were still issues in close relationships, the movement away from ego-domination resulted in far fewer conflicts than before the portal shift.

(Note: In a later chapter, we have gone into detail on the subjects mentioned in the preceding paragraph.)

Moving Beyond 2013

As the souls on Earth continued their journey, the divergence between the three societies continued to become more noticeable. Those in the fourth density began moving more fully into a total commitment to their new way of life. Many chose to sell their properties in the cities and move to the country. Some chose to purchase a five-acre farm, complete with barn, corral, pasture, and in some cases, animals. Others went in together, pooling their finances, and acquired larger acreage with the intention of building individual homes and collective meeting facilities.

It became obvious that the things of greatest value were: inner wisdom and a knowingness of One's connection to God, the cultivation of healthy human relationships, the ability to share fertile land, and knowledge of how to create and maintain alternative energy sources.

Although the specific arrangements, financial structures, legal agreements and such that were necessary to acquire the land and energy resources varied from person to person and community to community, the Lightworkers used their inner creative power to work out the details and move forward with the building of their intentional communities of Light. This process was not straightforward. Below, we have gone into a bit more detail regarding the all-important task of learning how to truly live and create together.

Challenges in the Enlightened Communities

Up until the 2012 portal, attempting to live in an intentional community was a very arduous task for the enlightened souls of Earth. Often, the ego would get in the way of even the most simple of tasks.

Usually some form of struggle would beset the evolving community, whether it pertained to financial and legal issues, or involved intimate relationships. There were issues with physical and emotional boundaries. Without a high degree of intuitive awareness, souls would often have ulterior motives for joining a community. Many had hidden agendas behind their actions and intentions. Some wanted to be taken care of by others, and there were those that were bossy and demanding. Imbalances would show up after souls had made a financial commitment to a particular place, so it was not easy to simply move out.

For example, a thriving community would need a balance of labor, skills and areas of expertise. It would not do well if you had, say, 100 plumbers and no electricians, or 10 administrators and no money.

Eventually the communities emerging on Earth would need to learn self-sufficiency, meaning that they would not rely at all on the old world monetary or global distribution system. That was almost unheard of before the portal shift and was still rare on Earth in the year 2013. Of course, they had a lot of motivation to become self-sufficient due to the rapidly deteriorating global distribution system in third density.

So the evolving souls on Earth quickly discovered that they must come together in prayer, meditation and intention, using advanced healing modalities and creative manifesting skills in order to attract exactly the right souls to each location. They needed to maintain a perfect balance, not just in labor expertise, but in consciousness. Not every soul would be at the same level of awareness. There would undoubtedly still be some karmic lessons to learn that would draw souls together, as well as those who would have no sense of direction or purpose. Others would be there simply to co-create with the enlightened beings and would "go with the flow" to assist wherever needed.

Above all else, Love was the glue, the common thread holding the fledgling communities together. The enlightened souls discovered that it was essential to meditate together and hold visioning meetings, often daily and sometimes for hours, as long as they took enough time to complete their basic tasks, such as emptying the compost, or stopping the water leak. As things unfolded, the enlightened souls started to see that the power of group consciousness was enough to overcome the most difficult of challenges, whether they were financial, social, geological, or otherwise.

The Year 2014

As the calendar marched towards 2014, several factors began to enter into the equation for the various groups of souls on Earth. The rapidly rising vibration of the planet was now sufficient to allow exciting new technologies to be introduced.

In the past, and especially before the opening of the portal of 2012, inventors of zero-point energy machines and other technologies were unable to overcome the mass consciousness of lack, limitation and scarcity. The negatively-oriented masses emanated a polarized quantum field that exerted an imbalanced level of energy on the Earth's grid system, thus penetrating the positively-polarized electromagnetic field of the inventors and their machines. This prevented the machines from working correctly. In the rare event that a machine continued to function properly in the zero-point field while amongst negatively-oriented souls, the sheer magnitude of the opposition was still enough to prevent production and distribution of the device.

Now, in 2014, the opposition was waning. The third density "powers that be" were losing control, and fast. It seemed hardly a day went by where there was not some catastrophe or malfunction in their military machines, computer systems and government interfaces. It was as though anything that could go wrong would go wrong. And so the positively-oriented inventors encountered less and less opposition to bringing forth the fruits of their creative endeavors.

As the souls in the enlightened communities continued to grow and evolve, healing old emotional issues, releasing limiting beliefs, and eliminating toxins from their lower bodies, a brilliant and strong force field of light began to form around each community. This positively-oriented quantum field matched the energy of the zero-point devices and allowed them to function correctly and efficiently. It also acted as a shield to prevent negatively-oriented souls from encroaching upon the settlements of the enlightened ones.

Eventually, such force fields became tangible enough to prevent *all* negative souls from even entering the property. Not only would groups of malevolent souls march right on past the property line, but in the unlikely event that one of the dark souls did manage to venture into the enlightened community, something would invariably befall that soul, preventing him from doing any damage. In some cases, such soul would be taken in by the community, healed and restored to a balanced state. This could only happen with souls who were ready. If they were too deeply embedded in darkness, being exposed to the loving vibrations of the community would be too much. In a few cases, such souls could be seen fleeing in terror to the relative safety of their egocentric comrades in third density. In other cases, mysterious illnesses would befall them and force them to retreat.

It became more and more obvious that the gulf between the enlightened New Earth and the old world of misery, poverty, suffering, malice, greed, oppression and control, was widening. Many of Earth religions had been calling this phenomenon, the "separating of the wheat from the chaff."

(Note: We in the higher realms do not use terminology such as "separating the wheat from the chaff," because it implies judgment that some souls are more worthy of ascension than others, and that is simply not the case. Natural laws are at work here. The law of attraction suggests that souls with an extreme variance in vibration cannot and will not work together unless there is a strong karmic bond between them. Since karmic lessons are coming to an end on Earth over the next several years, fewer and fewer of these kinds of relationships are manifesting in the evolving souls.)

(Further Note: The law of attraction and the law of karma actually work hand in hand. There are essentially three ways souls are attracted to one another. (1) For co-creative purposes, souls of similar vibration will come together, as described in this narrative; (2) you may attract souls of a lesser vibration who have a karmic contract to learn from you – in other words, you are the teacher, they are the students; and (3) you may attract teachers to you who are vibrating at a higher level because your soul wants to learn how to attain that higher frequency.)

As the awakened ones worked daily to clear themselves of primal fears and ego control, the gulf between these souls and the third density world continued to grow, until the force field of Light around the community became so great that it was completely and totally protected from all negativity.

Before the portal of 2012, the awakening souls still had too much unresolved emotional and mental baggage to be able to create such a powerful force field. Now, with their deep commitment to healing and help from the multitudes of guides in the heavenly realms, the enlightened souls finally had the beginnings of what they had been working long and hard for – a beautiful new world, still fragile, but filled with certainty, knowingness and balance.

Chapter 1 – A Future Timeline Overview

The Emergence of the Councils of Light

There were councils of Light that formed from the membership of the various intentional communities evolving on Earth. These councils consisted of members of the communities that volunteered to be in those roles, coupled with those who were voted in by the members at large. Council members would listen carefully to the people and make wise decisions based on the will of all the enlightened souls in the community.

The councils were not based on any existing form of third density government, but borrowed from the most enlightened ideas inherent within those structures, along with brand new ideas brought forth from on high.

Some communities explored the idea of consensus, while others practiced majority rule. However, it quickly became apparent that there was another way of making decisions that transcended consensus and majority. Council members would go into meditation, become One with each other, and simply *know* how to proceed.

(Note: We, the Founders, have observed that almost all higher dimensional worlds and systems use a form of enlightened councils for making decisions. This body of Light beings does not coerce, demand, or dictate the laws of the worlds to which it is entrusted. As you evolve, such a structure is possible because every soul becomes a master, able to discern and determine the highest and best course of action for all concerned. We have devoted Chapter 12 to an exploration of various social and political systems on other worlds that are more evolved than Earth.)

The Period of 2014 – 2016

As Earth continued to go through the Galactic Shift and divergence, the communities of Light depended on one another for supplies and technology. Souls would travel, using whatever means were available, between the communities of Light scattered across the globe. Although conventional means of transportation were still available, it was becoming increasingly difficult to depend on automobiles, buses, trains, boats, and airplanes to get around on Earth. This was due largely to the rapid destabilization of currencies and monetary systems among the major countries. Fossil fuel costs were astronomical and few could afford to replenish their supplies.

The cost of goods and services also skyrocketed, and spot shortages of so-called basic commodities began to become apparent, even in the most technologically advanced places within the third density structure.

The enlightened souls used trade and barter primarily, and relied as little as possible on sources of transport based on fossil fuels. Those that still interacted with the third density world discovered that the currency in use, whether dollars, pounds, yen or Euros, would seldom remain stable long enough to depend on as a means of trade.

Things of real value would fetch a very high price in the open markets. There was a lot of chaos in the bigger cities, particularly those located in places that depended heavily on global transport, such as metropolitan areas in the deserts and along seacoasts. The coasts were largely fished out, so sustenance usually came from distant lands that grew crops with inferior nutrition, mostly with depleted soil. The few factories that could produce the necessities of third density life were having trouble receiving enough raw materials to stay open.

The third density governments were painfully aware of these problems, but due to their identification with ego, spent long hours arguing, debating and rarely resolving their differences. As the Earth continued to rise in vibration, more and more negativity would surface in the governing bodies of the major countries. Unable to handle the rising tide of anger and fear, it was commonplace to witness assassinations, blockages, embargos, regional wars, and work stoppages. Although many of the workers competing for jobs in the few remaining functioning factories were critical to the success of the operations, their bodies were weakening under the constant stress of living in a world with too many people and too few resources. The air, water, food and buildings were heavily polluted, and this pollution was taking a toll on the immune systems of the third density souls.

From a deeper perspective, souls stuck in third density knew they could not keep pace with the rapidly accelerating changes occurring with Mother Earth herself. Earth was now a fourth density planet and the third density souls realized they were like fish out of water. Their level of vibration was no longer compatible with the basic frequencies of the Earth herself. Something had to give and it was the immune system. Incidents of illness continued to rise until the sick filled hospitals to overflowing. Lack of medical supplies and inability to pay doctors and nurses due to the failing economy resulted in long waits for medical care. In countries with government-sponsored medicine, the high cost of rendering assistance to the sick was bankrupting the system.

When enlightened souls returned to their respective communities after venturing forth into such a world, a period of detoxification would be necessary. Members of the fourth density spiritual communities would come forth to offer healing and counseling to returning souls until the negativity was sufficiently cleared. The enlightened ones had great compassion for the suffering happening in the third density cities, but there was very little they could do about it except to continuously send prayer and loving thoughts far and wide. They had long ago realized that attempting to rescue struggling humanity and to save them from themselves was a losing proposition, akin to having a Messiah complex. Furthermore, it often violated the free will of the dying souls, who likely needed to learn about the relationship between consciousness and their circumstances.

It had taken the enlightened ones years to learn these lessons themselves. For a long time, many of them had pleaded with the extraterrestrials to come pluck them off the Earth in their gleaming mother ships and take them to a world without war, poverty and suffering. This was not to be. The fourth density souls did not volunteer to come to Earth, only to leave at the first opportunity. They were here to do the hard work of healing and resurrecting higher truth principles, one step at a time.

Despite the beautiful picture painted by some souls, regarding the emerging new communities, life was not easy for a lot of the enlightened souls. Old addictive behaviors ran deep, and while the 2012 portal had advanced their consciousness immeasurably, it was not a magic pill instantly eliminating the old self. In fact, it was a little like a young bird being pushed out of the nest and being forced to fly or die.

Souls could no longer have second thoughts and try to go back to the way things were before. That comfortable little world no longer existed. It was unraveling day by day.

The Dying Realm of Third Density

As the year 2015 came and went, the situation in the third density realm became even more turbulent. Sea levels were rising and erratic weather patterns were causing crop failures and devastation on a scale never before experienced. Those who still clung to the idea that they were in control would introduce new currencies and trade regulations, but the problems remained. The soldiers started refusing to fight in the endless conflicts staged by one group or another in a vain attempt to remain in control.

Some countries tried to instigate mandatory enlistment, but were met with tremendous opposition from their own people. Protestors lined the streets and walkways leading up to the institutions of government. Many had long ago lost their employment and some were homeless and had nothing better to do than camp out near the locations where the leaders met and quarreled endlessly about how to handle the situation.

A few relatively enlightened leaders would propose radical solutions, only to be shot down (sometimes literally) by those who were trying vainly to return to some semblance of the world they had once known. Civil war broke out in the larger and seemingly more organized countries. Attempts were made to overthrow the existing rulers, but usually when such actions were successful, the new leaders found they were equally unable to resolve the immense problems faced by everyone.

Dwindling natural resources became the primary reason for going to war, and all so-called civilities and rules of war were abandoned. In a sense, it was every man for himself (and every woman for herself).

Some time around 2015, the world's population reached its peak, at around eight billion humans (at the time of this writing, the population was about 7.3 billion and was estimated to rise to 7.8 billion within a few years). The depletion of natural resources, coupled with massive pollution and immune system failure, raised death rates in most areas while simultaneously lowering the birth rate.

Many of the genetically modified substances being consumed on a regular basis, along with toxic metals in the water supply, contributed to partial or total sterility amongst women of child-bearing age. Add to this a contribution of bioterrorism agents from extremist groups, including adulteration of medications and vaccines, and you could understand why this birth/death situation was occurring.

Seeing no way out of the mess, many souls began getting their affairs in order in preparation for exiting the Earth plane and reincarnating somewhere else. Mysterious, unexplained illnesses were now so common as to barely garner mention in the nightly news.

Yet still, many remained in denial, reassuring each other that things would return to "normal." The young people were a bit more rebellious and started refusing to obey the strict mandates being handed down from the so-called controllers.

Every night, violence would erupt in the larger cities, usually between youth and police or soldiers. However, increasingly, the military and police forces were also becoming disillusioned and disheartened. Many joined the opposition forces and tried to overthrow their own authorities.

The so-called "entitlement" programs designed to help the less fortunate were also being abandoned as the stark reality of financial and moral bankruptcy began to sink in. Not knowing where to turn, souls resorted to basic survival skills, often barricading themselves in their homes after storing what little food they could find.

Chapter 1 – A Future Timeline Overview

Although war expanded during the years 2012 to 2015, the Divine Dispensation preventing the use of weapons of mass destruction meant that only a small percentage of humanity actually died in battle or from dropped bombs. Many soldiers during that period simply refused to fight, while others dropped out of the military due to deteriorating immune systems. A few were able to raise their vibration sufficiently to find their way into the enlightened communities, but this was becoming quite rare.

The New Earth Begins to Emerge

The fourth density souls were thriving. They were developing new modes of transportation and agriculture. They were starting to use electromagnetic motors that consumed almost no natural resources and cost almost nothing to operate.

Another important factor was the return of the star beings. Although many had been waiting for what seemed like forever to reunite with their brothers and sisters from the heavens, the actual meetings were quite unlike the expectations of most.

First of all, the ETs were not going to save anyone or take away the pain and challenge of growth. Initially, they would come tentatively for brief visits to some of the evolving communities, never staying very long, lest they get caught in the vibrations of Earth. They chose their witnesses carefully, making sure the fourth density humans were emotionally stable enough to be in their presence. To a few humans they would leave explicit instructions on how to perfect a technological device. To others, they would offer a plan for resolving conflict in personal relationships. They did not sell tickets to Arcturus. The new humans were simply not ready for that.

A select few members from each community were solidly on the path of ascension into the fifth density Light Body. They were allowed to interact more freely with the ETs. Most of the space visitors came from the Pleiades and Arcturus, with a few Sirians. The humans quickly learned that there are strict protocols for intervention in the affairs of Earth. If it is not your time to interact with ETs, then try as you might, you will not see them.

The beautiful ET souls visiting Earth had learned a long time ago the true meaning of "Do not cast your pearls before swine." They knew that only certain human beings could use the sacred knowledge of the stars wisely and for the good of all. They also realized, after many past mistakes, that it is not always easy to understand human free will. They had to humble themselves and recognize that interacting with humans and having respect for free will are difficult and tricky operations. If you are an ET visitor to Earth, you do not simply go to a weekend seminar in how to understand human free will. It takes a lot of diligence and determination to grasp, on a deep level, the whole psyche of humanity.

As 2016 came and went, the divergence continued, but another major event was looming on the horizon.

The Comet of 2017

Although the energies stayed very high on Earth following the 2012 portal, with rapid change continuing relentlessly, some things had begun to settle down a bit since then. The axis of the Earth had now moved slightly away from the scalar electromagnetic frequencies streaming forth from the quasars near the central sun of the galaxy.

One of the curious side effects of the portal had been the compressing of time. To many humans, a day seemed to be only about eight or nine hours long during the portal shift of 2012. Now, as the Earth changed her position, the days became seemingly longer, back to about 12 hours in length, but still perceived as much shorter than they were prior to the year 2000.

However, a new energy was beginning to be detected among the clairvoyants and prophets. Scientists had discovered a comet entering the solar system and predicted it would pass fairly close to Earth. This celestial object had a period of approximately 10,500 years and it was noted that the last time it came through, there were disruptions in the geology and life forms on the planet.

The enlightened ones already knew that this comet heralded the arrival of the "second wave of ascension," meaning that those fourth density souls who were ready to move to the next stage of evolution would get a giant boost.

The third density world was deteriorating rapidly. Deaths were now outnumbering births in all but a few places. The combination of radiation from nuclear reactors, coupled with pollution from fossil fuels, and exotic viruses and bacteria, were too much for the failing immune systems of the third density humans. For those souls, the arrival of the comet would signify further disruption of their lives. A few of them would use the event to boost themselves out of the third density spiral of destruction and onto the fourth density path of redemption. They would come flowing gently into the New Earth and be welcomed by the intentional communities that now numbered well over 10,000.

Throughout the enlightened communities, a small percentage of the souls residing there were preparing for ascension into their fifth density crystal Light bodies. It was obvious to the general membership of each community that these souls had moved to a new level of understanding and hence, they were usually given positions on the high councils of the communities of Light. Some were quite mobile, seeming to be unaffected by the transportation difficulties of the third density world. They were rapidly developing their more advanced psychic and intuitive abilities, and a few were now able to teleport themselves from one location to another, although the majority still relied on conventional means of transport. Some used new electromagnetic motorized devices, while others were ferried about by the ETs.

The ascending ones offered workshops and seminars in personal development and provided healing and counseling for fourth density souls who needed extra help surmounting their emotional and psychological issues. There was still a lot of grief to be integrated around the loss of family and friends. A few third density family members were able to communicate with their fourth density spouses, sons, daughters, cousins and the like, but the majority had broken off all communication quite some time ago. Nevertheless, as the comet approached, a few fourth density family members hoped and prayed that some of their loved ones in third density would be able to "ride the tail of the comet" into the New Earth.

As the comet approached, souls noticed a change in the air. Things became translucent and sound waves were different. Energy seemed to crackle and pop, and the atmosphere appeared to be more tangible, as if you could see the colors and textures of the individual gases. The aurora borealis became brilliant almost every night, even at low latitudes. To some fourth density souls, it felt as though sound waves were traveling through water, or hollow pipes, or even cellophane. Surges of electricity would go through their bodies, and sleep became almost impossible.

When the comet passed, the Earth felt very different. In some ways nothing had changed, but in other ways, it was as though the world had entered yet another dimension, different from the one it had entered during the portal of 2012.

The electromagnetic interference from the comet had destroyed many of the telecommunications devices and satellites utilized by the third density humans, even though it had officially missed Earth by several million miles. This, along with the widening gulf in vibrational states between third and fourth densities, essentially stopped the flow of communication between the two realms. The New Earth was now truly separated energetically from the old Earth. For all practical purposes, the two existed in completely different dimensions with almost no overlap between them.

Conventional travel became nearly impossible and so the fourth density souls released their final attachments to the old world and occupied themselves with the monumental daily tasks that confronted them – gardening, building, organizing, meeting, and most importantly, communing heart to heart with each other.

The Years 2018-2020

The communities of Light prospered and thrived. Agricultural methods were perfected, and although the climate of Earth was in a great state of flux, the locations of the centers of Light were exactly right for good yields of a variety of crops. Energy efficient buildings powered by electromagnetic generators became the norm. Holistic healing modalities were a way of life. New children came forth from expectant mothers and these children were already highly advanced in their soul evolution.

Schools were built to accommodate the children, but they were completely unlike the third density schools that had crumbled and decayed. The enlightened schools recognized the unique needs of the new children. Emphasis was placed on self-examination and self-awareness, as well as harnessing creativity. These children grew up knowing that they lived in a friendly Universe filled with beings of all shapes and sizes. They witnessed unconditionally loving adults and a world of plenty.

By now, things had deteriorated so much in the third density world that entire areas were essentially quarantined energetically from the communities of Light. The fledgling fourth density souls knew that they could not remain for long in the lower levels without becoming contaminated by the constant barrage of negative thought forms and pollution. Only those ascending into fifth density could walk openly among the third density cities and be unaffected, though they rarely did so because by now there were almost no souls remaining in the decaying cities that were open and receptive to the enlightened teachings. The dominant consciousness of the third density was one of survival, something that was becoming more difficult every day.

The fourth density adults taught the new children about the world that had once been, and many of them had a hard time believing such a world could exist. Some had never incarnated on a world where war could take place, and the thought of human beings killing one another was completely foreign to them.

These new children would travel with their parents to visit other communities of Light, but in almost every case were not allowed to venture near a decaying third density city. These young souls needed to stay pure and build strong bodies free of discordant thought forms. Of course, some brought issues from past lifetimes to be healed, but because they were raised by an enlightened group of souls, this healing process occurred rapidly. These children did not forget their past lifetimes, nor did their psychic and intuitive abilities wither and atrophy as they grew up. They were the first generation to grow up in the new Golden Age.

The Years 2020 – 2030

During the next ten years, the third density civilization deteriorated further until only a few souls remained in that level of vibration. Mass plagues and pestilence spread across many of the heavily populated areas and, due to the decreased immune function of third density humans, most were unable to resist the invading viruses, bacteria, fungi, heavy metal contamination, hydrocarbons and radiation. The population dropped from nearly eight billion to scarcely more than two billion. About half of the deaths were the result of immune system failure and the resulting invading organisms and chemicals. The rest of the deaths were from a variety of factors, including starvation, dehydration, extreme hot and cold, war, flood, earthquakes, volcanoes, and violent weather.

After 2020, war became nearly non-existent on Earth. The only violence was from scuffles between individuals or roving gangs where physical survival was at stake. The economic failures and political upheavals had made it nearly impossible for third density souls to travel using airplanes and modern transport systems. Countries no longer had the money or natural resources to manufacture armaments. In many cities, transportation was only possible by foot or bicycle due to extreme shortages of fuel.

In the enlightened communities of the fourth density Earth, a whole different picture was unfolding. Great harmony was spreading forth as more and more enlightened ones resolved their negative emotions and psychological blockages. New farming methods and alternative energy sources were now firmly in place, creating a level of prosperity that had scarcely been dreamed of even by proponents of utopias.

Increasingly, the teachings of the day were about ascension into fifth density – what it is, how it works, and when souls can expect to enter the immortal, crystal Light body. The souls already firmly on the path of ascension were having experiences of the etheric Earth, including the wondrous realms of nature spirits, faeries, devas, sprites, gnomes, and all manner of animal and plant spirits.

To the ascending souls, the world was a place of indescribable beauty. Everything sparkled and shone with a radiance formerly only seen clairvoyantly. The eyes, ears and senses of their bodies were changing. They could now see and hear broader frequencies. The visible and auditory spectrums were expanding. Physical strength was also increasing. They found they could tolerate great extremes of hot or cold. Their bodies rarely, if ever, experienced injury or discomfort. Radiant life force energy coursed through their veins. Sleep became less and less necessary. The need to eat dropped slowly away until many of them became breatharians, living solely on oxygen and prana (pure etheric life force energy).

The ascending ones were the teachers of the New Earth. They gathered together with the fourth density evolving souls and led seminars, workshops and healing circles on a regular basis. They were the wise counselors and holistic practitioners that kept the fourth density communities healthy and vibrant.

The 2030 Passage of Nibiru

As the decade of the 2020s drew to a close, excitement rose once again as amateur astronomers among them had detected a significant heavenly body heading for the solar system. It was about one-third the size of Earth and appeared lifeless to those with physical eyes, yet to clairvoyants and the ascending souls, this planetoid revealed itself to be anything but lifeless.

The return of Nibiru meant the reappearance of the Annunaki, the wise elders of ancient civilizations that had brought both enlightenment and ruin, depending on the occasion.

The wise Annunaki already knew about the state of affairs on Earth. In fact, some of the highest level teachers of Nibiru were able to journey to Earth using pure consciousness, even though the planetoid itself was still outside the orbit of Pluto.

As the Annunaki came into the energy field of Earth (though still millions of miles away physically), they saw the death and destruction of the third density world. Of course, the wise ones of their race had already shared their wisdom and knowledge of the Earth changes with the people of Nibiru, but it was still quite a shock for the average Nibiruan to behold the scenes of destruction. To their relief, they saw, through their clairvoyant lenses and sophisticated technological equipment, the blossoming fourth density communities of Light and the ascending ones shining brightly.

The Annunaki organized the brightest and best of their race and prepared them to interact cautiously among the members of the New Earth.

During the passage of Nibiru, which came within 25 million miles of Earth at one point, many visitations occurred between the fifth through ninth density members of the planetoid and the enlightened human race. The Annunaki shared their wisdom and technology with the New Earth much more freely than they had in the past with the Sumerians and Egyptians. This time the Nibiruans knew that the humans would not misuse the higher technologies.

In addition, the people of Nibiru had evolved considerably since their last visit to Earth. The minority of Annunaki that had caused trouble before on the Earth were now healed and willing to assist in compassionate ways with the rebuilding of Earth.

The electromagnetic fluctuations that occurred on Earth with the close passage of Nibiru served to once again accelerate the evolution of enlightened humanity, resulting in a third wave of ascension. Now, millions of surviving souls on planet Earth were solidly on the path of ascension into fifth density.

The third density population of Earth was essentially non-existent by now. The fourth density population numbered somewhere between one and two billion. They were spread out across thousands of intentional communities, ranging from homesteads with just a few people, to well-organized new cities with as many as 100,000 souls residing in each one.

In 2030, the last of the third density humans who had evolved sufficiently to enter the new Golden Age came straggling in to the fourth density intentional communities. They were welcomed with open arms.

The Galactic Shift: 2030 – 2100

The Galactic Shift, which began in about 1950, reached its peak around 2025. This shift affected the entire solar system and many areas of the Milky Way galaxy in the same general vicinity as the solar system. (The mechanics of the Galactic Shift were detailed in the book, *"Earth Changes and 2012."*)

As the Earth continued to move through the electromagnetic null zone, the quarantine around the Earth began to be lifted. With almost all of the darker human souls now departed and the negative ET races removed from the astral realms of Earth, benevolent beings from all over the galaxy were able to come to Earth and interact with the more enlightened members of the human race. Because the overall vibration of Earth was now high enough, they no longer needed to take the extraordinary precautions that were necessary prior to this time period.

During 2030 to 2100, the ascending souls reached a level of vibration whereby they were no longer visible to beings vibrating at third density. Already psychologically invisible, they became undetectable by the instruments of third density scientists. Of course there were very few third density souls around to witness this anyway, perhaps a small number living in caves or underground, though the ones that had fled underground to escape the plagues and pollution had experienced the same immune system issues as their brethren on the surface of the planet. Therefore their numbers were extremely small and the lack of sunlight and fresh air had mutated their bodies, often in strange ways, causing some of them to resemble earlier humanoid forms.

As the ascending souls began completing their ascension process, they radiated a beautiful golden halo or aura of Light that was clearly visible to the fourth density souls. Their telepathic and psychokinetic abilities continued to increase and they were now completely impervious to conditions in the Earth's environment. They walked in two worlds, the fourth density one of enlightened spiritual communities where they taught higher truths and were instruments of healing, and the fifth density world of the nature spirits, where they communed with various beings from all over the galaxy.

As the century drew to a close, the Earth began to settle down, with fewer climatic disruptions and a more stable atmosphere. By now, the communities of Light had stabilized as well and most had discovered the highest and best possible form of government. Usually this involved enlightened councils of 12, with each member responsible for a particular aspect of the new society. These governing members were sensitive to the needs of the community and took great steps to minimize egoistic behavior. Education and the attaining of wisdom were the top priorities for members. The young children demanded this, for they were not about to rest on their laurels or involve themselves in petty distractions. They wanted to explore the Universe and they asked all the hard questions that can only be answered through deep inner investigation.

The agricultural systems had matured and the evolving souls had plenty to eat. Their system of trade and barter was now highly refined and nobody went without the basics.

Souls on the New Earth thrived, living with a very high standard beyond what even the richest members of the third density society had achieved. Most of all, they were genuinely happy. Love was the central focus of their lives. Service was integrated into every aspect of their society.

Gradually, with the help of advanced technologies and ET groups, they were able to expand their communities to embrace the empty skeletons of the third density cities. They resurrected the houses and buildings (where such resurrection was possible). They cleaned up the waterways and remodeled the factories. Where third density infrastructure was no longer needed, they turned the Earth back into the pristine paradise it was before the dark ones had destroyed the balance.

The Earth was once again a jewel in the heavens and a place that welcomed celestial travelers with open arms.

CHAPTER 2
The Nature of Time

The story you have just read was given from the point of view of the fourth density enlightened humans and their experience of spiritual community. The story would have had a very different flavor if it had been told from the perspective of the third or fifth density humans.

To each of the three main groups of humanity, their experience feels like the one valid reality that supersedes all other versions or perceptions of time and space.

Each group uses the Earth as a staging point for the next step in spiritual evolution. For the third density souls, life on Earth becomes harder and harder until they finally leave their bodies and take up residence on other worlds more suited to their level of vibration. To those still able to perceive third density Earth, it will look somewhat like a barren wasteland with very little life remaining.

Yet to a fourth density human, the world will return to the verdant green paradise it was before the industrial revolution, and a new, more responsible stewardship approach will prevail regarding the air, water, soil, etc. For a time, there will be an overlap of realities. Fourth density humans may temporarily be able to travel to what is left of the third density cities, though most of them will likely lie in ruins.

The fifth density ascended souls will have a "birds-eye" view, so to speak, being able to walk in the world of enlightened humanity as well as the world of the nature spirits. They will have the ability to perceive the ruins of third density Earth, but their vibration will be so different that to them it will seem as if they are watching a grade B movie with a black and white projector every time they look at third density.

You had a book and film come out many years ago, one of your Hollywood products, no doubt. The channel informs us that it was called "The Langoliers," and was written by one of your sci-fi writers, Stephen King. In this film, a "sub-world" was discovered that was slightly out of phase to your "normal" world. In this sub-world, sound, movement and color were lower, slower and faded. To add an element of Hollywood horror, the writer invented some bogeymen who would literally chew at the edges of this pseudo-reality.

Another sci-fi show that aired for a while on your television was called "Sliders." It portrayed parallel dimensions of Earth (although the dimensions in

Sliders were separated by physical portals generated by an electronic device). In both of these sci-fi scripts, there are similarities to the three parallel Earths.

The parallel realities we are speaking of here are generated by states of consciousness, which have the power to change physical reality. Not only do you see what you want to see, but the world rearranges itself to accommodate your viewpoint of it. If the collective viewpoint is strong enough, a dominant parallel reality is formed. Realities created by large numbers of souls all having similar beliefs are called "dominant timelines" or "probable realities."

The Nonlinear Earth and Her Levels of Being

From a nonlinear point of view, the Earth already has seven dimensions of reality existing simultaneously in the here and now. Your passage through the doors of these dimensions rests within your consciousness. For example, if you are vibrating at seventh density, you have access to the seventh density Earth and its beings of Light. This version of Earth has indescribable beauty and entities with virtually unlimited power that are able to come and go from her at will.

Each of the vibratory levels of Earth has unique characteristics. The seventh level Earth, commonly called Gaia, is the domain of supreme consciousness, love and compassion. This Earth is a member of the lower celestial heavens. While the lowest realms of Earth have been quarantined for millennia, the soul level (seventh density), known as Gaia, has never left her cosmic family of beautiful planetary Beings.

Sixth level Earth is also a beautiful place, and corresponds to the causal level of reality. We will simply call her upper Terra for now. Upper Terra is a crystal-like world similar to what is portrayed in your sci-fi movie "Superman." It is interesting to note that the lower realms are often a mirror of the higher realms. In this case, your third and fourth density Earth's crust is composed primarily of silicon-based minerals, including quartz, the most common form of crystal.

Your fifth density Earth, or lower Terra, is the etheric realm equivalent of the crystalline structure, and this is the level where the ascended crystal light body form of humanity will emerge in the years to come. You are already familiar with the lower four levels (mineral, plant, animal and enlightened human).

Just as Gaia has seven levels of Being to her planetary soul, you have seven levels of being to your individual soul essence. Your home level is seventh density. It is the level where you started out as individual souls, emerging from the Godhead many millions of years ago.

Although we are not entirely comfortable with the concept of "older" and "younger" souls, we will often refer to those souls that have experienced hundreds of millions of years of exploration of the lower worlds, as "old" or even "ancient" souls, and those that have only been exploring the lower worlds for a few million years or less, as "young" souls.

Earth has been a place where souls from all levels of experience and vibration have come to learn a variety of lessons. In linear time, this is about to change. The Divine Dispensations that have been granted by the Godhead (and which are described in detail in *"Earth Changes and 2012"*) include the opportunity for souls to graduate to the next level of evolution very quickly.

Put another way, Earth has been a melting pot for all types of souls, but things are getting a bit out of control and the darker ones have brought Earth to the point where her very life seems to be threatened. While this is not ultimately true, the dispensations have been granted in order to correct this imbalance. Earth and other planets are being set up to allow all souls to find their true place where learning can be maximized.

In earlier writings, this was likened to taking a one-room schoolhouse (Earth) with grades from primary through intermediate and high school, and finally constructing two new buildings, one for primary grades (new 3rd density planets) and one for high school (5th density and above involving the ascended Earth and other ascended planets), and letting the intermediate grades (4th density representing the New Earth) take over the original one-room schoolhouse.

The Relationship Between Consciousness and Time

Let us now return to our discussion of the levels of awareness and how they fit into the nature of time.

Higher levels of awareness are more inclusive. For example, if you have a seventh density consciousness, you can perceive all the levels below your level of vibration as well as the qualities unique to seventh density. However, if you are vibrating at third density, you only have access to first, second and third levels.

You, dear humans, are exploring the third, fourth and fifth density realities of Earth. Each of you has some of the qualities and characteristics of all three of these levels of being. The one level you are most focused on will become your dominant level of reality in the coming years.

Consciousness "activates" what it perceives. In previous dissertations, this has been likened to paintings on a canvas. The non-activated levels are like blank canvases waiting to be painted. Once you focus on a specific level, you bring life to that level or density.

If there are beings or entities already vibrating at a specific level, then those beings activate that level in their own way. For example, the nature spirits and elementals existing in the lower fifth density realms of Earth have created a beautiful reality that fifth density humans will be able to witness as they move into that realm.

Your Earth is an experimental world. Many of the conditions present today are different than on any other world in your galaxy. Because you have free will, there are many variations within the overall framework of multidimensional reality. This means that no two planets will ever evolve in exactly the same way. That said, you have 11 other planets in your galaxy that have reached a similar situation to what is taking place on Earth.

Let us now look at some of the physical and psychological changes that seem to be happening with time.

Changes in the Nature of Time

Many of you have asked us to address your sense that time is speeding up. While this is not true from a third density perspective (the Earth still rotates once about every 23 hours and 56 minutes), there is a profound psychological shift taking place within almost all human beings.

Some of the experiences you are having at this time are related to the Galactic Shift, and this includes the speeding up of time. Although there are still 23 hours and 56 minutes to one Earth day from a linear third density standpoint, within the fourth density realm, psychological time is changing. As of the year 2000, those 24 hours really felt more like 16 hours to many of you. As you move through the 2012 portal, a day will seem to have shrunk to about 8 to 12 hours in length. Due to your changes in level of vibration, along with changes in the base frequencies of Earth, the time harmonics are being altered.

The base frequency of Earth used to be about 8 hertz. Now it has increased to about 13 hertz (as of the end of 2011). It will peak around 14 hertz by the year 2015 and remain relatively stable at around 12 to 14 hertz through the duration of the Galactic Shift.

As you go higher in vibratory state, what seems to you to be perhaps a few seconds can be a few hours to someone in a lower state of vibration. At very high frequencies, a few seconds to someone in that high vibration can seem like hundreds of years to someone in a much lower frequency. This is called "natural harmonic time compression."

There is also a phenomenon known as "harmonic time expansion." An interesting ability afforded those in the higher realms includes the idea of "manufactured harmonic time expansion." This reversal of the natural time compression normally experienced in the higher realms allows time and space travelers from higher dimensions the option of exploring the lower realms for days, weeks, months or even years, and then returning to their own realm wherein only a few seconds have elapsed.

An example of time expansion occurs almost nightly during the dream state. Some of your dreams may span years within one dream, but when you awaken, you might find that only 60 to 90 minutes have elapsed.

Natural and artificial vortex sites often have expansion or compression of time as one of their features. Generally, "positive" vortexes have time compression, while "negative" vortexes have time expansion. This is consistent with the principle of consciousness that says, "Higher states of consciousness promote time compression, while lower states promote time expansion." In lay terms, this means if you spend time in a positive vortex, time seems to fly by. When meditating in a negative vortex, time may seem to crawl.

Just as you can compress and expand time, you can do the same with space. This is how extraterrestrial beings are able to come and go from the Earth plane without having to traverse the great distances described in Newtonian and Einsteinian physics. You have sci-fi authors and filmmakers who have introduced the idea of hyper-space, with spacecraft capable of hyper-drive, or warp speed.

Where do you think all these ideas came from? While they are certainly embellished with your typical Hollywood dramas and themes, the central ideas are based on actual mechanics of time and space inherent to higher levels of reality.

We will return to our discussion of time and space expansion and compression a bit later in this book, in our section on future technology.

One more psychological time anomaly that is worth mentioning involves the idea that the lower dimensions of the Universe represent the past and the higher dimensions the future. Because you as human beings are capable of perceiving both linear and nonlinear time, and because you are evolving from lower to higher dimensions in linear time, from a nonlinear perspective, the lower dimensions are part of the past and the higher dimensions are part of the future.

Said another way, from a higher perspective, you can see your entire linear timeline laid out before you stretching from past, through the present and into the future. As you move along your timeline from past to future, your vibrational state increases. This is why you will find the higher dimensions positioned along the future segment of the timeline.

So during time and space travel, if you dial into higher dimensional frequencies, you are, in essence, moving into the future, with respect to linear time. From a nonlinear perspective, all of time happens at once, so you are merely shifting your lens of perception to another part of the time/space fabric. We have given a more detailed explanation of this below.

A Discussion of Possible and Probable Timelines

It is the nature of your world, dear Creators, that it serve as a "scratch pad" for your creative endeavors. Like us, you are Creator Gods, created in the image and likeness of your Creator. You have all the abilities, talents, skills, and potential that we have. What you do with your abilities is up to you because you have free will.

Chapter 1 used a retrospective approach to see the dominant timelines of your world as we see them. They are not set in stone. They can be changed and are changing moment by moment. In our millions of years of evolution and understanding of human affairs, we have portrayed the most likely outcomes as we see them. Chapter 1 gave you the scenarios with the highest probability of being played out on your world over the next few decades.

In fact, you are an integral part of these dominant timelines, adding your own creative energy to the visions set forth in this book. The presentation given in Chapter 1 is helping to create the very things it describes.

You might say, "Well, if that is the case, then why can't we save everyone instead of only 25% of the human race?"

Therein lies the paradox of free will. For within the many possible realities is one in which everyone wakes up to the reality of their magnificence and immediately ceases all forms of negativity upon your world. Yet, knowing what we do about the levels of evolvement of souls on your world and the reasons they came to Earth in the first place, it is almost inevitable that some souls will choose to fall back into darkness once again, for they have not yet integrated their Original Cause issues. They are still reenacting the Fall from Grace that seemed to happen eons ago. This root cause of humanity's suffering will be approached in many different ways throughout this book in an attempt to help you understand the primal issues that are responsible for the rise and fall of civilizations.

The following chapters of this book will go into a detailed explanation of the many changes that are likely to come to your world in the years ahead. We have provided a broad overview, but a practical and sensible question to ask at this point is, "How do we get there from here? What tangible steps can I as an individual soul take to help bring about the visions you have described?" Of course, you are referring to the fourth and fifth density scenarios and not the third density one.

For most of you, the time will soon arrive when you will find that letting go of third density is the sanest approach. We urge you to start today by releasing your remaining identification with that realm. To help you do this, we suggest re-reading Chapter 1 several times and talking to others who share your visions of a peaceful, enlightened world. We will also be giving specific techniques (in Chapter 3), designed to help you heal your psychological and emotional issues.

Facing the Truth of What Is

Coming back to our central topic, multiple timelines, it is important to remember the "activation principle" of consciousness. *What you focus on, you become.* This is true for collective groups of humanity as well as individuals. Right now would be a good time to observe where you are placing the emphasis in your lives. What is getting the most energy? What is receiving the most attention?

We realize there is a fine line between consciously choosing to become a positively-oriented ascending human, and putting on an artificially happy smiling face and going into denial about what still needs healing within you. There are many humans obsessed with remaining positive, at the expense of denying major parts of themselves that are in pain. It is not about avoiding pain, or wallowing in it, or identifying with it. The true healing is contingent upon how you interact with it.

You can be focused on the magnificence of your spiritual Being while seeking to fully understand and integrate fear, anger, sadness, grief, resentment, worry, anxiety, dread, terror, rage, judgment, guilt, and all manner of negativity. The key is to look at these things *from* the Oneness of your all-wise, all-knowing, all-powerful God Presence. Because of the existence of nonlinear reality, or the eternal now, it is not only possible to do this, but ultimately your God Presence is the only true reality and so there is no way you cannot come from that part of yourself.

In many of your writings, the analogy is used as follows: *You are Gods dreaming of mortality and limitation.* Indeed, this is the case. Your task, beloved Creators, is to recognize when you have become identified with the world of form and all its traps and pitfalls, and to withdraw your energy from the world and return to the One True Reality of your God Self.

Creating a Timeline that Empowers You

Let us return again to our discussion of timelines. In nonlinear time you are already enlightened and free and are creating powerfully from the vantage point of your God Presence. Spread out before you is a tapestry of time/space possibilities and probabilities. The level of validity of a particular timeline depends on two factors: (1) How much energy and focus you place upon it; and (2) how many of you decide to adopt that particular focus. For example, if you believe in and focus on war as a way to get what you think you need, and millions of others believe and focus in the same way, you will end up creating war on your planet.

Conversely, if enough of you adopt the fourth density timeline proposed in Chapter 1, you become a powerful force for creating prosperity and joy on Earth. Anything you enthusiastically adopt as your desired reality gets merged into the collective reality being created on Earth. The extent of your ability to focus on your desired reality depends on how much you have healed your psychological and emotional issues and cleared your core negative beliefs.

As you focus on the reality you desire to create and seek out others who have similar desires, you become an undeniable force on the planet. While it may only take one enlightened individual to change the world, several enlightened souls all working together to create a dominant timeline of peace and prosperity will do just that.

Past, Parallel and Future Lifetimes

You do not have in your language the words to adequately describe the relationship between the nonlinear Self and the myriad of linear selves that thread through the tapestry of possible and probable timelines. We will do our best to keep this subject simple and easy to understand, but we cannot guarantee you will grasp what we are saying here.

In linear reality, you have your emergence from the Godhead, let's say 100 million years ago, followed by a series of incarnations in various lower worlds, occasionally followed by a period of respite in the higher dimensions before descending once again to commence the lessons you did not learn completely in previous lifetimes.

Many of you, in fact most of you reading this, have been all over the galaxy in your various incarnations and manifestations. A typical enlightened soul may start out in seventh density Pleiades and then drop in vibration to incarnate for several lifetimes in fifth density Pleiades, followed by a few lifetimes in fourth density Sirius A, then a couple of pleasant interludes in sixth density Arcturus, followed by a challenging round of several lifetimes in fourth density Orion, then a brief visit to one of the early civilizations on Earth as a third density being, then on to more fourth density Pleiadean lifetimes, etc., finally coming back to Earth at this time.

Most souls on Earth have been here before, on average 50 to 100 times, although for a few this is their first lifetime on Earth. Some souls have been here hundreds of times. Starseeds are those souls whose linear timeline consists primarily of lifetimes on other worlds. They may have come to Earth only a few times, usually during the heights of civilizations or during pivotal times around a period of Earth changes.

After this incarnation on Earth, you will either (1) go through physical ascension, (2) die and be reborn in the new Golden Age on Earth, or (3) choose to journey on to some other planet. As you complete your Earthly lessons, you will spend more of your time in higher worlds and less time incarnating into the lower worlds. When you do incarnate on a lower world, it will be for the express purpose of helping souls awaken in that place, just as most of you reading this now have come to Earth from higher worlds to help humanity.

The True Nature of Karma

Each planetary system upon which you incarnate presents a unique series of soul lessons and when you have completed those lessons, you no longer have any "karma" or unfinished soul business on those particular worlds. You are then free to come and go as you will from those worlds, depending on the level of your desire to help other souls there who are still stuck on the wheel of karma.

As we have mentioned many times before, karma has nothing to do with reward and punishment. That is an elaborate scheme set up by guilt to convince you that you are worthy or unworthy of enlightenment. In this respect, many of the Eastern religions merely promote guilt from a different angle than the western religions.

For example, if you were born into poverty in this lifetime and have recall of being wealthy and abusing your wealth in a previous lifetime, this does not mean you are being punished for your past transgressions and are destined to remain in poverty for the balance of this lifetime. More likely, it means that your soul simply desired to understand the duality of wealth and poverty from both points of view. In your past lifetime, you were the oppressor and now you get to experience what it feels like to be the oppressed.

Once you have completed a soul lesson, you are free to create your life in a very different way. That means that if you were born into poverty in this lifetime and have learned everything there is about that state, you are free to create wealth once again, perhaps this time with greater love and compassion for others.

For many of you, it seems the journey through your Earthly lifetimes has been long and harsh, and from a strictly third density point of view, it has been. Up until the Galactic Shift, Earth had been one of those planets where finishing your karma and moving into ascension was reserved for a few yogis who lived high in the mountains and meditated several hours per day. Now, with the recent Divine dispensations, ascension is available to any soul who sincerely desires it and is willing to work on clearing the negative aspects of self.

More on Parallel Lifetimes

Before we take a deeper look at ascension, you may be asking, "What about parallel lifetimes? I get the feeling I have other selves in other dimensions living lifetimes in other worlds, or even in other bodies on this world."

We can go quite deep with this question, perhaps too deep for your intellectual minds, but let us make the attempt to explain. First of all, your past and future lifetimes are parallel, from the standpoint of nonlinear time, because they are all unfolding right now in this eternal moment, despite appearing to happen sequentially. They are not set in stone. Your past lifetimes are mutating, diverging, converging, and in general changing moment to moment, just as your present and future lifetimes are.

You do have what is called the Akashic medium, which records every soul experience, and from that standpoint, your past lifetimes are fixed. But every time you journey back in time and change something, you create a new timeline. In effect, you jump from the original timeline into the new one created by your actions of going back into the past and making changes.

The simplest example of this, which is mentioned in detail in the next section in our discussion of healing techniques, is when you perform a timeline healing, which means to go back and give one of your past selves a healing. Unlike the paradox demonstrated in your science fiction movies, you cannot go back and, for example, kill your grandfather and then return to the present and find out you no longer exist as a result.

You can only change your *experience* of the past, which includes making energetic changes to the way you experienced events. By doing this, the original timeline remains intact and you do not violate the free will of other souls having experiences in that timeline. Imagine the dramatic change that would occur to those who burned you at the stake if you were to be rescued by future versions of yourself and carried off into the woods just as the burning ceremony begins.

However, you can create an alternate timeline that includes a visitation by future selves and you can receive a healing from them while in your past lifetime. In the "burned at the stake" lifetime, you now have an alternative timeline in which your condemned self was visited by future versions of himself/herself. In this alternate timeline, your soul can avoid the trauma originally experienced in association with being burned alive because your future selves can come back in time and lift your spirit out of your body before you have the experience of being burned. This is usually allowed because it does not affect the consciousness of those who condemned you to die. They do not know that you consciously bypassed the burning experience.

From a nonlinear perspective, all these alternate timelines are part of the eternal now, and you can access any of them at any time. So they will seem like parallel lifetimes because in fact they are. Every time you change some aspect of linear time, you create a new thread in the fabric of time/space, and these fabrics are all accessible from nonlinear time.

There is another type of parallel lifetime that involves what is commonly called soul families and oversouls. You have, usually, six members of your soul family on Earth or other lower density planets, and six in the higher dimensions, at any given time, and it is possible to meet the six Earthly souls while in human form and feel a deep connection with them. It is also possible to become aware of their life experiences while at a physical distance.

You have an oversoul, which consists of the 12 souls described in the preceding paragraph. You can tune into the oversoul and realize that he or she is one aspect of a larger monadic or atmic Self, the oversoul of your oversoul, also called your master oversoul. Each of these 12 oversouls that form your master oversoul, in turn, have 12 individual souls attached to them, and from a ninth density perspective, you are intimately connected to all 144 souls in your master oversoul. The structure of souls and oversouls is explained in depth in *Earth Changes and 2012*." For now, we are bringing up this subject to help explain why you might feel you have other selves living other lives in other places.

Finally, there is the God perspective itself, which is beyond anything your mind can conceive, but let's go ahead and take it to its extreme. Fasten your seat belts, please.

Have you ever wondered, if you are truly One with Everything, why that Everything chose to come through *your* body, in *your* unique circumstances, at this moment in time? Why did it choose to experience itself through *you*, and if you are truly One, then why can't you decide, at any given moment, to experience it through your sister, or friend, or someone down the street? Why do you seem locked in this one physical body?

The answer is simple, but not easy to understand. If God is everything, then there is no differentiation between any two or more aspects of Creation. There only appears to be differentiation because of the existence of linear time.

From the perspective of God, you can rewind the linear "tape" of time and experience every aspect of Creation, one at a time. Or you can choose to experience all aspects simultaneously. As God, the choice is up to you. That means that this lifetime, you could choose to be Sal in the USA, and in another parallel lifetime, you could choose to be Steven down the road, then in another parallel lifetime, you could choose to be Sarah in Bath, England, etc.

From a linear perspective, it seems absurd that you could experience every life form everywhere in the Universe, one at a time, but this is how God perceives its Creation, because time is infinite from God's perspective. To overly simplify, that means that God has unlimited time on his/her/its hands to personally experience every individual aspect of Creation. Then, while God is experiencing itself individually, it can zoom out to the nonlinear realm and experience everyone at once.

While this ultimate viewpoint is available to all aspects of God's Creation, it is not possible, while in human embodiment, for you to spend very much time in this state of consciousness, so we will now return to our discussion of the dominant timelines of Earth. We hope you have enjoyed our journey into the profound state of God consciousness.

Earth's Three Dominant Timelines

Coming back down to Earth, let's take another look at the three dominant timelines being created by humanity. Please keep in mind that there are other individual soul realities besides the following three descriptions, but over 95% of humanity will likely fall (or rise) into one of these three realities in the years to come on planet Earth.

The Dominant Timeline of Third Density Death and Destruction

As we have discussed in the Introduction and again in Chapter 1, not every soul is ready to enter fourth density with Mother Earth. Going back to the classroom analogy, there are some students who are simply not willing to do what it takes to graduate to the next level.

They are not to be judged or condemned or thought of as less than, dumb, stupid, bad or wrong. They are simply learning at a different pace than the more enlightened members of humanity.

The vast majority of souls on Earth have, as their dominant DNA, the Orion strains. This is a result of extensive interbreeding that occurred nearly half a million years ago when the star systems of Rigel and Betelgeuse invaded the Earth. At that time, there were no safeguards in place to prevent such occurrences. The souls on Earth were primarily Pleiadean prior to the invasion, and one of their difficult soul lessons was to experience being taken over by a more warrior-like, aggressive, domineering race.

We know that most Pleiadean souls on Earth did not consciously choose to become Orions, but on a higher level, this was part of the natural outcome of the original separation and reflected the lessons that came out of the primal beliefs that arose after the fall. Invasions and interbreeding are frequent occurrences in the lower worlds and on some level the incoming souls to Earth during that time knew that this could happen.

Nevertheless, the negative programs, in the form of emotional scars, etheric imprints and astral implants, have remained with humanity throughout several ages. Those souls that are still caught in this cycle of Original Cause and victimhood will experience one final disaster here on Earth (or several related disasters, such as wars, famine, flood, earthquakes, etc.). They will exit during the Earth changes and take up residence on other worlds specially designed to assist them in finally overcoming the reenactment of the fall.

After the destruction of Lemuria and Atlantis, a few souls were able to balance their various aspects. They made a commitment to completing the soul lessons surrounding the fall and the resulting experience of having their free will violated, so they could finally move off the wheel of reincarnation and onto the spiral of ascension as fifth density consciousness.

Another group emerged that was not quite ready to complete all karmic lessons. These souls grew tired of endless wars, conflict and misery and began moving into fourth density consciousness.

The souls stuck in third density, the ones who are working to overcome their remaining karma, and the ones ready for ascension, are all in embodiment on the Earth today and represent the three dominant timelines.

The Dominant Timeline of Enlightened Communities

About 20 to 25% of humanity has evolved to the point where continuously re-enacting the fall (and experiencing the resulting constant pain, misery, suffering, abuse, control and oppression) is no longer a soul lesson that needs to continue. This group is ready to complete all negative karma and enter the new Golden Age. They will get to have what they truly desire, a beautiful radiant Earth that no longer experiences constant wars and environmental degradation.

Most of this book is dedicated to this group and centers around the "how-to" regarding navigation through the difficult transition period and the rebuilding of the Earth after the third density souls have completed their embodiment here and have moved on.

The Dominant Timeline of Ascension

Approximately 15 to 30 million humans (about 0.3% of humanity) will likely choose the path of physical ascension in the years to come. As described many times throughout our writings, the ascension is instantaneous from a nonlinear perspective, but takes many years, or decades, from a linear time frame. Basically, ascension occurs through a quantum jump at the atomic level. However, because you have trillions of cells in your physical body, and bodies do not like sudden change, there is a master template program that gradually converts your cells into the crystalline light form. Therefore, the complete process of physical ascension will take 10, 20, 30 or more years to complete, depending upon your unique soul path.

As stated in "*Earth Changes and 2012*," physical ascension is vastly different than spiritual ascension. Almost all of you have experienced spiritual ascension, some of you many times. Spiritual ascension involves leaving the body behind and ascending in consciousness into the celestial planes. The celestial planes are the true heavens spoken of in your scriptures. Do not confuse them with the upper astral and lower etheric planes that can mimic the heavens in some respects.

Spiritual ascension happens when souls have completed their Earthly soul lessons to the extent that they no longer have a reason to reincarnate on Earth except to be a teacher and help souls awaken. Many yogis and saints have chosen spiritual ascension, such as Paramahansa Yogananda and Swami Muktananda.

Those souls who do not take their body with them into the higher realms during physical ascension may choose spiritual ascension instead. Because of the critical situation on Earth now and the anticipated transitional period of about 20 years, souls who choose spiritual ascension will likely elect to either assist humanity as spirit guides, or reincarnate on Earth during the new Golden Age with the specific purpose of helping the fourth density humans rebuild and grow.

Chapter 2 – The Nature of Time

The majority of you reading this book will become part of the ascending humans in the years to come and are in one of the three waves of ascension described earlier. Even if you choose not to transfigure your body into light and instead leave your present body behind with the intention of reincarnating in the New Earth, you will find the following chapters to be of immense benefit. At least, you will understand what the ascending souls are experiencing because one day you, too, will go through these stages of evolution.

In the following sections, we will describe in detail not only the physical ascension of humanity, but the changes to the structure of your society that were briefly visited in Chapter 1. This book is a "How To," as much as it is prophecy.

Remember, dear Creators, you have free will and are powerful, creative, spiritual beings. Therefore, do not fall into the trap of simply believing that everything described herein is inevitable. We encourage you to take an active part in the unfolding dynamics of the New Earth. This story is about you, the meek that are inheriting the Earth. If you were not already a member of the new humanity, you would not have been attracted to this material.

Once you embark upon this path, you cannot turn back. You have reached a critical stage in your unfoldment. Any attempts to return to comfortable, familiar territory will be unsuccessful. You will no longer desire your old way of living. None of it will appeal to you. It is as dead as last year's leaves. Let it go. Let it float silently into the void to be recycled into another wondrous creation.

We are the Founders. Good day.

CHAPTER 3
The Changes Within

Greetings, beloveds, we are the Founders. Now that you have had an overview of some of what to expect in the coming years, and have been briefed on the nature of time, we will go into detail on what you may experience in the years to come.

To recap, we are making some assumptions as we begin this chapter. First, we are assuming you are all members of the enlightened humans who are inheriting this beautiful planet. Second, a great many of you are also on the path of ascension. However, you will find that many of the issues described in this and the following chapters will relate to you regardless of your level of vibration.

Note: You have, by now, noticed that we often repeat ourselves. This is not bad editing on the part of the channel, but an intentional move designed to reinforce the more important ideas. Now, let us proceed.

The Catalysts for Change

In spiritual terms, a catalyst is a trigger mechanism for moving evolution forward. In some cases, a catalyst will trigger a mutation in the DNA or radical transformation in the consciousness of a species. On virtually every level of human experience, you have, at this time, catalysts prompting you to make changes at a fundamental level of your being.

From a purely third density perspective, your species cannot continue on its present course. The story given in Chapter 1 illustrates what will happen to the third density world if you repeatedly ignore the warning signs inherent within your lifestyle choices. To review briefly:

You are running out of pure, clean water and fresh organic food. Your climate is changing, partly from interference by humankind and partly from natural cycles. Your population is currently unable to feed itself and provide a basic standard of living for about one-fourth of its people. You continue to use fossil fuels and nuclear power even though you have had recent major accidents involving these products. You have fouled your air and water to the point that your beloved Earth is having difficulty correcting the problem. Your food is contaminated and contains dozens of chemicals your bodies do not know how to process. Your physical bodies have compromised immune systems due to stressful lifestyles. These stressors include constant noise, electromagnetic pollution from radio and mobile phone towers, bombardment with media and advertising, a pop culture that promotes consumerism and violence, a political system bought and paid for by special interests, corporate monopolies that genetically alter crops and promote excessive spraying of pesticides, a corrupted medical system that values profits over people, weapons of war that spray radioactive chemicals into the air (depleted uranium, etc.), weather modification substances sprayed into your atmosphere, hydraulic fracturing of shale to produce natural gas that pollutes the groundwater, constant small spills of petroleum products along with a few major spills, leaking nuclear reactors, depletion of the ozone layer, and exhaustion of natural resources to satisfy the ever-increasing cravings and desires for more, more, more.

The above paragraph ought to be enough of a catalyst to trigger major changes in behavior among human beings, but most continue to march off the cliff, perhaps taking quick note of a problem and occasionally considering a solution, but then rationalizing the issue away and going back to sleep. Souls are conditioned to believe they are mostly powerless and have very little say in what takes place in the world. This sense of powerlessness stems from identification with the body and ego mind complex. This identification with form, which began during the soul's descent into matter, is the primary reason nearly three-fourths of humanity will likely leave the Earth over the next 20 to 30 years.

From a fourth density perspective, your own souls are the catalysts behind the changes you are seeking to make. Many of you are what is commonly called "old souls" and have had enough of war, poverty, misery, suffering, control, oppression, etc. You want to learn new lessons of love, unconditional acceptance, responsibility for Mother Earth, and living harmoniously with the environment.

Even without the specter of environmental disaster, you would be unable to continue living a third density lifestyle. You are no longer interested in which brand of shaving cream or deodorant is best, or how to make more money than your neighbor. Long ago you put away the insane idea that the one with the most toys somehow "wins" in life. The things that excite you now involve personal growth, spiritual unfoldment and entering into deep, bonded, truly loving relationships with others who are also committed to their soul evolution.

As an enlightened human, you seek out experiences that will bring to the surface those patterns and issues that need to be healed and integrated. Of course, your human ego might still resist and even complain at times, but the dominant force in your life is the desire to grow into greater wisdom through compassionate service.

From outside the Earthly drama, there are a number of catalysts contributing to the changes. These catalysts go all the way to the Source of everything. You could say that there is a Divine fiat or commandment that all life on Earth shall evolve or go elsewhere. This is in answer to the call of Mother Earth herself, who is a living, conscious being existing on seven dimensions.

As the three portals of 2012, 2017 and 2030 (discussed earlier) begin to factor in to the equation, you find all these catalysts for growth converging in the present time period.

The Cause of the Darkness On Earth

The cause of darkness on Earth goes back to Original Cause. Because Earth has been a third density planet for millions of years, souls that incarnate here usually forget their Divine nature and become identified with materiality, at least to some extent. This has been part of the desire of souls exploring the lower densities – to become temporarily enmeshed in such worlds in order to experience them to their fullest. Unfortunately, many souls who desire to free themselves from identification with the material are finding it quite difficult. A lot of this difficulty stems from the fact that "laggard" souls have come to Earth and have kept the overall vibration here very low due to their slow learning curve or outright refusal to learn.

Our Creator, being infinitely compassionate, has given souls millions of years to learn lessons on Earth, but now the very life of lower density Earth is threatened by those souls who have refused to turn away from destructive behaviors. These are the dark ones who have been stuck in a negative view of reality for eons. From their distorted perspective, God is the enemy to be overcome through force and might. Deep within their consciousness is rage and terror associated with the original descent into matter (Original Cause). As a consequence of identifying with form, they have come to the erroneous conclusion that they are small, helpless, powerless beings all alone in a hostile universe. As a result of this belief in separation from God, they feel they must control and manipulate others in order to feel powerful and meaningful.

Most of you have been on Earth during the rise and fall of the significant civilizations, such as Pangaea, Lemuria, Atlantis and the present. Every time you have climbed to the heights of personal achievement, something has come along and seemed to sabotage your efforts. Sometimes this has been a so-called "natural" disaster, but more often it has been the result of invasion by negative extraterrestrials, or decay from within the culture itself. Usually, the so-called "civilized" world descended into warfare and oppressive, dictatorial regimes designed to keep people locked in fear and servitude.

Why do you think things fall apart just when it seems they are getting good?

The answer lies in the nature of denial and suppression of primal experiences. Most of you never completely resolved the feelings that arose during Original Cause. Fearful of reenacting the descent into darkness and compression, you locked that fear deep within your subconscious mind and pretended everything was just fine. Having this suppressed negativity did not make it go away. It still worked behind the scenes according to the law of attraction, meaning that your soul would attract negative experiences in order to mirror what was unresolved within the psyche.

Dear Creators, if you did not have unresolved psychological issues lurking within, you would not attract negative ETs, natural disasters, or leaders that betray you or try to control you.

Attempts by Avatars to Turn Things Around

How are these issues resolved? Until recently, it was very difficult to heal Original Cause and its myriad of associated disorders, such as fear of abandonment, guilt, shame, depression and despair.

Seeing the predicament you were in, teachers were sent to Earth to help you remember that you are more than a body-mind personality. They reminded you that you are powerful, creative, spiritual beings, capable of remembering your true magnificence and manifesting it on this planet.

These teachers became some of the strongest catalysts for change, even though many of them were met with great opposition. They became mirrors not only of that which you had carefully concealed within and were afraid to look at, but also mirrors of your greatness. However, instead of seeing your own greatness reflected in the avatars and holy men and women of times past, you fell to idolatry and worship, thinking that salvation comes from the blessing of the guru or whimsical granting of pardon or forgiveness by the master, as in the adage, "Christ died for your sins."

Believing that one manifestation of God in the form of a human soul is the key to salvation, you refused to look within for the answers and once again, you failed to move forward significantly along the spiral of evolution.

The Intricacies of Free Will

Most of the industrial and technological achievements made by humanity during the four great civilizations (Pangaea, Lemuria, Atlantis and the present) occurred due to intervention by ETs, and often by those star races that did not fully understand and respect human free will. In other words, they interfered with human evolution, often out of concern for your well-being, but with disregard for your soul lessons.

Due to the Creator's infinite compassion, it would not have made sense to deny some souls their lessons in order to save other souls. After all, many souls are young and immature and actually want to learn about war, poverty, misery, suffering, oppression, control and identification with materiality. A compassionate God would not deny them the privilege of using their free will to learn about these things. Therefore, a plan was set in motion to give all souls what they truly desire.

In order to achieve this, several new worlds have been set up to receive the souls who can no longer match the frequencies of the New Earth. As souls exit their human bodies, they will reincarnate on these other worlds and continue learning about war, poverty, misery, suffering, oppression, control and materiality.

Those souls who desire to live in true peace and prosperity will remain with the Earth, or in some cases ascend and go to other planets that accommodate peace and prosperity.

A small number of souls are ready to complete all their soul lessons as mortal humans, and these souls will go through the spiral of ascension in the years to come.

This is the most exciting time ever on Earth because the catalysts for change are converging and causing a major shift in all areas of life. Within a few short years, many of the hallowed institutions of the old ways will crumble, and new ways of life will be welcomed by those choosing to remain on Earth.

Spiritual Awakening

Those souls moving on into fourth and fifth densities will undergo a profound spiritual awakening. Since about 1950, at the start of the Galactic Shift, a lot of souls have been experiencing higher states of consciousness. For the most part, very few have been able to hold the higher frequencies due to the tremendous amount of negativity present on Earth.

You must remember, dear Creators, that Earth has been a melting pot for souls from all over the Universe, including many of the renegades and rejects from other worlds. Put another way, souls that do not fit into the order and structure of a particular world have often been sent to Earth because up until the 2012 portal shift, Earth had accepted souls from all levels of vibration.

Yes, you have souls from every conceivable level of consciousness here, from extremely ignorant to sublimely enlightened. You also have souls who have dedicated themselves to paths of darkness and so-called "evil." In this case, the word "evil" means, "Having a conscious intent to hold souls back on their spiritual evolution."

Because Earth's own survival is now threatened (from a lower density point of view), a series of Divine Dispensations (detailed in *"Earth Changes and 2012"*) have been granted, allowing the Earth to move into fourth density. This implies that only those souls vibrating at fourth density and above will be allowed to incarnate on Earth from this point forward (from December 21, 2012 onward).

Those souls who do decide to remain with the Earth are going through a spiritual awakening. For some, it begins with coming to a realization that there is more to life than the nine to five workplace and raising a family. The popularized rite of passage known as the "mid-life crisis" is an example of a partial spiritual awakening that occurs in much of your population. Simply put, after working hard for 10, 20 or 30 years and making their way up the corporate ladder, or perhaps raising a family and now the kids are grown up and out of the house, such souls start to ponder the meaning of it all.

The job that seemed so promising in the beginning now fails to fulfill an inner longing that the soul just cannot quite put his finger on. The one raising children might have a wonderful relationship with the grown kids, but feels there is now another purpose calling her. (We have used the traditional male and female roles here, but we are quite aware the roles can be reversed.)

Distractions from Your Spiritual Path

In some of your earlier tribal cultures, there was a time set aside for men and women to begin their spiritual paths (usually after working and raising children). Typically, there would be some rite of passage or ceremony honoring the various phases of tribal life. Often at a very early age, the men and women would go to work, hunting, gathering, or creating useful things for the tribe, and then at some point they would marry or bond and raise a family. Once the children reached a certain age, they would begin their spiritual rituals and rites. For women, it was often at menopause. In your modern cultures, you have lost much of the tribal ceremony and rites of passage.

In place of rites of passage, you have endless activities to keep you busy and focused on "getting ahead in the world." You might combine spiritual activities with other tasks or try to cram them into your busy schedule. It is not uncommon for us to meet students who are going to school at night, working during the day, raising a family, and going to church or some spiritual group whenever possible.

This, combined with constant media bombardment and social engagements, makes for a very stressful lifestyle.

Perhaps you take an hour or two off every Sunday to contemplate God or the Universe, and then it's back to the "daily grind" for another week.

The Soul Nudges the Personality Back Into Alignment

For many, spiritual awakening comes in a most unexpected way. As the body begins to rebel against the stressful lifestyle mentioned above, illness may result and force the soul to slow down and reprioritize.

Many a near-death experience has triggered spiritual awakening. Such souls often dedicate their lives to service after being given a "second lease on life." In most cases, near-death accidents and illnesses are the soul's last-ditch effort to awaken the soul to his or her true purpose and mission on Earth. Often such a soul has failed to listen and acknowledge the more subtle approaches the soul may have used in the past to get his or her attention.

Whether it is through mid-life crisis, sudden accident or illness, or near-death experience, a significant percentage of such souls begin to realize there is a greater purpose underlying the endless busyness of life.

Very advanced souls may not need to create such dire circumstances in order to begin the awakening process. They might be predisposed toward the more esoteric sciences. In some cases, they may have been fortunate enough to be able to choose parents who were already metaphysically inclined and thereby grew up around holistic healers and trance mediums. In other cases, they naturally gravitate toward individuals and groups who are on a spiritual path.

The Earth changes now taking place offer an exceptional opportunity for awakening. Some souls are "seeing the writing on the wall" and are realizing a radical new approach to life is being called for at this time. In desperation, they turn from the crumbling third density world, looking for a way out of the mess. This is where the Lightworkers of the world come in handy. Just as confused souls are looking for the Light, the Lightworkers are often looking for their unique way of expressing their gifts in the world.

Before we go into more detail on the ways the Lightworkers can help, let us take a look at some of the ways Mother Earth will be healing herself in the years to come.

The Purging on Earth

Virtually all of your major religions portray a time of tribulation, apocalypse, Armageddon, or judgment day. Many erroneously postulate that God is going to separate the righteous from the sinner, or wheat from the chaff, or meek and mild from the aggressors. It is understandable that in your limited perception, you would believe that some outside force is capable of passing judgment upon your species.

The natural laws of the Universe, which include the higher spiritual laws as well as the laws of Newtonian physics, Einsteinian time/space, quantum theory, superstring theory, metaphysics, genetics, etc., are all part of the workings of the multidimensional Omniverse, or Multiverse, or Universe of Universes.

While it is overly simplistic to say that disobedience of God's laws is the cause of suffering, it is certainly true that ignorance of natural laws is a major contributor to the misery of the majority of humanity.

When your human body gets sick, its defenses generate antibodies and all sorts of biochemical reactions, such as fever, to repel the invading organisms.

When your Mother Earth gets overrun with ignorant souls who seek to plunder her resources and dominate her life forms, she mounts defenses as well. Life seeks balance. When things get too far out of balance, correction must be made. This is not the wrath of God, but is the consequence of ignoring or fighting against natural laws.

A soul that has not yet learned how to levitate and fly is subject to the law of gravity. If he falls off a building and hurts his body, does he blame God? Does he believe God is angry with him and is punishing him? Or does he simply need to learn about the law of gravity and have respect for it until such time as he learns other laws that supersede it.

Such is the case with humanity. The following is a list of the catalysts and causes for the purging which is now in the process of occurring on planet Earth:

Table #1 – Reasons for the Purging Taking Place on Earth
*Mother Earth seeks to balance herself *The Lightworkers desire to live in peace and harmony *Souls are completing their lessons of karma/reincarnation *Divine Dispensations have been granted *The Earth is moving into the three portals *The Galactic Shift is underway *Benevolent ETs are interacting with Earth *Natural periodic mutations are being triggered *Souls desire to be free of misery and suffering *Humanity has discovered how to destroy itself/the planet

Your Mother Earth has fourth density as its dominant mode of expression starting on December 21, 2012. That means all souls who reside upon her must be aligned with the fourth density principles of co-creation, cooperation, harmonious living, respect for the environment, desire to grow and evolve, and awareness of themselves as conscious beings on a spiral of evolution and ascension.

Souls who are not able or willing to embrace the above qualities will have a short time in which to get their affairs in order before exiting their third density bodies and taking up residence on another third density planet through the process of death and reincarnation.

This period of time will likely encompass the three portals concluding in 2030. In a few cases, souls may be granted additional time to get their affairs in order, but all incoming (reincarnating) souls from 2012 onward will already be vibrating at fourth density or higher. In other words, Earth will only accept those souls who have a vibratory state above 3.50 on this channel's frequency scale.

The changes in the chemical composition of Earth and her atmosphere, along with solar storms and flares, and the electromagnetic fluctuations entering Earth from the center of the Galaxy, will all contribute to mutations in the cells of human beings. For those who have raised their vibration and kept their immune systems intact, these mutations will be welcomed and accepted as the catalysts for change that bring the soul to a higher state of being. For those who refuse to grow and evolve, who are deeply attached to materialism, or who do not feel ready on a soul level to embrace the New Earth, the mutations will cause immune system failure, opening the body to attack from exotic viruses, bacteria, molds, fungi, toxic chemicals, radiation, etc.

Our compassionate Creator is truly giving every soul what it desires. Souls who are not ready for fourth density Earth will not have to suffer as they vainly try to learn lessons they are not ready for. The only suffering involved in this plan is that incurred as a result of resistance by the ego. Those who are already in fourth density will finally get to experience the joy of living in a world of plenty where human well-being is the highest priority along with the well-being of Mother Earth.

Immune System Failure in Third Density Souls

As you know, dear Creators, the immune system is your body's defense mechanism against harmful organisms, including viruses, bacteria, molds, fungi, parasites, toxic chemicals, radiation and electromagnetic pollution. In your modern world, you have plenty of invaders ready to take up residence in your body.

Immune systems are depleted through many factors, including stressful lifestyles, poor diet, lack of exercise, associating with negatively-oriented people, and especially holding within the self core negative belief systems and unresolved emotional issues.

You are, perhaps, familiar with the concept of *default*. Spiritually speaking, to default means to go along with the prevailing energy and consciousness of that which surrounds you. In most cases, that means that you will become more like the third density negative souls because they are still the dominant group on your planet.

If you do nothing, meaning that you do not meditate or engage in holistic healing practices and do not surround yourself with positively-oriented people, then most likely your vibratory level will drop to near the average level of humans on Earth. Therefore, you must be proactive on your spiritual path. This means seeking out those who have a high level of vibration, consciously surrounding yourself with beautiful, high-frequency places, objects and energies, such as melodious classical or New Age music, positively-charged crystals, flower gardens, flower essences, vibrant trees, etc.

It is not absolutely necessary to have a structured meditation practice, but there must be some quiet time each day when you can retreat from the busy world. A walk in nature is a wonderful and easy way to get centered. It not only gives you exercise, but also helps quiet the mind.

If you are aware of negative psychological patterns, core negative beliefs and traumatic emotions from your past, then some form of daily therapy or healing is called for. This does not mean you must spend every free moment processing or analyzing, but it does mean staying conscious every time one of these patterns asserts itself and interferes with your enjoyment of life.

It is important to watch feelings as they arise, without judging them. Simply allow them to be. Do not label the feelings. If you go deeply into the now moment with a feeling, you recognize it as a unique pattern of energy. It might be a very strong energy that ripples through the body, or makes it tingle, or creates fatigue and soreness. Again, be careful not to label the feelings. Try to remain with the energy movement itself, rather than the descriptive words.

As you take care of yourself daily, your immune system will increase in strength and remain strong and you will survive the Earth changes physically. In fact, you will thrive. As the portals come and go, each one will strengthen your immune system if you are aligned with the frequencies coming into the Earth from the higher dimensions.

For those souls who do not take care of themselves, the constantly increasing stresses of the modern world will take a toll on the immune system. In addition, the mutations associated with the opening of the portals will greatly accelerate this decline.

Many souls will decide that they cannot make the transition into fourth density, and illness or disease will manifest in the body as a precursor to departing the Earth plane a few weeks, months or years later. This is the soul saying, "It's time to get your affairs in order. We have a new assignment for you somewhere else."

Often the ego/personality is not in agreement with the soul's decision and fights it. In the case of a third density soul with a declining immune system, this will often take the form of lingering chronic illness and gradual deterioration of bodily faculties. The body and soul are in conflict. The will of the ego/personality may try to force the body to heal because it does not want to die. Yet the soul gently keeps pushing at the body to give up the fight.

Due to free will, a soul can change its mind and decide to stay, but the longer the ego/personality and soul are at odds, the harder it is to reconcile the situation.

Your world is not set up to handle large numbers of souls with declining health conditions. Already, your medical institutions are on the verge of breakdown. The cumulative effects of many drugs exacerbate the problem, as does the financial drain on individuals and governments due to the need for constant care of souls from doctors and nurses.

In the years to come on third density Earth, it will become harder and harder to find clean air, food and water, and this, coupled with large-scale immune system failure, will create a negative spiral, especially in the cities where people live in close quarters. Diseases that once seemed non-contagious will spread due to the declining immune function. Viruses will mutate prior to, during and after the opening of the portals. Toxic metal and radiation buildup will take their toll.

Due to free will, we cannot say with certainty exactly how many souls will exit the Earth and how fast they will go. It appears that the population of Earth will reach a peak of slightly less than eight billion, sometime around 2015, and then start declining. This will be due not only to a higher number of deaths, but also to declining birth rates. Many of the same factors that destroy the human immune system will also create partial or total sterility in young females. Included are many of your genetically modified grains and the pesticides used to grow them as well as many of the chemicals used in processed foods. These pollutants have a cumulative effect and many scientists are not yet aware of the long-term consequences of genetic modification and certain commonly used chemical food additives.

Since 1950, about five percent of humanity has turned away from the third density path of deterioration and into the fourth density path of enlightenment. While that may not seem like much, it involves over three hundred million souls. A few million more are likely to make the transition from third to fourth density during the portal openings.

If you live in the country, the slow-motion cataclysm of immune system failure will not be all that noticeable. Of course, many of your neighbors will get "terminal" illnesses or complain of chronic conditions. However, this is already occurring to some degree. You might simply notice that a lot more people are coming down with unexplained illnesses or new forms of cancer.

For those in the cities, the effect will be a lot more dramatic. In some cases, dead bodies will pile up in the streets because hospitals, morgues and cemeteries will become overwhelmed.

It is important to remind you, dear Creators, that this is only a tragedy from a third density point of view. The departing souls will be getting what they truly desire – a fresh start on a planet more suited to their level of vibration. The transition period will be a bit rocky as their egos slowly give up the battle to stay alive.

Your response as enlightened souls is to give them as much love and compassion as you can. Forgive them for not taking better care of themselves. There is no fault or blame here. Just affirm that every soul on Earth is taking the right steps to ensure his or her highest and best soul growth and happiness.

Chapter 3 – The Changes Within

The Healing of Fourth Density Souls

Many of you in fourth density have had nagging health issues that just do not seem to go away. There is a common reason for this, but it is not easy to explain in your language. Nevertheless, let us try at this time.

You may have heard the expression, "You are surrogates for the birth of the New Earth." What does this actually mean?

Some of you have used the expression, "I am taking on the karma of Mother Earth and that is why I have been unable to lose weight or clear these health issues."

These are true statements from a fourth density perspective. To some extent, you are acting as mirrors for other souls to help them see what is taking place within the self. Because you are all connected, you cannot really be separate from those who are suffering and so you do take on a small piece of that suffering. A part of you aches when they ache and hurts when they hurt. While you cannot separate yourself from suffering, you can stop identifying with it. A healthy way of stating it is thus:

I am a powerful, creative, healthy spiritual being temporarily experiencing the suffering of humanity.

You are aware of the suffering, you feel it, you know it, and to some extent you become it. But you never forget that you are much more than the suffering. In other words, you can fully experience something without believing that it is the truth of who you are. Instead of saying, "I am suffering," you would say, "I have chosen to experience suffering."

The way to heal the suffering of the world and the maladies within your own body/mind/personality is to shine the Light of compassion directly into the darkest places within and without. As you expose the dark places to Light, they will either depart or move toward the Light and become absorbed by it. If they depart, then bless them on their way and return to your Self. Ultimately, all dark negative beliefs are illusions and will disappear in the bright Light of Truth.

Table 2 below details the most common blocks to enlightenment. You will note that most of these are related and are often the same state of consciousness expressed in different ways.

Table 2 – The Most Common Blocks to Enlightenment

--Belief in Separation from God or Source
--Identification with the Ego (or Physical Body/Mind)
--Self-Judgment (Belief that Something is Wrong with Self)
--Guilt and Shame
--Fear of God (Fear of Life)
--Belief that One is Not Good Enough
--Belief that One is Unworthy
--Belief that Life is a Struggle
--Fear of Death
--Belief that One is Not Safe (Demand for Outer Security)
--Fear of Harm or Physical Pain (Fear of Darkness)
--Belief that There is Not Enough (Belief in Scarcity)
--Need for Approval from Others
--Fear of Rejection (Fear of Being Alone)
--Resentment (Holding Grievances)
--Emotional Attachments
--Habits and Addictions
--Fear of Disappointment (Unrealistic Expectations)
--Blind Acceptance of Doctrine or Dogma
--Attachment to Religious Beliefs
--Distractions of the World (Laziness, Amnesia)
--Possession by Negative Entities
--Possession by Negative Thought Forms of the World
--Etheric Imprints and Implants from Past Lifetimes
--Childhood and Past Life Trauma
--Lack of Discipline & Motivation

We are sure you can add more of your own to this list.

Chapter 3 – The Changes Within

Recommended Healing and Therapy Techniques

There are many techniques for healing, and we will not go into detail on every one of them, but we will share a few of our favorites at this time. Keep in mind that the optimal frequency of application of these techniques will vary from soul to soul, so feel free to experiment with the regularity of practice.

In some cases, these techniques can be practiced on your own, while in other cases, you can purchase a CD or Mp3 file and listen without the need to employ a health professional. In other cases, the techniques are best conducted by a licensed or trained therapist or healer. We encourage you to use all these approaches to maximize your well-being.

Alpha-Theta Meditation

This is a basic technique that is at the root of guided visualization and hypnotherapy. The idea is that by taking a soul into a deeply meditative state, the brain waves of that soul will enter the alpha or theta range. It has been shown that souls emanating alpha and theta brain waves are much more creative and able to direct energy than souls emanating beta brain waves. During an alpha-theta meditation, the client is taken into deep meditation using a hypnotherapy technique commonly known as "standard induction." Specific autosuggestions are given to help the client relax, including the visualization of a favorite place in nature.

In more sophisticated versions of this technique, the client is instructed to interact with a human version of his or her own higher self that acts as a spirit guide during the process.

While in this deep state of mind, a number of additional techniques can be administered, including the visualization of specific goals and objectives as well as spiritual healing. Emphasis is placed on the safety of the technique and portions of the induction are specifically targeted toward maximum safety. Often an intention is stated before the session. Always included in the intention is that the experience will be for the client's highest and best soul growth, happiness and well-being.

Reprogramming the Subconscious

This is a specific application of Alpha-Theta meditation whereby the client goes into a deep state and consciously uses reprogramming techniques to clear out negative core beliefs from the subconscious mind. One such technique involves the use of a computer screen to bring up negative programming. The user then hits the "Delete" key to remove the beliefs that no longer serve him or her.

To some, that may seem like an overly simplistic approach, but remember, dear Creators, that the subconscious mind takes things literally. If it is being instructed to delete a program, it does so faithfully (under the right therapeutic conditions).

Once core negative beliefs are removed, positive autosuggestions are added. Affirmations must always be in present tense. The present tense can be in the form of active or passive verbs. An example of an active autosuggestion would be: "I am now experiencing my true innocence." An example of a passive autosuggestion would be: "I am innocent."

Most reprogramming techniques should be repeated often to increase their effectiveness since clients usually receive constant reinforcement of negative programming from the world that can reintroduce the old negative beliefs (remember our discussion on "default").

Forgiveness and Release

This is another simple technique, but very powerful. The client is instructed to think about one to three people that he or she may not have completely forgiven. The litmus test for knowing whether or not complete forgiveness has been achieved is simple: If you feel anything other than pure unconditional love for a person when you think of him or her, then you have not completely forgiven that person.

Pay particularly close attention to the way you feel in your body when you visualize the person you are seeking to forgive. Look for tightness in the chest, a sinking feeling in the stomach, energy patterns of sadness or regret, or perhaps just a slight irritation. Also look for egotistical arrogance, such as an inner response, "I am so glad to be me. I would not want to be this person for all the tea in China." While that may be true, usually thoughts of this nature are laden with judgments that you are somehow superior to the person you are forgiving. In this case, you might really be thinking, "I forgive the sorry wretch." If your forgiveness is not genuine, go back to deep breathing and ask your God Presence within to help you reach true forgiveness. Then return to the process.

In the forgiveness technique, clients visualize the souls they are forgiving and imagine such souls are sitting in front of them at about arm's length. Then there is a withhold process and the soul in front of the client is lifted into the heavens on a golden beam of light.

After the processes with others are completed, forgiveness is directed toward the self. This process is done differently and involves declaring your forgiveness in front of everyone you have ever known in this lifetime or in past lifetimes.

Remember, forgiveness is to benefit *you*. If it also benefits the souls you are forgiving, that's great, but those souls have free will and can choose to accept or reject your forgiveness.

In some cases, you can do this process face to face with other souls, but in a lot of cases, the recipients of the forgiveness will not be aware that you are doing the process, nor should you tell them. Their higher selves will be aware of your intentions and will either respond or not, depending on free will. It is not your concern whether or not the recipients actually benefit from your forgiveness or not. Your concern is to release yourself from emotional attachments, psychic "hooks" and etheric and astral "cording."

Ultimately, all forgiveness is self-forgiveness, for ultimately all souls are reflections of your one shared Self.

Gestalt Therapy with Spiritual Healing

This technique is a combination of traditional therapeutic psychology (psychotherapy) and spiritual healing. The therapist asks the client to remember a time when the issues that are being worked on were particularly apparent. This usually involves trauma from early childhood, but it could involve an event from young adulthood as well. An example would be sexual abuse during the period from age 7 through 10. The client then "creates" or "personifies" a version of the self that experienced these events, and dialogues with that self. That self is given various spiritual healing techniques, as well as general psychological counseling, including affirmative statements such as "You are totally and completely innocent. You have done nothing wrong. You are a beautiful, creative being of Light."

Depending on the level of advancement of the soul undergoing therapy, it might be possible to include forgiveness processes and the sending of God's golden, radiant, loving Light to the perpetrator of the abuse and witnesses who failed to intervene.

This technique is not a substitute for counseling with a qualified professional psychologist or psychiatrist, but often helps speed up the recovery process and gives the client a broader, spiritual perspective on early lifetime trauma.

The gist of this technique is that very often the "inner children" of a soul's past did not receive the love and nurturing they truly wanted, and so the adult self in therapy takes the role of a loving, nurturing parent and gives the inner children the love they so desperately wanted during childhood (and still want as an adult).

Rebirthing

Rebirthing is a conscious breathing process based on Kriya yoga, which was first brought to Earth by the ascended master Babaji (known in various places by various names). This 9th density avatar taught a series of breathing rhythms and disciplines designed to raise the frequency of the physical body. Rebirthing is a somewhat diluted, but still highly effective, offshoot of Babaji's work that was brought to Earth by Leonard Orr and later modified by various practitioners.

Rebirthing involves deep, connected breathing rhythms that often trigger cellular memories from the birth process because a soul's first traumatic experience of life on Earth usually involved coming through the birth canal into physicality.

Personal sessions with a trained rebirther are typically 60 to 90 minutes and may include affirmations and other basic guidance techniques in addition to keeping the client breathing in "circular" rhythms.

You can practice a short form without a therapist, simply by closing your eyes, relaxing, and breathing fully, freely and deeply with no pauses between inhale and exhale. Do this for a couple of minutes. If you start to experience intense energy, slow the breathing down a bit and come out of the process. If you get sleepy, speed the breathing rhythm up until you feel energized. The important thing is to stay aware of your breath and the energy patterns moving through your body. If your mind gets too active, simply watch it as you move your attention back to the breath.

Resistance to life force energy is the main cause of psychological pain. When you resist this natural breathing rhythm, the intense energy generated by the increase in the flow of prana through the body can be experienced as painful. If this occurs, temporarily slow down the breathing rhythm and see if you can perceive the pain as simply intense energy hitting blockages in the body. Learn to detach as much as possible from the patterns. Just observe them without judging or labeling. One form of rebirthing has you change your perception of intense energy into a feeling of pleasure instead of pain. You will discover, if you go deeply enough, that pleasure and pain are two sides of the same phenomenon.

Chapter 3 – The Changes Within

Soul Retrieval and Integration

There are various soul retrieval techniques being taught by counselors worldwide. The simplest of these involves reconnecting with those souls that may have triggered fragmentation of pieces of the client's soul. These might include family relationships, traumatic interactions with intimate partners, rape, incest, and any experience whereby the soul experiencing the trauma dissociated parts of the self in order to escape the extreme pain associated with the trauma.

The simplest form of soul retrieval literally involves projecting the mental body to the time and place where the "perpetrator" is currently residing (whether or not the conscious mind knows the location and circumstances), and asking for those soul fragments back. The "perpetrator" holding the fragments cannot actually refuse to give them back because that would be a violation of free will, but if the "victim" believes he or she is powerless to take the fragments back, it will be more difficult to do so. Various visualizations can often accompany this technique.

After retrieving the soul fragments lodged in other souls, the client will then seek to return the fragments of other souls that are lodged in the client's own body.

Sometimes soul fragments are held in the chakras (as etheric body imprints) and at other times there can be concentrated areas of physical energy (implants) usually associated with the astral body, which are essentially traumatic events embedded in the cells. By breathing deeply and visualizing the returning of these fragments, areas that are physically inflicted can begin to improve.

Etheric and Astral Body Depossession

Release of soul fragments in the astral level of the self is akin to depossession, or release of entities, thought forms and negative energy patterns. Letting go of cords, filaments, threads and hooks of energy belonging to other souls can be done through visualization, affirmation, invocation, chanting, and energetic movement (such as aura clearing and chakra balancing).

Not all depossessions are simple and straightforward. If the client has a karmic connection with the entity or entities involved, they will not be easily removed. In that case, it may be necessary to investigate the present and past life connections between the souls involved in the karmic relationship.

There are various ascended masters and archangels that specialize in soul integration and healing. You can, for example, ask Archangel Michael to clear all negative energies, entities and thought forms from the astral and etheric bodies.

If you are experiencing repeated attacks by astral entities, there are more forceful techniques available. You can contact the channel for more information on astral depossession.

Timeline Healing

This is a process whereby certain aspects of your self go back in time to heal other aspects that have experienced trauma or negative programming. All timeline healing therapies are based on the quantum physics principle of nonlocality. One way of stating this principle is as follows: You have an infinite number of selves, one for every moment in Creation, and there are an infinite number of moments. All these selves exist in this eternal now moment.

Some scientists have postulated that the Universe blinks on and off millions of times every second, which is essentially true. Every "blink" contains a soul experience, however brief it might seem to third density consciousness.

Those "blinks" or past life selves that experienced trauma have received emotional scars, astral implants, etheric imprints and causal body blockages that tend to carry over into future lifetimes (or in the case of early childhood trauma in this lifetime, they carry over into adulthood).

In timeline healing, the soul is guided into a deep meditation and is taken back in time to heal the traumatized selves. This is accomplished by using a standard induction process similar to hypnotherapy, along with guided imagery and affirmative statements. The aspects of self that go back in time are the meditative Light body and the golden radiant God Presence. To the past life self, these two higher aspects appear as shimmering beings of golden light, similar to angels. In some cases, the aspects of the self traveling back in time might choose to identify themselves as angels sent by God to give a healing to the past self. (Often, the past self has no way of conceptualizing the idea of future versions of itself going back in time to give it a healing.)

Various healing techniques are included during the visitation with the past self. It is important to note that the aspects going back in time are not changing the physical details of the past self's experience, as this would be a violation of the free will of other souls involved in the past self's creations. Instead, the purpose is to change the past self's experience of what happened and to remove the emotional scars, astral implants, etheric imprints and causal body blockages that resulted.

Once the healing is complete, the higher aspects of the client return to present time and the soul now has a new timeline that includes the healing that was received by the past self.

Chapter 3 – The Changes Within

If the process does not go deep enough, it still works because the superficial version of this technique is the psychological process of "reframing," which is often used by therapists to give people the happy childhood they always wanted but never received in the original third density linear past.

When the timeline healing process does go deep enough, it is possible for the soul to "remember" receiving the healing, especially if the timeline visited involves early childhood in this lifetime. This is called "closing the time loop." This channel has had a number of clients exclaim "A-ha!" when it finally becomes clear who the golden beings were that appeared when he or she was a young child. Now, later in adulthood, the timeline healing process has answered that question.

Reverse Timeline Healing

This technique is essentially the opposite of regular timeline healing in that the journey back in time undertaken by the meditative Light body of a soul is to a period in that soul's experience that was particularly enjoyable and empowering, rather than traumatic. The idea here is to bring the happy, powerful, successful self that was experienced at some point in the past, forward in time to the present, so that the energy can be accessed in the present.

This is more than simply recalling a pleasant memory. The meditative Light body and God Presence actually go back in time and retrieve some of the wonderful energy of a past experience and then bring it forward in time and overlay it on the present physical body of the client.

The client then uses this powerful, creative, happy energy to project forth his or her desires into the world. The technique is particularly useful for creating/manifesting specific things in life, such as the best possible career or business, or more loving relationships. Reverse timeline healing is based on the law of attraction. By putting out happy and loving energy into the world, it will return to the soul in various ways.

Also emphasized in this technique is the fact that the most powerful and creative energies are emanated from the heart and solar plexus, rather than the mind. The mind is simply the mechanical device used to carry out the desires of the soul (or ego as the case may be).

Part of reverse timeline healing involves ways of dealing with the ego when it tries to interfere with the intentions of the soul, as it invariably will.

Future Timeline Linking

This is a relatively new technique given to this channel by the Arcturians, in which a link is created to specific future selves. Once again, it is based on the principles of quantum physics and specifically, the uncertainty principle. Until free will directs a soul's intention toward a specific goal or outcome, there are an infinite number of possible future timelines spreading out from the present moment like branches of a very large tree. As soon as the soul decides on a desired outcome, the possible timelines are narrowed down to a specific optimum path. Of course, there are still an infinite number of possible paths to the intersection point of manifestation in the future, but now the intersection point is established, meaning that there is a discrete and very real future self with which the soul can interact.

Once the future self is established, dialogue is opened between the present and future selves. The future self, in essence, gives the present self advice on how to reach him or her. For example, if there is a specific goal of the present self, the future self will essentially say, "This is how I achieved that goal. First I did this and then I did that," etc.

There can be an ongoing relationship between the present and future selves to keep the present self on course. The future self becomes just like a spirit guide or benevolent ET and can be invoked in a similar manner. This is similar to shamanic techniques in some traditions.

Each of the above techniques can be facilitated by this channel, or he will be glad to refer you to someone who is qualified to guide you through these processes. As always, it is not our intention to make you dependent on a therapist or healer. You have the greatest healer within you already. The purpose of a practitioner is to help you get in touch with your own inner healer, your God Self.

As the fourth density souls clear their negativity, many will be ready to move onto the ascension spiral. The following section is specifically for those souls who are already on the path of ascension. For the rest of you reading this (who are vibrating at fourth density), sooner or later you will also begin the following processes.

Biological Changes in Ascending Souls

We are going to detail the process of ascension from a biological point of view. While ultimately no outer event can or will determine the outcome of your ascension, the portals of 2012, 2017 and 2030 will have a tremendous positive impact on your progress. You could say, at the risk of being overly simplistic, that 2012 will be about a fundamental psychological shift in consciousness, 2017 will be more of a cellular shift, and 2030 will accentuate the societal shift. All of these catalytic or trigger events will propel the ascension process forward at great speed.

Many of you are understandably doubtful about the claims being made that suggest you will be able to resurrect your physical bodies, make them disease free, and end the aging process. You are even more skeptical about youthing, the ability to make the body look and feel younger. Yet even your mainstream scientists have acknowledged that these things are possible. What they fail to realize is that no amount of tinkering with genetics or introduction of anti-aging drugs will make much difference unless the soul truly desires to participate in the New Earth.

Your bodies are already changing. The first thing you will notice is that there is a direct correlation between how you feel emotionally, and the physical state of your health. While this may seem obvious to some, usually there has been a time delay between how you feel and what your body manifests as its state of health. That delay will shorten dramatically as you move through these portals.

For example, if you think a positive, uplifting thought, your body usually feels better immediately, but any illness or imbalance you may be carrying in your cells usually takes a lot longer to dissipate as a result of your positive thoughts. If you have a lot of negativity in your subconscious mind, it will take a great many positive thoughts to have much of an impact on your physical health.

As you go through these accelerating experiences, your subconscious mind will rapidly empty itself of old programming and conditioning. It will no longer take months or even years to reverse an illness or create a new state of physical health. While this is wonderful news to most of you, it also means that the adage, "You cannot afford the luxury of a negative thought," will be truer than ever.

This channel has often responded to the question, "What will actually happen as we move through the portals?" with the following: "Your state of consciousness will be magnified hundreds, if not thousands of times." You could say that this is a corollary of our above discussion. Your thoughts and feelings will manifest not only more quickly than ever, but with much higher amplitude and magnitude.

Changing Your Consciousness and Healing Your Body

The most important task facing you as Lightworkers is to do whatever is necessary to create a powerful, positive state of consciousness as you move through the portals. So how do you actually achieve this? The following exercise will assist you in creating the state of consciousness you truly desire to magnify and amplify.

To keep this practical, imagine going through your day and having a variety of different experiences. People come and go from your sphere of influence. Some are positively-oriented and some are negatively-oriented. As you encounter each one, you either remain clear, calm and centered and do not let their state of consciousness affect you, or you might be swayed, ever so slightly, by their energy fields. If you spend the day alone, you are still subject to your own thoughts, as well as the psychic "soup" in the atmosphere of Earth. Those are the thoughts continuously bombarding you through the astral and etheric planes. So no matter where you live, your emotional state and quality of thinking will vary, usually from extremely happy to extremely agitated. It is important to keep track of the ups and downs you experience in an "average" day. Notice not only your base feelings, but your reactions to how you feel and what you think about how you feel.

Begin by resolving to eliminate ALL judgments or negative reactions to your daily experience. Refrain from labeling your state as "good" or "bad." It just *is*. Once you have entered a state of complete acceptance for what you are thinking or feeling, just observe your level of vibration. Ask yourselves, "Does this level of vibration serve me and my mission and purpose for being on the Earth? Am I allowing my natural unfoldment and evolution to happen, or am I fighting, resisting, or trying to control my evolution in some way?" Remember, dear Creators, pure awareness is an active state, not passive. At any time, you can actively observe what is taking place within your own consciousness.

Once you have determined, with no judgment whatsoever, that your present state of consciousness has a lower vibration than what is desired by your soul, then immediately begin connecting with your golden, radiant, God Presence within, your 12th density Self that exists at all times and in all spaces right now. Ask that Self to take over the situation and direct your life. Ask it to purge the body of all discordant vibrations, negative thoughts and undesirable feelings. Remember, you are not judging these feelings. You are merely observing that they no longer serve you. In fact, most of these thoughts and feelings are probably not yours. They likely belong to your parents, spouses, friends, or the disgruntled employee across the room. Almost all of the negative things you experience are fed by the constant stream of negativity permeating the astral planes of Earth.

Place a golden shield of Light around your body and see every cell cleansed, purified and healed of any and all negativity. Send unconditional Love to all parts of yourself. Pay particular attention to any places in your body that feel tense, tight, numb, tired, or in any way out of sorts. Use the affirmation, "*Every day and in every way I am bringing more and more Divine Loving Light into my physical body.*" Another good affirmation is, "*I am fully and completely releasing everything that is not in accord with my highest and best soul growth, happiness and well-being.*"

In the beginning, you will likely forget to do these exercises. The amnesia and negativity on planet Earth has been here for millions of years. It takes a great deal of patience and persistence to overcome the negative inertia. However, as you go through this book and practice these techniques, you are doing just that.

You are making tremendous headway. Every day, more and more Light is indeed streaming into this little planet, this little jewel in the heavens. In addition to our collective group (the Founders), there are millions of beings in the higher planes directing their love and wisdom into your astral and etheric planes. This high vibrational energy then percolates down into the physical Earth.

Once you have done the exercises given herein, notice once again how you feel. Let go of any belief systems that no longer serve you, including the belief that enlightenment requires years of struggle and sacrifice. Let go of the belief that you cannot heal your own body. It matters not the nature of the illness, disease or disability. Even birth defects can be healed, but it requires a radical shift in consciousness in most cases. Entertain the possibility that you *can* and *will* be free of any maladies that seem to beset you.

As you go through the portals, the doubts will fall away. You will become certain that you are on the right path. You will simply *know* that your requests for healing are being granted. You will see positive, tangible results on every level of your being. Healing *will* happen. You can be sure of it. Not only are you coming to the end of your own karmic journey, but the entire planet is purging and clearing old karma at a record pace. Every day you spend on Earth is lighter than the day before, despite appearances. You have many teachers on your planet correctly postulating that the reason things look more and more negative is because all negativity is coming to the surface now to be healed. How could hundreds of enlightened teachers be wrong? They are not. You are healing. Ask your God Self to remove ALL doubt regarding this wonderful fact.

In order to move yourself out of misery and suffering, you must end denial and face squarely the issues in front of you. If any person, place or thing seems to anger or upset you, give thanks that the lesson is right in your face, ready to be healed. Resolve to heal it, no matter what. Call forth all your strength and resolve. Ask your spirit guides to help. Know that you are now making a choice to release the anger, fear and sadness (or various forms of these feelings) around this issue. Send Love to yourself. Be compassionate. Bring in a little humor if necessary. Lighten up.

Does this mean healing the physical body is easy? No. In most cases, it is a difficult challenge. But your success in doing this is inevitable because of the path upon which you have placed yourself. If you were not ready to heal yourself, you would not have attracted this lesson. Even if it appears you have failed, or do not feel you are ready to confront the issues, or simply want to run away and forget the whole thing, make sure you still have compassion for yourself. It is really okay. No, you cannot put off the lesson forever, or even for very long, but accept the fact that you might feel overwhelmed and not ready to heal completely. Then resolve that tomorrow will be different. Of course, do not use this strategy every day, or it will always be tomorrow. After a couple of days of putting it off, resolve that today will be the day. You *are* ready. Welcome your new-found willingness to be healed and done with it. It is time to move on to greater things.

Note: There will be some of you that are not able to heal your physical bodies during this cycle. This does not mean you are failures, only that your soul wants an additional lifetime to complete its lessons and enter into enlightenment. If you lose your body during the Earth changes, you will likely reincarnate into the new Golden Age and experience childhood during a far gentler and wiser era. That means you will likely receive much better education, filled with love and compassion, than you received in this lifetime.

For the rest of you, there will be a sense of two steps forward and one step backward. Some aspect of your lower bodies will be healed, only to have another aspect rise up to challenge you. Although it might seem like there are an endless list of things to be healed, you will eventually get to the point where your healthy self will be the dominant force in your life and your unhealed parts will be a small minority of your One Holy Self. Then it will be easy to send love and compassion to those aspects that are still going through challenges. You will be able to welcome them back into your One Being.

Chapter 3 – The Changes Within

The Merkabah Vehicle of Light

Let us now discuss one of the most misunderstood topics among the Lightworkers, that of the Merkabah Vehicle of Light.

The Merkabah is a geometric pattern of Light energy that forms around ascending souls at various stages in the process of converting their form from a mortal carbon-based to an immortal silicon-based body.

The Merkabah is already partially formed around fourth density souls. Its primary purpose is to protect them from unfavorable environmental conditions during ascension. It can be likened to a chrysalis around a caterpillar that is becoming a butterfly.

As the soul moves through the various stages of ascension, the Merkabah becomes more solid and easily recognizable to clairvoyants and those already vibrating at fifth density. Eventually, the Merkabah serves to enable ascended souls to travel through time and space without the need for a mechanical transport device such as a spacecraft. However, the fully-formed Merkabah does not manifest itself until the later stages of ascension.

It is not necessary to learn any particular techniques for building the Merkabah vehicle. In fact, it is rather useless because the building of the Merkabah is an automated process that occurs naturally during ascension. The only value we see in doing a Merkabah meditation or process is that it helps focus you on the ascension process and, after all, what you focus on you draw into experience. So being aware of the state of the developing Merkabah is likely beneficial even though it is not required, just as focusing on the state of your heart is beneficial even though you do not need to consciously keep it beating.

A healthy Merkabah is essentially one that is not interfered with through trying to hurry the ascension process or trying to escape the mortal human self because you have judged it as unworthy, bothersome or hindering of your spiritual progress.

The little human self is an integral part of your Being, but it is prone to judgment. By judging *any* aspect of Self, you hinder your own spiritual progress. Becoming impatient with your growth is usually due to subconscious or unconscious judgments you have placed on yourself, including negative attitudes toward the ego/personality. You might have a belief system that says if you don't meditate enough, or pray enough, or let go of your negative beliefs fast enough, you will not make the grade. Let us assure you that if you have read this far, you are definitely on the path of ascension, and most likely within this lifetime. You do not need to beat yourselves up if you have days in which it seems you have not made any progress.

Do not judge yourselves, dear Creators. Most of you have made far more progress than you realize. Even if you are facing some seemingly insurmountable blocks in the emotional body, or appear to have chronic health problems, you have a lot of help. Continue to ask your guides and God Presence for assistance. Open to receive it. Do not be so quick to judge the form the help comes in. Sometimes the most so-called negative experiences are actually the most beneficial to your soul growth and well-being.

Energetic Symptoms of Ascension

Resisting the process of ascension is the flip-side of trying to hurry the process. Below are some of the symptoms you might experience if you have resistance to the increasing frequencies coming into the Earth.

It is important to realize, dear Creators, that your physical bodies have accumulated a great many toxins and negative thought patterns in the form of crystallized misqualified energy, not just in this lifetime, but over numerous lifetimes. These patterns are carried from lifetime to lifetime via the causal body, or aspect of the soul that remembers multiple lifetimes. Not only are you clearing thousands of years of negativity from your lower bodies, but you are also living in a negatively-oriented world that is constantly bombarding you with thought forms based on belief systems that seem to oppose your spiritual progress.

In addition, your environment is quite toxic. Your processed foods introduce chemicals that your body does not know how to digest. Your soil is largely depleted of nutrients. Your water has heavy metals and toxic hydrocarbons in it. Your lifestyles are stressful because most of you do not take time out to relax, refresh and regenerate.

As the frequencies of ascension increase on the planet, these higher energies clash with the negativity in and around you, forcing it to the surface to be released. Ascension symptoms involve the body's resistance to the higher frequencies coming into the planet. This resistance occurs not only because of the aforementioned process of accumulated negativity, but also because the human body is comprised of trillions of individual cells, and the programs in those cells do not change easily and quickly for the most part. Physical bodies like gradual and gentle change, and this is not a time of gradual and gentle change. So it is quite challenging for the human body to cope with the rising Earth frequencies.

A great deal of patience, love and compassion is called for, as well as acceptance for your human nature. As you tune into your bodies more completely, you will learn to recognize when a symptom is due to your body's natural resistance to the increased energy, and when it is due to something harmful in the environment that needs to be dealt with. Included in the definition of harmful here are: viruses, bacteria, molds, fungi, industrial chemicals, radiation and electromagnetic fluctuations. Some electromagnetic fluctuations are helping your cells mutate toward ascension and some tend to interfere.

With the help of recent Divine Dispensations, negative fluctuations are being held to a minimum. Most are due to the extreme amount of negativity being generated on your planet by the 75% of humanity engaged in such activity. This negative vortex of energy enters the grid lines of the Earth's electromagnetic field and is distributed along the ley lines.

The Arcturians and others are actively engaged in balancing this negativity and that is why their spacecraft are detected primarily in sacred spots around the world.

The more sensitive souls on Earth can sense earthquakes, volcanoes and extreme weather before such conditions are actively manifest. Others will register these events in the physical body as they are occurring in different parts of the world. Another way you might feel the negativity is when you pick up on the collective fear and anxiety of humanity when large numbers of souls are located in the path of these events.

As your bodies attempt to balance the negativity on Earth with the incoming frequencies of ascension, you will tend to vacillate between illness and health. Chronic conditions will flare up during intense periods of negativity and then subside during relatively calmer periods. In addition, your natural soul cycles will trigger either healing crises, or so-called miraculous healings, from time to time.

Each of you has a natural soul cycle that vacillates between an urge to be more outward, and a desire to go more within. Even in extroverted people, there are quiet cycles, although highly active souls may not recognize and respect their souls' desire to retreat from the world periodically. Knowing your own soul cycle is valuable when deciding on the timing of a course of action. In general, major decisions should be made during active soul cycles, rather than quiet ones.

Returning to our topic of ascension symptoms, it is important to strike a balance between a true sense of urgency that tells you to deal with your emotional and psychological issues, and the tendency to try and hurry your ascension process because you want to clear negativity immediately. To put it another way, the biological changes your body is undergoing are hampered and hindered by impatience just as much as procrastination. If you are experiencing uncomfortable ascension symptoms, you must have both patience and acceptance for what is, and a willingness to move through whatever is blocking you.

Remaining clear, calm, centered and alert, while seeking out the appropriate healing, therapy, or rebalancing activity, is essential.

If you approach your healing crises with anger and frustration, telling yourself, "Oh no! Not that headache again!" then you are placing a block between you and the open acceptance of the higher frequencies that want to come in to your body.

On the other hand, the more you ignore your healing crises, or pretend they don't exist, or try to rationalize them, or resist the fact that they are an inevitable part of your process of evolution, the more intense the symptoms are likely to be until you deal with them. While it may be "normal" and "natural" to have ascension symptoms, it does not mean that they should be ignored or explained away. Remember that almost everything you feel in your body involves some form of resistance – that is the nature of physical bodies. A certain amount of resistance is necessary. Otherwise, you would have too much energy flowing through your bodies and they would literally burn out. The key to healing is in how you handle the resistance.

We recommend breathing, yoga, meditation, regular exercise, therapy, and holistic healing modalities to help reduce the amount of resistance to a level that is manageable. Psychologically, resistance is about facing your denials; the things you are unwilling to look at directly. Ask yourselves, "What areas of my life am I avoiding? What would I rather not look at? What part of my life experience am I still judging?"

We suggest you review the techniques given earlier in this chapter and find the ones that best help you cope with ascension symptoms and the resistance and denial that is usually a part of them.

Specific ascension symptoms, such as erratic sleep patterns and extremes of fatigue and restlessness, were covered in previous writings. There is a lot of material on specific symptoms available on the Internet, so we will move on to our next topic.

Youthing and Boundless Energy

As you move through the years 2012 to 2030 and heal your resistance to the changes, you will begin feeling light and clear most of the time. Your energy will increase and your need for food and sleep will decrease. You will no longer get sick and your body will stop aging. At first, you may go through temporary periods where you feel calm, centered and "in the flow," interspersed with times when you feel you have fallen back into your old, neurotic human self. Over time, the lapses will become less frequent and of shorter duration.

Chapter 3 – The Changes Within

It will be essential to surround yourself with ascending souls and those with whom you are similar-minded. Creating a resonant field in your immediate environment will greatly assist you in reaching an optimum level of resistance.

As you move into higher states of vibration, tangible changes to your cellular structure will result. To the trained scientific eye, the mutating patterns of DNA will eventually be detected. At some point before 2030, a few souls will begin exhibiting what your scientists would call "super-human DNA." Biological tests will reveal that the ascending souls will be acquiring more and more of the "immortal" strands and less of the "mortal" ones.

The genes responsible for aging will be replaced with those of eternal youth in the ascending souls. While there may be drugs designed to accomplish this in all souls, such chemical catalysts will be unreliable since souls are rarely free enough psychologically from negativity to keep from re-inviting free radicals and other cell-damaging mechanisms into the body. Your religious texts call this phenomenon, "pouring old wine into new caskets."

There are no shortcuts to enlightenment. That is why you will never have an "instant enlightenment pill." Even if you developed such a medicine, those vibrating at a high enough level to be attracted to the medicine would ultimately have no need for it. Others who managed to acquire it would experience a temporary "satori" experience, but would inevitably fall back into duality due to their unresolved issues.

Changes to your Cells – The Mechanics of Ascension

There has been some recent discussion among your biologists and geneticists regarding the conversion of your cells from a mortal, carbon-based structure, to an immortal, silicon-based design. Most of your present instrumentation is not designed to detect these changes. Since the mutation process is quite significant, they are noticing something, but they are at a loss to explain it, since the idea of biological life forms shifting their base chemical codes from one element to another is not yet firmly planted in the consciousness of mainstream scientists. In fact, your researchers have just recently discovered life forms with base elements of silicon and lithium. As the ascension process accelerates, the more forward-thinking of your biologists will discover what is taking place.

Already in some children, scientists have discovered extra sequences of DNA, or extra receptors indicating DNA compositions that are not within their existing database. These would be, of course, the enlightened souls coming into embodiment from other star systems.

There are Light receptors in your DNA. The actual coding sequences are contained within what your scientists call the "junk" DNA. These receptors are sensitive to higher frequencies and have many qualities of an extraterrestrial source. Many researchers have admitted that "junk" DNA must have some purpose and they simply do not understand it. We have been saying all along that your "junk" DNA contains not only these Light receptors (allowing prana or life force energy to stream directly into the cells of the body, activating the ascension template), but in addition, the "junk" DNA holds a record of the soul's other-worldly incarnations and contains links to various star lineages.

Returning to the subject of Light, the visible domain will change as the soul goes through physical ascension. This means that the eyes will be altered in such a way that they will be able to perceive a wider range of frequencies. In other words, the visible light spectrum will expand to include more of the infrared and ultraviolet range.

The Light receptors in the DNA of the ascending soul must tune themselves, like a radio receiver, to the incoming ascension frequencies. There is a complicated program, part of the ascension template, that calibrates the DNA to the incoming frequencies. You could say there is a built-in analyzer of the quality and texture of the signals, and a resonator that "matches" the incoming frequencies. The resonant field of the soul's consciousness consists of many factors, including overall state of soul evolution, level of receptivity, peacefulness of environment, influence of other souls, etc.

At some point, scientists will be able to calculate the resonant field of a soul using advanced mathematics (i.e., multiple variable nonlinear vector equations). To greatly oversimplify our explanation of the master template program, the DNA codes and keys keep track of the vibratory level of thoughts that go through the soul's conscious and subconscious mind. The template then produces a series of electrical impulses that match the unique frequency generated by the soul's resonant thought forms. The ratio of positive, life-enhancing thoughts to any negative thoughts and beliefs is an integral part of the "light quotient" that figures in the calculations performed by the ascension program. The result is a unique combination of energies often called the "soul signature." This signature is then "matched" to the appropriate incoming frequency.

If the frequency generated by the soul's DNA cannot be matched adequately to the incoming frequencies, then an imbalance results, literally creating a block in the auric field of the soul. When the frequencies are correctly matched, a resonant field is generated and the incoming ascension frequencies are encoded into the cells, activating that portion of the ascension template that resonates with the incoming signals.

For example, if the incoming program contains an instruction, "Insert an immortality strand of DNA into existing mortal cells and 'excite' the carbon atoms into producing an extra electron orbital resulting in a silicon configuration," then that program will attempt to create a resonant field with the level of consciousness emanating from the soul. If the frequencies match, the conversion will occur, usually to a particular number of cells in a specific area of the physical body.

The program has built-in safeguards to assure that only the proper number of cells are converted into the crystal light body format. If too many cells are converted at one time, the antibody and immune system response is triggered and the body will view the mutated cells as enemies to be attacked and/or repelled. This is one of the reasons the ascension process in the physical body is gradual, rather than instantaneous.

Although in nonlinear time the trigger event is instantaneous, the physical realm and its linear time sequences tend to lag behind the quantum jump, much like the delay between light and sound due to velocity differences between the two. Stated another way, just as the psychological state of a human being requires time to adapt to new surroundings, the physiological components of the soul also need time to acclimate to the new frequencies of ascension.

The more resistance present within the physical body, the more difficult this conversion process. Ideally, the soul simply allows the ascension process to proceed at its optimum rate, but souls rarely enter into a state of complete acceptance. You are programmed from an early age to have certain psychological characteristics. There are traditions, cultural beliefs and various societal conditioning, as well as ancestral connections, genetic and past life memories to contend with. Moreover, there are the medical "beliefs" of traditional mainstream practitioners, who may have convinced you that the body must go through certain "stages" of birth, decay and death.

These mortal programs are coded into your DNA, and immortality "triggers" must occur before the new ascension frequencies can be properly assimilated. In other words, you must embrace the idea of physical immortality, not to avoid death (or sublimate the fear of death), but rather, to understand the regenerative properties of the Universe (also known as "centropy") and how these energies interact with the second law of thermodynamics ("entropy"), which is the tendency in the lower densities for things to slow down, wear out and decay. (In technical terms, entropy states that energy moves toward a more disordered state over time, such as from electromagnetism to heat.)

Effect of the Portal Shifts on Ascension

As the portals of 2012, 2017 and 2030 impact the Earth, the magnitude, amplitude and periodicity of the incoming ascension frequencies will be such that these new frequencies will tend to "break down" the resistant barrier of old programming and conditioning. If the resistance is particularly strong in an individual, ascension symptoms will be quite severe. In some cases, the incoming frequencies will rapidly trigger suppressed negativity in such a way that disease will manifest.

A soul's ability to cleanse, purify and let go of resistance is crucial. Many souls are aware of the purification process and have evaluated whether or not they can withstand the increasing frequencies coming into the Earth. If souls have not adequately learned the lessons they came to Earth to learn and feel they need more time to process and learn from their mortal experiences, they will not make the shift into immortality. The resistance will cause blockages in the aura of the soul, preventing the immortality mutation from occurring. The ascension template program will then abort temporarily in that soul. As a result, such a soul may appear to regress to earlier forms of behavior as the old mortal programs come back to assert themselves, now being free of the "intruding" energies of ascension.

Most souls who refuse the new ascension energies will begin the process of rapid decay of the immune system, since it has become obvious to the soul that the lessons it needs to learn can no longer be found on planet Earth. It will then prepare itself to transition out of the body and reincarnate on another world more favorable to its perceived level of awareness.

For those souls who are ready for ascension, the new frequencies will start small and increase logarithmically over time. A soul whose ascension template has been activated might end up converting just one percent of the total body cells into the crystalline Light body structure over a ten year period. However, the next one percent might take only two or three years, and the next one percent only a few months, etc.

There has been a debate regarding how many Earth years it actually takes for a soul to fully ascend physically. Theoretically it is possible for a soul to ascend instantaneously, but almost always it takes many years. A typical time span would be 20 to 30 years, and for some souls, 40 to 50 years. It all depends on how quickly the soul can acclimate to the new frequencies.

Souls who spend a lot of time in meditation, but lead active lives, are the best candidates for a smooth and quick ascension. If you are unattached psychologically to the mortal mindset, then you have an advantage over those who still believe what their mortal physicians tell them.

Being unattached emotionally and physically from the traps and conveniences of your world is required. Once again, this does not mean you must live a monastic life. You can be in the world, but not of the world. Having no energetic link to the mortal ways of the masses of humankind, you are free to embrace the idea that your physical body can become younger and more vibrant.

To sum up the biological changes you can expect as you ascend, may we gently remind you, dear Creators, that your state of consciousness has a direct impact on your DNA configuration. There is no separation between the outer world and inner state, unless you believe this is so. If you do not see the Oneness inherent in both inner and outer reality, then you will fail to see the connection between the quality of your thoughts and feelings and the ability of your physical body to acclimate to the ever-increasing frequencies coming into the Earth.

Most of your biological processes take place below your conscious awareness, in what is often called the autonomic nervous system or automated subconscious. You do not have to think about your heartbeat or how to pump your blood. As far as ascension is concerned, it is part of your automated biological system and if you are aligned within your being, nothing is needed but to accept the process. In the psychology section below, we have outlined the emotional and mental processes that are likely to occur as you go through ascension, as well as the blockages that can hinder your natural ascension process.

Psychological Changes to Expect as You Go Through the Portals

As we stated in Chapter 1, the main psychological change you can expect as you move through the portals is a sense of finality, a feeling of certainty, that you can never go back to the way you were before. Until now, you have been vacillating between the old ego self and the God Self. While you will not have the more basic aspects of your humanity magically disappear overnight, there will be a definite sense that something fundamental has shifted within you. You will be unable to go back to the self that you were before the portal shifts. The old ways will simply not work anymore.

One of the conditions we are observing in this channel and other ascending souls is the tendency to become what they term, "more right-brained." This channel, for example, was raised in an intellectual, scientific environment, and used to pride himself on being logical, rational and down to Earth. However, in recent years, his left-brain intellectual side has seemed to short circuit more and more often in favor of a spontaneous, intuitive, right-brain approach to life.

In some more extreme cases, you have had scientists who appear to have a stroke and suddenly they are devoid of their intellectual prowess. At first this is quite alarming, but very soon these souls discover that they have great gifts of intuition and psychic functioning that were not apparent before.

This channel has correctly postulated that one of the reasons why this effect is occurring is because you have multiple selves that are working at different levels to help you accomplish the shift. For example, fragments of your soul may be dispatched to different places on the Earth in order to help with crises or resolve karma. After a particularly significant Earth change, it might be difficult to concentrate on tasks at hand, even if you are not consciously obsessing about that Earth change. In traditional terms, you say your mind is scattered and you are having trouble concentrating because you keep thinking about what happened somewhere in the world.

Although soul fragmentation occurs most frequently when there is immediate trauma here and now, it can also happen when the trauma is halfway around the world and happening to people you do not know personally. It might be a good idea to use a soul integration technique following a major disaster or upheaval even if you are not directly affected physically.

You are becoming more sensitive. This can seem like a blessing or a curse, depending on your viewpoint. As you evolve, you will have a greater ability to change your level of sensitivity at will, but in general, you will feel things more deeply. That includes the sorrow and pain of humanity. Sometimes this seems like too much to bear and so you withdraw, shut down, or seek escape. Instead, we recommend summoning the power and presence of your spirit guides, angels, archangels and ascended masters to help you move back into your center where you can radiate love and compassion to the affected segments of humanity.

You are One with all life, so naturally you will feel the pain of those life forms that are having a hard time with the Earth changes. The psychology of the shift includes learning how to experience this Oneness while at the same time detaching from it emotionally.

As we have mentioned many times before, embracing change is a cornerstone of ascension readiness. Being psychologically detached and even psychologically invisible to the world of third density is part of the process. With all judgment gently laid aside, you are free to embrace only those aspects of life that are truly uplifting in every sense of the world.

Although struggle was once an integral part of your soul growth, as a fully matured soul you realize the utter uselessness of clinging to the outmoded belief system that says struggle is necessary in order to reach enlightenment. Now you extend that realization to the realm of physical ascension. Just because only a handful of souls have achieved ascension since this world began does not mean it is almost impossible to attain. Perhaps that was the case before the recent Divine Dispensation, but now it is within reach.

Rejoice, dear Creators, for the entrance requirements into the world of true freedom have been relaxed. You are not meant to run through the wheel of reincarnation forever like a hamster in a cage. Your time of death and rebirth is drawing to a close. Take good care of your physical body, nurture your heart and cleanse your mind. Let go of all belief systems that paint a picture of lack, limitation and death. You are created in the image and likeness of your Creator, who is unlimited and free.

Past Life Recall

As you grow and evolve, your ability to remember past lifetimes will increase significantly. You are completing karmic patterns. This is a culmination lifetime. It is like the end of a play where all the actors come out on the stage together for a final bow. This is why in the years ahead you will meet souls from thousands of years ago that played an important part in your evolutionary spiral. These are people you had long forgotten, that participated in situations from early on in your soul's journey.

It will not be necessary to remember all your past lifetimes, just the ones that are relevant to what you are learning now. Usually, memories will come flooding in just when you need understanding in a particular area. As you grow in awareness, you may have flashes of multiple lifetimes where you instantly see your incarnations lined up like pearls on a string.

For example, you might flash on all the lifetimes where you were persecuted for your beliefs. Instead of reliving each one and getting caught in the drama and emotions of the time, you will have the capability of seeing instantly the entire pattern spreading through each lifetime and into the present. You can then use various timeline healing techniques to clear all remaining karma and stuck energy around those experiences.

One of the biggest psychological hurdles to overcome is the fear of failure. This is often engendered because of past life memories of seemingly failing your mission. This channel has counseled hundreds of souls who were present during the end times of Atlantis. The predominant negative psychological pattern present in these souls involves the idea that they did not do enough to prevent the destruction of their beloved homeland. Many of them feel responsible and guilty for their part in the collective karma of that period. They find it necessary to repeatedly forgive themselves for their part in the drama.

Atlantis is part of a bigger issue that goes all the way back to Original Cause, or the Fall from Grace. To review, the rise and fall of civilizations on Earth is due to a fundamental blockage in the consciousness of humanity. During the fall (which is really nothing more than getting enmeshed in the lower worlds and identifying with them, forgetting your true Divine nature), the experience was so traumatic that humanity has done everything possible to never again repeat that experience.

If you perceive that we talked about the fall earlier in this book, your memory is serving you correctly. This is not the first, nor will it be the last time we discuss Original Cause.

Refusing to look at what happened during your original descent into the lower worlds is the primary cause of the seemingly endless re-enactments of self-sabotage and perceived mission failure that gave rise to the collapse of advanced societies on Earth.

The guilt experienced by many souls is so uncomfortable that it remains hidden in the unconscious self. That means many of you are denying and suppressing the part of the self deemed responsible for the fall.

Keeping that fragment of the soul separated from consciousness takes enormous energy, resulting in a draining of overall vitality from the soul. This disempowerment of the soul means that humanity has not had enough energy to clear the old karmic patterns associated with the fall and, therefore, every time humanity has reached the heights of civilization, they have been unable to go beyond a certain point. The channel calls this seeming barrier, the "spiritual glass ceiling."

The outer manifestation of this primal psychological pattern is to attract some condition or event that sabotages the successes of the civilization. In some cases, it might be a negative ET race coming to Earth and interbreeding with humanity, diluting the DNA to the point where the frequency and vibration drops below the level necessary to sustain the civilization. In other cases, it manifests as not having enough energy and insight to be able to overcome the effects of the precessional alignment of the axis, or the mutations associated with the passage of a comet, or the fluctuations associated with the passage of a planetoid.

Souls with a lot of Original Cause denial will tend to become complacent and lazy as life gets better. They become comfortable in their relative wealth and luxury, and stop seeking out experiences to help them grow and evolve. This can be likened to stagnant water beside a river.

These collective "plateaus" eventually cause decay and disintegration, just as a stagnant pond eventually dries up and the life within it dies.

The fear of facing the primal feelings associated with the descent into the lower worlds has kept humanity from achieving physical ascension in all but a tiny handful of souls. The fear is far worse than the actual experience of facing the primal feelings. Once these feelings of separation and abandonment are faced, the lost soul fragments are returned to the soul and he or she then has enough energy to overcome the entropy associated with the lower worlds, thus moving back onto the path of ascension.

Humanity has once again reached this point. Due to multiple Divine Dispensations, the story is different this time. There are a sufficient number of souls able and willing to move through Original Cause to allow for a mass ascension. There is also a large body of souls not ready for ascension. Nevertheless, many souls have as their primary soul lesson the desire to live together in relative harmony and peace on Earth. These souls will, together, build the New Earth spoken of in Chapter 1.

Metaphysical and Spiritual Understandings

Early in the study of metaphysics, souls on Earth discovered that their thoughts were energetic transmissions capable of changing outer reality. Simple demonstrations of this principle by teachers were illustrated through reminding students that virtually everything in the world of humankind started as an idea in the mind. A few metaphysicians carried this idea to its extreme and suggested that *all* outer reality was a projection of thoughts held in the mind and that simply changing these thoughts would change the outer reality. There were a number of misunderstandings in this approach, which led to this channel's revision of the way the law of creative thought is now stated, as follows:

The quality of your consciousness determines your experience of reality.

At humanity's level of evolution, the natural world and the heavens are not direct products of human thought. Although souls influence their outer reality, a lot depends on the level of energy generated by their thoughts, and whether or not the thoughts are collective or individual. Individual thoughts primarily influence the individual timelines of souls, while collective thoughts generate collective timelines. A few individual souls are powerful enough to affect the collective timelines significantly, but at this point in the evolution of humanity, the number of such souls is only a few thousand.

If enough souls believe something strongly enough, they create a dominant timeline, meaning one that supersedes all others and ends up manifesting in the physical world as part of the linear sequence of events. Because Earth is a fairly large place and has a wide variety of souls, it is possible to manifest simultaneous realities, each with different manifestations. An example is war and peace. If one group of souls desires peace and this group visualizes it intensely and projects thoughts and feelings of peace continuously, very likely the region of the Earth where these souls reside will become more peaceful. Henceforth, if another group is hell-bent (pun intended) on war, they will likely find themselves in a state of conflict.

Because humanity is ultimately One Being, the different states of consciousness of various members of humanity will influence each other. If a group of peaceful souls visualizes and prays for world peace and directs this peaceful energy to a distant part of the planet that is in conflict, it can have a significant positive impact on the warring factions. Unfortunately, this can also work the other way around. If the peaceful souls have not sufficiently cleared their own negativity, those souls at a distance that are engaged in war can have a negative influence on the Lightworkers praying for peace.

Ultimately, the ability of negatively-oriented souls to hinder humanity (whether residing on Earth or influencing Earth from space or the astral realms) depends on the degree to which humanity has cleared their own negative aspects of consciousness. There is a reason some of the news items broadcast on Earth hold fascination for you while other stories mean almost nothing. You will be drawn to those dramas and traumas that trigger your own unresolved issues. In some cases, you have just enough empathy and triggering of your own memories of similar experiences to effect compassionate action. This can obviously be a good thing. The thought forms around this level of triggering go something like this: "I understand how hard it is for Uncle John right now because I was in a similar place myself just a few years ago."

In such a case, you might be able to demonstrate to Uncle John the steps you took to extricate yourself from a similar drama. More importantly than the "how-to" is the resonant field you are able to create with Uncle John by temporarily matching his level of vibration. Yet because you have cleared the majority of the negativity relating to Uncle John's predicament, there is a relatively low risk of getting caught up in the details of Uncle John's life. In other words, the ability of Uncle John to trigger you has decreased due to the fact that you no longer have a "charge" on many of the details of his situation that are similar to what you went through.

Chapter 3 – The Changes Within

Your purpose in helping your struggling relative in the above example comes partly from pure love and compassion, but it also serves to welcome him into the new vibration you have discovered so you can experience the joy of ascension together. You do not have a personal investment in his progress, but nevertheless, you rejoice when he responds to your offering of assistance.

Your Aunt Sally may be a different matter entirely. After carefully listening to your inner guidance and feeling the unease in your body as you approach the situation, you might determine that one of two conditions is occurring here. (1) You have not cleared enough of your own psychological effluvia to effectively help Aunt Sally because her condition is triggering you intensely and you are unable to detach from the drama enough to truly be of help; or (2) You determine that you are not the right person to effectively communicate with Aunt Sally and help her integrate the unresolved negative patterns. Perhaps there is not enough similarity in experience, or you do not have the necessary understandings of her predicament.

So you graciously bow out of a potential entanglement with her and suggest a therapist or healer who may be able to achieve results with Aunt Sally. This third party will have true detachment since he or she is an independent observer. You might also be able to find someone who has been through a similar experience and has reached a higher level of understanding than you have.

Knowing when to intervene and when to let things run their course is one of the major spiritual lessons on the path. It is one that we, the Founders, have had to learn on many levels and dimensions. All of your spirit guides work hard to make sure they are providing the optimum level of support and encouragement. There is a perfect balance point between trying too hard to help, which means being codependent and enabling, and being too detached, which often means giving advice from your head and not your heart.

If you factor in the variabilities associated with free will, it can be quite challenging to find that perfect balance.

You are walking in two worlds (actually three for a short time). Part of each day is still devoted to taking care of what you call your human business, which includes basic activities such as getting dressed, paying bills, answering phone calls, running errands, etc. Another part involves your fourth density pursuit of education, enlightenment and higher understanding. The majority of your relationships will likely have, as their primary goal, the pursuit of these higher qualities. A portion of your day might be spent activating your ascension template through meditation, sacred toning, breathing, visualizing or connecting with others who are on the path of ascension.

You will vacillate between the three main aspects of self (human ego, enlightened mind and ascended being) perhaps several times a day, depending upon what is called for in any given moment. If you are fully dedicated to the path of ascension, you will set aside some time, however brief, to do your spiritual practice. You will have determined by now what works and what does not. Some activities will leave you feeling uplifted and inspired, while others will feel more like drudgery. More and more often, you will choose those activities that nourish and sustain your higher Self.

The most important aspect of being spiritually enlightened on this Earth involves your ability to come from the reference point of your God Self. You are a powerful, unlimited, creative spiritual being living in the material world. This is your identity. Your spiritual Self is vast and your human self is tiny by comparison. Yet your human self is no less important than your spiritual Self because it is an integral part of that Self. Would you judge your right hand to be less important than the rest of your body just because it is a relatively small part of it?

True transcendence means to move beyond the identification with the ego or human personality. From a higher perspective, you still have a human ego, but it has become a rather small part of the big picture. To quote this channel, it has become your humble servant, dutifully carrying out the will of the master, your God Self.

Balancing the Role of Spirit Guides

We observe the two extremes of codependency versus aloof isolationism, occurring in your relationship with spirit guides and teachers from other realms. Some of you rely too heavily on your spirit guides, while others fail to take advantage of the help that is freely offered you.

Once again this is a situation wherein you must straddle different worlds. The human self needs help, whether directly from God or through spirit guides or other members of humanity – usually all three are called for at some point in your process. Learning to accept help when appropriate is an integral lesson on your path.

Going back to the quicksand example, if your best friend falls in and you have no knowledge of how to help him, you would quickly run and get help from someone more experienced, or you would summon your inner courage and ask for guidance to come to you from on high.

If you are the one in the quicksand, you would not simply shrug and say, "Go on ahead. I'll find my way out. I don't need any help."

Conversely, if you are not in a life threatening situation and simply feel a bit challenged, you do not want to be too quick to run for help. This might be a time to take responsibility for your own actions and learn some new ways of coping from your own inner wisdom. As a child, you might have relied on Mommy to make the hurt feel better, but now you are on your own and the world expects you to attend to your own little hurts.

Sometimes the hurts are too big or all-consuming and you need outer help. Learning to effectively ask for such assistance is an art. You might be challenged financially and seem to be temporarily unable to simply walk into a therapist's office and book a session, so you do some research and find a spiritual counselor who can accept you for little or no money. Or perhaps you seek out professionals and decide, after visiting three or four different types of therapists, that a particular one is perfectly suited to help with your specific emotional patterns.

The same is true of spirit guides. There are millions of them. Most are eager and ready to assist. Some are too eager, and you will need to do some inner research here. You do not want to go running to your spirit guides every time some little aspect of your life goes out of balance. On the other hand, if your primary guide lovingly reminds you, "I am here for you. How can I help?" you do not want to ignore him or tell him to go away and leave you alone.

You have a contract with your spirit guides. It is their job to determine, to the best of their ability, when to communicate with you and when to remain silent. Some souls have spirit guides that are very "hands on," while others tend to have spirit guides that only show up in dire situations. To determine the best response to spirit guides and the best level of involvement with them, you need to overcome any past patterns of pride or arrogance that say, "I am a mature person. Now I rely only on myself. I don't need anyone else." This can be as destructive as expecting Mommy to rescue you every time something adverse occurs in your life.

Most souls have a variety of spirit guides that specialize in different forms of help. Knowing who to call on is part of the process of discernment. In addition to us, this channel has several other guides and groups that work with him. We are not always the best choice for any given situation. Typically, his higher self will make the determination who to call. Occasionally, one of his guides or groups will be proactive and contact him first, but it is always with a suggestion, never a demand. If you have any spirit guides that demand change or obedience, it's time to kick them out of your aura. Contact this channel or another respected healer for help with this.

As you go through ascension, you will find that your sources of help change periodically. You may outgrow some of your spirit guides and it might be necessary to end the relationship. You have a right to refuse service from spirit guides and you have a right to remove any guides that are no longer serving you on your journey regardless of whether or not they are happy to go. When dismissing them, it is best to say, "*Go in peace. I release you into the Light*," or something similar.

You may acquire new guides as you are ready for them. Be sure and welcome your new guides and express your gratitude for having them in your life.

It is not absolutely essential to know your spirit guides. If you do know them, it is not necessary to know their names. Names of spirit guides will vary, depending on your language and level of awareness. The only real value of a name is that it sets up a resonant sound frequency when you say the name and it triggers a conscious memory of the guide being called.

Do not be overly concerned if you do not know your specific guides. You can use a general invocation, such as, "*I now call forth my benevolent spirit guides to assist me. Come forth, beloved beings of Light. Thank you, wonderful beings.*"

Many of you have asked, "How do I tell the difference between my own higher self and my spirit guides?"

Generally speaking, spirit guides will identify themselves at the onset of communication. They will have a specific "energy signature," which may consist of a feeling, series of thoughts, visions, impressions or intuitive knowing that has a certain quality. In this channel's case, his regular guides always appear in the same general location within his etheric field, with a consistent energy and presence.

The more you practice contacting your spirit guides and working with them, the easier it will be to recognize imposters. Unfortunately, there are a lot of mostly well-meaning entities that want to help so badly that they will make false claims in order to get your allegiance. In a few rare cases, very dark beings will claim to be of the Light. Pay close attention to how you feel when you call in your spirit guides. If you feel heavy, confused, anxious, or angry during the process, visualize golden light surrounding your body and clear your aura. Tell your guides you will work with them later when you feel more centered. Ask that only those beings that are 100% of God's Loving Light be allowed in your space. Command that all others leave your space immediately. Contact this channel or another teacher for additional spiritual and psychic protection techniques.

There are a lot of teachers on Earth available to help you contact your spirit guides, so we will refrain from spending any more time on this subject.

We will now turn our attention to the subject of soul psychology.

Chapter 3 – The Changes Within

Two Steps Forward, One Step Back

As you go through the portals, you will *know* that you are moving forward and that there is really no turning back. Nevertheless, it is the nature of the spiritual path to go through what this channel calls periods of rapid soul growth, followed by plateaus. The ideal soul path looks somewhat like a stairway to heaven. You have surges of momentum forward, called periods of rapid soul growth, where everything is moving quickly, manifesting easily, and resolving wonderfully. Then you have those periods where it seems nothing is working, energy is sluggish, and there is little or no momentum. In this channel's earlier book, "*Earth Changes and 2012*," there is a section on the psychology of soul growth, discussing integration, consolidation, purification, etc. We suggest you re-read that section thoroughly.

Basically, for those who have not read our prior work, it states that some parts of you evolve more quickly than others and often it is necessary to stop and wait for the slower parts to catch up. In addition, you have your soul cycles, the cycles of humanity and the natural rhythms of the cosmos. It is important to be aware of these cycles and use them to your advantage.

Do not make the mistake of attributing undue power and importance to them, however. Some souls will refrain from taking action because "Mercury is in retrograde," or "It is the wrong time of the month." If you are truly experiencing an inward soul cycle, then perhaps it is best to postpone action. But make sure you are listening to true inner wisdom and not simply making excuses because of an unresolved fear of acting.

Learn to recognize your natural soul cycles. Learn to see the "stairway" nature of soul growth. Much of the time, you will want to simply allow your soul to express its cyclical nature and structure your life accordingly.

One of the major issues souls are having at this time on Earth is the feeling of overwhelm associated with busy lives. Stressful lifestyles seem to be in fashion on the planet right now. This is not a requirement for living here. You can learn to say "No" to those commitments that just do not feel right. You can let go of the negative belief that says you must work hard every day just to make enough money to put food on the table. That may have been true in some of your past lifetimes, but things have changed. You have technological advances and spiritual energies coming into Earth right now that can propel you out of survival mentality very quickly.

Regardless of how hopeless or overwhelming your life might look, you *can* change it. You *can* make time for your spiritual practice. In fact, you *must* make time for it. That does not necessarily mean sitting in meditation for hours every day, but it does mean taking time out from your busy schedule to remember why you are here in the first place.

If you do not heed your inner advice to slow down and let go of stress, your body will find a way of getting your attention and it will likely not be pleasant. Eighty percent of all illness is emotionally based, and even the ten percent directly caused by stressful lifestyles is usually emotionally based as well because if you did not have unresolved emotional issues and core negative beliefs to clear, you would likely not believe you must work so hard every day just to survive.

For some of you, survival is not an issue, but you still find people and situations distracting you at every turn. A simple process is to stop what you are doing and ask, "What is the purpose of this activity? How is it assisting me in my soul growth?" This does not mean you must forgo pleasurable activities and spend all your time processing emotions or meditating. Your body will tell you when you get out of balance. If you are tired all the time, something needs to change. If you have so much energy you cannot sleep at night, you may be out of balance in a different way. Balancing quiet time with activity, sedentary time with exercise, and alone time with social interaction, is essential.

Diet and Nutrition for Ascending Souls

A question many of you have asked involves diet and nutrition. How do your eating habits change as you ascend? How should they change?

Our usual response to this question is to ask you to tune in more deeply to your body and pay attention to how it feels when you eat, and especially, after you eat.

As you increase your vibration, dense food will tend to drop away naturally if you do not have any emotional attachments or addictions involved. Bodies do not like sudden change. This is one of the reasons most diets do not work. The body feels as though it is being forced to adhere to a strict standard and its usual response is either to rebel or shut down.

The emphasis with diet should not be focusing on what to avoid, but rather, to ask the question, "What does my body need for maximum vitality and energy?" Then concentrate on devising a way of acquiring those things that make you feel the lightest, clearest and most energetic. By energetic, we do not mean a sudden rush of energy followed by a crash, as in the case of most sweets, but rather, sustained energy over several hours.

Chapter 3 – The Changes Within

You will need to experiment a bit. Certainly, it is wise to do some research. We suggest reading about blood types, Ayurvedic philosophy, herbs and natural remedies to correct nutritional imbalances. This channel acquired information about blood types and then realized he was already eating 98% in alignment with what is recommended for his blood type. That is because he tuned into his body and discovered what felt good and what did not.

It is important to recognize the difference between cravings stemming from unresolved emotional issues and genuine hunger and bodily desire for a certain type of food. In rare cases, these will overlap, but usually you can tell the difference in retrospect by how you feel after eating. When indulging in a craving you might later feel lethargic or tired versus the satisfied feeling after eating a food your body really wants.

After giving some general nutritional advice in this section, we will follow up with a brief discussion on habits and addictions in order to address the issue of cravings and self-destructive behavior. We will take a brief look at several popular addictions, with our recommendations on methods of healing. Here is our general nutritional advice:

About three-fourths of humanity has a body structure that desires the basic hunter-gatherer foods, which are: simple carbohydrates, simple fats and regular protein. Only about one-fourth of humanity can tolerate complex carbohydrates such as grains, bread, pasta, pastry and such. If you feel bloated, tired, gassy, or suffer from heartburn after eating these foods, you are probably among the three-fourths who cannot tolerate wheat, gluten or large portions of complex carbohydrates.

For you, we recommend a diet with lots of fresh organic vegetables, a moderate amount of fresh fruit (not juiced), and regular protein, in the form of organic meats, fermented soy and supergreen powders, such as spirulina and chlorella. Meat consumption should be moderate, with emphasis on poultry and seafood. If you are vegetarian, make sure you have adequate amounts of protein at each meal. If you eat soy products, make sure they are fermented and organic (tempeh, miso, etc.), since almost all soy that is not certified organic has been genetically modified. Tofu and soy margarine can clog the system and elevate estrogen levels. Isolated soy protein is not recommended.

Generally speaking, the less processed the food, the better it is for your body. Processed food is usually high glycemic, which means it converts very quickly to sugar in the body. This wreaks havoc with insulin, which regulates blood sugar levels. Both hyperglycemia and hypoglycemia can be caused by too much or too little sugar in the diet. Some doctors recommend only 15 to 25 grams of fructose from organic fruit daily. Avoid all diet and regular soda.

Choosing a diet full of raw vegetables, with minimal processed food and little or no sugar, can put type II diabetes into remission within a few weeks, in the majority of cases.

Another problem with processed foods is the nature of the chemicals used to preserve or enhance the flavor. Be especially wary of MSG (monosodium glutamate), often disguised as autolyzed yeast extract, hydrolyzed vegetable protein, and "natural" flavors. Even Bragg's amino acids, which has natural glutamic acid, converts a percentage into glutamates. About half of the population is allergic to glutamates and most do not know it.

Other chemicals to avoid include high fructose corn syrup, aspartame, sodium nitrite, sodium benzoate, BHT, BHA, propylene glycol, and many others. In Europe, it is important to avoid E321, E322, E323, E621, E622, E623 and most of the E900 series where artificial sweeteners are found.

In addition to the more obvious advice above, it is important to dispel a few myths about food. Let's start with the myth of dairy products.

Milk is the perfect food – for baby cows. In fact, we note that humanity is the only species that drinks the milk of other animals. In its raw state, there are some beneficial properties to cow's milk, but generally speaking, dairy products create excess mucus, leading to enhanced and aggravated head colds, influenza and various other maladies. This channel gave up dairy products almost 20 years ago and has not had a bad head cold or flu since that time. If you do use dairy products, avoid pasteurized ones, since the heating of these foods kills most of the nutritional value and makes them difficult for the body to recognize and digest properly.

While giving up of mucus-producing foods can greatly reduce the occurrence rates of certain illnesses, there are, of course, other factors that contribute to the general well-being of the body, including your attitudes about food and whether or not you eat only when you are truly hungry. Most humans eat out of boredom, for social reasons, or because the food is there in front of them. If you go to potlucks, buffets and smorgasbords, it is very easy to overdo it, not only eating too much, but taking items that are not good for your body.

A further word about soy: Eating natural organic soybeans in moderation is okay, but in general, soy is best consumed in its fermented state, which includes tempeh, miso and a few other dishes. Regular tofu, soy milk, soy margarine and soy protein isolate are not recommended. Make sure your soy is free of genetically modified ingredients. Do not buy anything that lists soybean oil as an ingredient unless it specifically indicates the oil is GMO-free.

The best drink is natural spring water, served in glass containers. If you want variety, use a bit of lemon, or green tea, or make up a batch of natural sun tea (in summer).

A small amount of full-bodied beer or ale, or a glass or two of red wine on occasion is okay, but pay attention to the level of acidity in your body, as alcoholic drinks can quickly lower your overall pH. You want your body to be slightly alkaline. We do not recommend drinking high pH waters put through some fancy machine. If you do use one of these expensive alkalinizing filters, choose the setting closest to the 7.0 to 8.0 range, and drink plenty of natural spring water in addition to the high pH water. A small amount of alkaline water will help neutralize over-acidity, but a large amount will trigger the body's acid-producing response as it seeks to restore balance. Your stomach needs to be at a low pH in order to digest food, so go easy on highly alkaline water.

The best way to alkalinize your body is through consumption of dark green leafy vegetables, such as chard and kale, along with supergreen powders. Make sure your supergreens do not have a significant amount of added sugar.

Speaking of sugar, a small amount of natural cane juice or honey is okay. Avoid any forms of processed sugar and all artificial sweeteners. Probably the best sweetener is stevia.

We promised to keep our answer brief, so let us finish up with a few comments about mineral balance. We observe that a lot of female problems, such as prolonged and painful menstrual cycles, are due to imbalances of minerals. Copper, zinc, calcium, magnesium and selenium are the five biggest contributors to hormonal health.

We strongly suggest avoiding all forms of synthetic calcium. The body does not know what to do with it, and as a result, you may go from calcium deficiency to over-abundance with just a few doses. Synthetic calcium builds up in the joints and actually promotes osteo-related imbalances, including arthritis. If you use a calcium supplement, make sure it is derived completely from whole foods. Avoid calcium carbonate entirely (the active ingredient in most antacid medications). Almost all heartburn will cease when you reduce or eliminate complex carbohydrates and eat a balance of carbs, fat and protein at each meal.

You can get most of your minerals, in proper balance, from eating moderate amounts of raw nuts and seeds. Use naturally processed (virgin) olive and coconut oils, as well as cold pressed flaxseed oil. Flax, chia and hemp seeds are the best sources of fiber and are also rich in essential minerals. If you take a mineral supplement, make sure it comes in powder or liquid form, not tablets or capsules, which are harder to break down.

Okay, we are not quite done. A word about chocolate: Small amounts of dark chocolate with minimal sugar and processing can actually be beneficial. Avoid milk chocolate. Use products with a cacao number above 70%. You can buy raw organic cacao at health food stores. If you make your own chocolate candy, use a little agave syrup for sweetness (but not too much, as agave is somewhat high glycemic).

Finally, let us mention the subject of portions. There are many conflicting levels of advice on this topic. We recommend several small meals throughout the day because this way the body's survival mechanism does not get triggered. When you go several hours between meals, the body often feels it is not getting enough nutrition and so it sends a signal to the brain to store the next meal as fat in case it is the last one for a while.

You can pay close attention to portion size and know when you have had enough. If you feel tired after a meal, or especially two to three hours after eating, it is either because you overate, or because you included too many complex carbohydrates with your meal.

Do not eat anything of significance within three hours of bedtime. A light snack is sometimes okay, but experiment a bit and see what arrangement best contributes to a good night's sleep.

Remember the adage, "Everything in moderation, including moderation." Balanced eating is much more beneficial than strict dieting. If you feel deprived, your diet is likely not going to work. If it requires sudden changes and strict adherence, your body will probably rebel. Once you do have a good eating regimen in place, it is okay to cheat a little here and there, as long as it does not get out of hand. When traveling, go ahead and have a chicken salad or lightly breaded fish at a restaurant once in a while, but when you get back home, go back to free range organic chicken and broiled fish.

As you move through ascension, heavier foods will naturally drop away. This does not mean you should beat yourselves up if you are still eating meat and are under the belief that ascending souls must be vegetarian. Your body probably needs to stay grounded to the Earth, and for a while, meat is a good way to stay grounded.

All right, we're still not quite finished with this topic. One last word, this time about genetically modified organisms: It is not a simple matter of just stating that GMOs are bad for you. This may be the case more often than not, but really it is about whether or not your body recognizes the molecular configuration of a food or nutrient and can process it. Some GMOs are relatively stable and do not differ substantially from their natural counterparts, while others use exotic grafting, splicing and hybridization that the body cannot recognize.

In addition, the primary reason for genetic modification is to create resistance to certain pesticides so that crops can be grown without interference from weeds. The relatively high concentrations of toxic pesticides used on many GMO crops are not completely eliminated during processing of the food.

We conclude (finally) our discussion of diet and nutrition with Table 3, a list of diet types and how they fare in the vibrational scale. The ones at the top of the list are consistent with higher vibrations, while the ones at the bottom of the list are the densest and tend to hold back soul evolution.

Table 3 – Dietary Stages on the Path of Ascension
(Highest to Lowest)

--Pure ingestion of prana life force (no air, water or food)
--Breatharian (ingestion of air only, no food or water)
--Water only (no ingestion of food)
--Liquid supergreens, liquid vitamins and minerals only
--Raw vegetable juice fasting
--Raw vegan diet (fresh vegetables and some fresh fruit)
--Vegan unprocessed (fruit, vegetables, nuts and seeds)
--Vegan processed (includes grains, sugars, caffeine, etc.)
--Vegetarian (includes dairy and eggs)
--Partial vegetarian (no red meat or dairy products)
--Mostly omnivore (everything except red meat)
--Omnivore (all types of food)
--Junk food diet (fast food, mostly fried and processed)

It is only logical to follow our discussion of diet with some words on addiction. Many of you have asked, "How do we change bad habits and heal addictions?"

Addictions and How to Heal Them

Addiction occurs because you believe that some process or substance is going to fulfill needs that have not been met in a healthy way. An example might be addiction to sugar. Perhaps you received sugar as a reward for good behavior when you were young and, as a result, came to equate sugar with receiving love and attention. Then, during periods when you perceive a lack of love and attention, you turn to sugar for solace.

Below, we are going to list several addictions, along with our advice for healing them.

Part 1 – Process Addictions

These are addictions to certain behaviors or states of consciousness that do not directly involve substances ingested into the body. We have listed them in order of prevalence among your society.

■ *Addiction to the Ego (also rational mind, intellect)*

This is by far the most common and hardest addiction to heal. Even when a soul knows that it is not healthy to identify with the ego, such identification continues to happen. It takes a strong resolve and usually therapy and lots of healing before detachment from the ego is possible.

The "I, Me, Mine" mentality gives rise to selfishness, self-centeredness and narcissism, and is responsible for clinging to a false sense of self-importance. Closely related is our next addiction.

■ *Addiction to Power*

Those who are attached to ego will have a deep-rooted sense of inadequacy. To overcompensate for this perceived sense of lack, souls become obsessed with power. Typically they will seek to dominate other souls, or amass great wealth, or seek positions of responsibility where they can be the boss over others in order to feel a sense of power. The fear of powerlessness is at the root of this addiction.

■ *Addiction to Money*

This is, of course, related to the addiction to power (above) and the addiction to material things (below), but in addition, money represents potential energy or the ability to be free and independent. Souls who feel powerless or helpless to change their circumstances may falsely believe that money alone will change things in their favor. While this might be temporarily true, an inner feeling of imprisonment has very little to do with actual independence, financial or otherwise. More than likely, such feelings stem from unresolved trauma in this or a past life where the soul was actually imprisoned or lived in a highly controlled environment (such as being a slave). Often, souls will over-achieve in order to prove themselves worthy to authoritative parents, or to win their approval.

■ *Addiction to Material Things*

This addiction is closely related to ego and power addictions. The soul that feels empty inside will tend to fill up his life with all manner of physical distractions ("toys") in order to avoid looking at the perceived state of emptiness. In this category would be addiction to shopping, addiction to spending money, and addiction to "keeping up with the Joneses."

■ *Addiction to Excitement and Entertainment*

Avoiding loneliness is one of the ego's primary motivations and because souls who perceive themselves as separate can never feel satisfied, no matter how many friends, family and activities are crammed into their busy lives, they will continuously seek new forms of excitement and entertainment. Thrill rides that pump adrenaline are a favorite, along with horror movies, news of catastrophes, gossip, and preoccupation with pop culture icons. People in this category worry more about the wardrobe of their favorite celebrity, or who she is dating, than with their own lonely state of mind. A subset of this addiction involves gambling and also criminal activities (the excitement of winning or losing, or avoiding or getting caught provides an adrenaline rush).

■ *Addiction to People (the socialite lifestyle)*

Some people can never be alone because then they would have to face their own issues, so they fill up their lives with superficial relationships. There is always a party to go to, or a social function to attend. While some of this can be healthy, the socialite depends on getting noticed by peers, wearing the right dress or business suit, and in general being approved of by others. This one could be reworded, "Addiction to Receiving the Approval of Others."

■ *Addiction to Sex and Relationships*

Souls who do not feel connected to their God Presence within will seek to feel complete in the arms of another. Pop culture is based on the idea that a soul needs to find "his other half" in order to be complete. Souls in this category run the gamut between impersonal sex in order to maintain the illusion of intimacy on the one hand, to clingy, codependent relationships in order to avoid feeling lonely, on the other hand. There are a lot of good books on this subject, so we will keep our discussion here brief.

■ *Addiction to Religious Beliefs*

Underneath blind allegiance to a faith or way of life is usually a deep fear of the unknown, sometimes reinforced with guilt and the threat of punishment if one does not rigidly follow scripture. Those who feel separated from God hold a deep fear of being abandoned by the Divine and may cling to a religious belief in the hopes that their image of God will somehow reward them in some way. Many souls have a distant memory of being persecuted for straying from the prevalent beliefs of the time and are fearful of the consequences of thinking for themselves.

■ *Addiction to Being Right*

We could have placed this one under "Addiction to Ego" or "Addiction to Seeking the Approval of Others," but there can be a lot of different reasons why a soul might become addicted to being right. Humans are conditioned to strive and succeed in school by getting the answers right. Unfortunately, a lot of the deeper mysteries of life do not involve right or wrong, and therefore, this leads to the "Addiction to Duality." Having a black and white viewpoint of life creates tunnel vision. Such souls are likely to be satisfied with simple answers, never using critical thinking to investigate deeper meanings.

There are many more process addictions, but these are the basic ones. Some of the solutions to healing process addictions can be found in the section on therapy techniques given earlier in this chapter. We suggest you go through the list of tools offered in this book and apply your process addictions accordingly. Of course, the first step in healing is self-awareness, which includes admitting you have the addiction. Obtaining the help of family, friends and professional therapists and healers is essential. In some cases, a 12-step program might be appropriate, but we urge caution for the reasons given below under "Addiction to Alcohol."

Let us now turn our attention to food and drug addictions.

Chapter 3 – The Changes Within

Part 2 – Substance Addictions

The definition of substance addiction involves the idea that in order to attain a certain state of consciousness, one must depend upon ingesting a certain food or chemical into the bloodstream.

■ *Addiction to Food (Overeating)*

We have already talked about this to some extent in our section on diet and nutrition. Overeating usually stems from "stuffing emotions." By filling yourselves with food, you receive a feeling of fullness that often masks uncomfortable feelings. Frequently, the emotions being sublimated with food involve feeling deprived, neglected, rejected, lonely, or abandoned. Other times overeating is centered around boredom (which is a negative emotion related to suppressed frustration) or apathy (suppressed helplessness or powerlessness). Refusing to eat (anorexia), or purging after eating (bulimia) are variations on a theme. Often with anorexia there is a deep feeling of self-disgust (self-judgment or self-condemnation) buried under the militant desire to forego oral satisfaction. While on the surface, anorexia might masquerade as a fear of becoming overweight (fear of disapproval from others or fear of illness and death), without self-judgment or self-condemnation the soul will eventually cease the destructive behavior and start eating again.

■ *Addiction to Sugar*

This is the most common food addiction. About half the souls in western societies are addicted to sugar or one or more of its derivatives. Some sugar addictions are quite serious, while others are mild. Sugar addiction is the number one cause of type II diabetes and is a major contributor to heart disease and many chronic illnesses.

We have already mentioned one of the causes of sugar addiction – equating sweets with love – but there is also a physiological component. The body starts to crave the "high" temporarily created by sugar before the inevitable "crash". Sugar is extremely physically addicting. After only one meal with dessert, the body may start "expecting" to have a dessert after every meal, salivating excessively in anticipation of such. The difference between a molecule of sugar and one of alcohol involves the rearranging of one hydroxyl ion. In fact, sugar is a necessary ingredient in the production of alcohol.

■ *Addiction to Alcohol*

This is generally considered to be the most destructive of the substance addictions. Every year alcohol directly or indirectly kills hundreds of thousands of humans, whether through automobile accidents, murders, or liver failure. Small amounts of certain alcoholic beverages can be beneficial to the human body, but there is a fine line.

Souls who drink in order to be more social or to loosen up, may be depending on a substance to become more extroverted or less self-conscious. While this is the psychological component of alcohol addiction, the physiological factor kicks in and is compounded by the tolerance factor. This means that the more you drink, the more you need in order to attain the same level of "high."

As with sugar, the high is followed by a crash. Usually the addict, during the hangover, swears he will never touch another drink, but as soon as the hangover wears off, he is back on a binge.

The Alcoholics Anonymous program has produced many beneficial results. However, we agree with this channel that many recovering alcoholics keep affirming they are alcoholics far beyond the point where such a declaration is helpful. At first, denial is an issue. The whole purpose of the first principle (step 1 of the 12 steps) of AA is to help the addict out of the state of denial. However, once that is achieved, it is important for the recovering addict to focus on positive, creative behaviors that enhance life, rather than starting each meeting with, "My name is Alan and I am an alcoholic." If denial is faced directly, with increasing self-awareness, the recovering addict will learn to recognize the difference between a healed soul and a "dry drunk." A dry drunk is someone who will, under just the right conditions, begin drinking again (which means the underlying emotional issues have not been completely healed).

The underlying issues may include an unwillingness to face the harshness of life, refusal to acknowledge one's own shadow self (dark side), attempts to cover over unhealed grief and loss from the recent or distant past, and a desire to acquire a false bravado to cover up deep feelings of inadequacy.

Alcohol addiction involves both physical and psychological dependency. Heavy drinkers often need to dry out over a period of time to reduce their physical dependency before they are ready to face the tough psychological issues that drove them to drinking in the first place.

Chapter 3 – The Changes Within

■ *Addiction to Caffeine, Amphetamines and Stimulants*

You may be wondering why we have lumped these together, since you probably consider a cup of coffee to be a far cry from popping speed or injecting crystal meth. Again, this dissertation is not a handbook on how to overcome addictions. We are just hitting on the main points to round out our discussion on the blocks to spiritual progress.

Our point here is to detail why people use stimulants. Their use stems from a general dissatisfaction with the state of human affairs, both personally and planetarily. It can be as simple as wanting more energy because your life is too stressful. How easy it is to pop a pill to keep going when it is ten o'clock at night and you have not yet found time to study for the exam tomorrow. Or you are on a long drive and need to stay awake. The list of excuses is long, but the process is the same. You begin to depend on caffeine or another stimulant to keep you going when your energy starts to lag.

The biggest causes of energy drain are unresolved emotional issues and stressful lifestyles. If you are eating a healthy diet, have cleared most of your negative emotions, and lead a balanced life, you will have plenty of energy most of the time.

Denial is the number one cause of turning to stimulants. Denial of anything takes a tremendous amount of energy. The next time you are tempted to reach for a stimulant, ask, "What am I denying in myself? How am I depleting my own energy field?"

Sometimes it is about having unrealistic expectations. You are working full-time, going to school at night, raising a family, and attempting to lead a spiritual life, getting four hours of sleep per day. Drinking coffee to keep up this lifestyle will temporarily seem to make it easier to cope, but eventually the bottom will fall out and you will either get sick or become disillusioned, and no pill or jolt will work when that occurs.

Restructure your priorities. Assume, for now, that you have finite energy and that it needs to be channeled according to your core values and long-term goals.

Begin eating a healthy snack or substituting decaffeinated coffee in place of your usual routine. Learn to say "No" to more commitments than you can handle. Seek help as appropriate.

■ *Addiction to Cigarettes / Smoking*

This soul has worked with numerous clients who are, or were, struggling with this addiction. According to many nicotine addicts, it is more difficult to quit smoking than to stop using heroin.

As with alcohol, there are two steps to stopping smoking. You must first deal with the physical addiction and then with the psychological one (we suggest facing these in a sequential manner rather than trying to heal both types of addiction simultaneously).

With nicotine addiction, the physical dependency must be addressed by gradually reducing the amount of nicotine entering the body. Yes, we know some have quit "cold turkey" but for many, this is just too sudden a change. Therefore, we recommend slowly reducing the number of cigarettes each day until the number reaches zero. It might be helpful to replace the cigarettes normally smoked with straws or chewing gum. A nicotine patch may be helpful for some people, but it is not a long-term solution since the body is still receiving nicotine.

Once the physical addiction is reduced substantially, work begins on the psychological cravings. During the initial reduction in cigarette usage, therapy sessions are helpful, but mostly so the client can talk about his or her experience with reducing the number of cigarettes. As the nicotine wears off, therapy can proceed with more dynamic techniques.

The most effective technique is called "awareness in detail" and involves staying centered and focused on the details of smoking. Notice the craving the minute it arises. What does it feel like? What color is it? How does it move in the body? Describe how the saliva begins under the tongue and moves into the rest of the mouth. Follow the process of acquiring the cigarettes. How do you light them? Which hand do you use? Notice how you hold the cigarette. As you bring it to your mouth, what thoughts are going through your head? Stay with the breathing process as you inhale the smoke. Imagine you can see the smoke entering your lungs. How does it feel to exhale? Where do you place the cigarette in-between puffs? How does it burn?

Some therapists recommend varying the way you hold the cigarette, such as using your non-dominant hand, or lighting it in a different way (matches instead of lighter, etc.) in order to stay more conscious during the smoking process.

For some clients, it is important to have a long-term goal and reward system in place once you stop smoking completely. An example would be to take the money you normally spend on cigarettes and put it in a piggy bank. At the end of a year, take the money out and reward yourself with a vacation.

■ *Illegal and Prescription Drugs*

Most illegal drugs are well-known for their addictive properties, but a lot of people are not aware of the addictive properties of prescription drugs. We cannot legally give medical advice, but we will say this. If a drug is prescribed for pain, use it for the smallest amount of time possible, which means until the pain is bearable. If you believe you can get by with a non-addictive substance to manage the pain, then forego the prescription.

SSRI drugs (antidepressants) are particularly controversial because they seem to be over-prescribed, especially in the case of children. If you are severely depressed and suicidal, your doctor may be justified in prescribing an antidepressant. In fact, these drugs do save lives. However, it is our observation that approximately 90% of the time, the patient can recover adequately without taking SSRIs.

These substances tend to clip both the low and high end of consciousness, making you a "middle person." This means you will be less depressed, but also less excited about life in general. You might find impairment of your psychic and intuitive abilities as a result of taking SSRIs.

Getting back to the subject at hand, these drugs are addicting, meaning that you will likely go through withdrawal if you take them over a long period of time and then suddenly quit. Withdrawal symptoms can be quite severe with some drugs. The mind gets used to being "prompted" to produce a certain amount of serotonin and when the prompt is taken away, its dependency becomes obvious.

After a severe illness, accident or situation involving pain, a prescription drug can be appropriate, but the idea is to get off them as quickly as possible without jeopardizing your recovery. Unfortunately the pharmaceutical industry depends on having a ready supply of addicts to keep their sales robust, and they subsidize doctors heavily for promoting their products.

Every year, thousands of patients die from prescription drug complications, side-effects and withdrawal. You can research this on your own, but take our word for it – these drugs are a last resort in most cases.

In Summary

This chapter has focused on the inner state of things as you go through the Earth changes. We have covered a great deal of psychology and behavior, as well as the more philosophical and metaphysical aspects of inner growth. Finally, we have gone into some depth in discussing the blocks to spiritual progress.

We hope this rather extensive discussion on self-awareness and the spiritual path has been useful to you. In the next chapter, we will explore some of the outer changes you can expect as you move deeper into the portals and Galactic Shift. We are the Founders. Good day.

CHAPTER 4
The Outer Changes

The changes you will see in your world over the next several decades will be a blend of free will and predestiny. To accurately predict the future requires an understanding of the predestined framework upon which the world of free will is built. It also requires the insight to recognize the limits and boundaries of free will and just how much you as humans on Earth influence the preordained events.

We and this channel are attuning ourselves to the collective vibration of humanity and we see the three dominant timelines spoken of earlier in this book. Our prophecy has changed very little since the predictions put forth in our previous transmission, "*Earth Changes and 2012.*" Below, we will detail some of the aspects we might not have adequately explained prior to now, along with some additional details based on the changes that have taken place in the years since the publication of the previous book.

To accurately see what is unfolding for the future, it is important to first take a non-distorted look at what is taking place now in your world, since the changes are already underway. This channel feels strongly that the most valuable information should be new, fresh and up-to-date, rather than a rehash of old reliable methods and practices. Of course, ancient traditions do have their place, but the world is changing very fast and you need to stay on the cutting edge of what is happening, so this is our goal in presenting this information.

Unless you have been living in a cave, you have no doubt noticed that both natural and man-made disasters have increased several-fold over the past decade. In addition, hardly a day goes by when there is not some new revelation about the corruption and decay of one or more of your so-called "cherished and hallowed institutions of government and finance."

In other words, many people, companies and organizations that used to be considered "rock-solid" and full of integrity are being revealed as corrupt or full of scandal. The underlying (and overlying) soul message here is for each human soul to learn how to go within and rely on inner guidance, rather than outer authority. For the Lightworkers, this is much easier than for the general populace.

All of you have grown up with an explicit understanding that there are experts in every field that will give you reliable and accurate information. You have discovered, however, that many of these souls are working for institutions that have been bought and paid for by special interests. This is unsettling at best and terrifying at worst.

Throughout our teachings, we constantly urge you to use critical thinking, investigative analysis, a willingness to look with non-bias perception, and openness to new ideas, when examining the conditions on your planet. Most of all, we urge discernment, no matter who is speaking, especially if the material claims to be from channeled entities. Because the information in this book is a blend of the channel's higher self and our group soul complex, it may be a bit more comprehensive and easy to understand than some channeled work, but that does not automatically make it more accurate.

We encourage you to check out the following information and compare it to other sources, both channeled and more traditional. Do some research. Find out for yourselves what is really happening. To assist you in this endeavor, we begin our focus with some scientific information.

Electromagnetic Anomalies in the Sun and Planets

Let us start with an assessment of the electromagnetic anomalies occurring in this part of the Milky Way galaxy as a result of the Galactic Shift. You will recall from our previous discussions that the Galactic Shift affects this entire section of your galaxy, including all the planets in your solar system, as well as your sun. During a 150-year period (roughly 1950-2100), the Earth and solar system are moving through an "electromagnetic null zone" or "photon belt" where the polarities of the EM field are considerably weaker than normal. Below, we have detailed some of the effects of the Galactic Shift and how the portal openings add or subtract from the electromagnetic null zone.

At the time of this writing (late 2011) your scientists were noting some very erratic behavior on the part of your sun. There were contradictory predictions. Some researchers were predicting exceptionally intense solar flares through the time of the 2012 portal, while others were predicting unusually quiet times on the sun during this same period.

One thing they all agree on is that the sun's magnetic polarities are weakening, as are the Earth's. We predict that the partial collapse of the polarities on Earth will drop about 40% from "normal," and the partial collapse on the sun could be as much as 50% weaker than usual, after averaging the periodic fluctuations against a broad time period. The peak of the electromagnetic null zone in the area of your solar system (when the absence of polarity is the most noticeable) will occur around 2025.

Although the precessional alignment of 2012 will affect the Earth dramatically, it will have a negligible impact on the sun. However, the interaction of the precessional alignment on Earth with the Galactic Shift makes for a rather confusing picture as scientists try to predict what will happen to the Earth's EM field. Add to this the typical imbalance within the Earth's iron core resulting in variable movement of the magnetic poles (the north pole is shifting more quickly than the south pole, for instance), and you have a very complex picture that your supercomputers are working overtime to map.

There are essentially four factors confounding your scientists that are making it difficult for them to predict accurately what is going to happen on your world: (1) the effect of the precessional alignment of December 21, 2012, (2) the long-term effect of the Galactic Shift (1950-2100), (3) the effect of thousands of beings in the higher dimensions assisting Earth and helping correct the imbalances fostered upon her by negatively-oriented humans, and (4) the effect of the Lightworkers on the electromagnetic grid system of Earth.

We could have included a fifth factor, the presence of negative ETs in or around the Earth, but their effects are being kept to a minimum, and besides, they will be leaving the Earth between 2012 and 2025 because their vibration will no longer be supported here.

Our discussion below will center on the various anomalies and fluctuations occurring in the EM field of Earth and particularly, the sun, as you approach the midpoint of the Galactic Shift (2015 to 2035, roughly).

Sunspots, Solar Flares, and Solar Storms

Your scientists have measured solar cycles that peak and decline regularly, approximately every 11 years, meaning that periodically the sun undergoes a heightened period of storm activity on its surface, followed by several years of relative quiet. While this is not entirely correct, it has been accurate enough for planning purposes among the technological community on Earth.

Although this relatively small cycle is expected to continue throughout the Galactic Shift, the magnitude of the fluctuations in the EM field of the sun will increase dramatically. By fluctuations, we mean increases and decreases of the intensity of sunspots and solar flares over a given period of time. To some extent, these erratic bursts of solar activity will create fluctuations in the polarity of the sun's EM field, but overall the polarity will weaken, as mentioned earlier.

The biggest fluctuations of the EM field intensity on Earth will occur not only during the portal openings of 2012, 2017 and 2030, but during the period 2015 to 2035 due to the influence from the sun's EM field. The radiation emanating from the quasars near the center of the galaxy on December 21, 2012, and the near proximity of other heavenly objects with significant EM fields in 2017 and 2030, will contribute greatly to the instability of the EM field of the Earth that is triggered by the Galactic Shift. As stated above, the Galactic Shift of 1950 to 2100 will be the biggest contributor to instability in the sun's EM field.

Effects of EM Shifts on the Human Body

How will these shifts in the level of polarization of the EM field and intensity of radiation from the sun and quasars affect the human body?

You have noticed, dear Creators, that your electromagnetic bodies are an integral part of your experience as humans. You call this EM body, "etheric," because it seems more directly connected to the ethers, or spiritual energy of the Universe than your dense physical body.

Everything in your physical Universe has an electromagnetic component. Your physicists have correctly identified electromagnetism as one of the basic forces behind the creative process. Because your body is electromagnetic, you will experience the fluctuations in the Earth's EM field quite dramatically. Most of you are also quite sensitive to the sun's EM field. Even now, some of you are aware enough to tell when a solar flare or solar storm is occurring without consulting instrumentation.

Of course, your sun is not the only object in the heavens that is affecting you. There are minor influences from nearby stars as well as the quasars near the center of the galaxy. Your bodies are continuously being bombarded by gamma and x-rays from dark matter, black holes, and other features of your galaxy.

Every cell in your physical bodies contains an energy matrix that consists of the light keys and codes that configure the DNA and genetic structure that creates the various attributes of the body. The light codes and keys that generate the specific DNA configurations are in turn directly connected to the fluctuating EM fields in your etheric body. The etheric body fields are directly connected to the EM fields of the Earth and sun (and all other heavenly objects).

Basically, pure undifferentiated Source energy gets stepped down through the different dimensions and is configured appropriately to each level as it descends in vibration. Once it reaches the fifth density realm of the etheric body, its primary expression shows up as "scalar electromagnetic impulses" emanating from the etheric realms of your Universe. In this case, the fifth density aspect of your sun emanates these energies into the fifth density Earth and is then stepped down into the fourth and third densities of your planet.

Chapter 4 – The Outer Changes

As this energy pulses out into space from your sun (and from the other stars and quasars), it reaches the Earth and mutates the DNA in the cells of living organisms.

Scalar pulses are quite different than polarized field pulses. When a scalar pulse reaches the Earth, the strength of the polarized field weakens considerably even though the intensity of the radiating field increases.

This partial collapse of the polarized EM field, and the new resonant field created by the scalar waves, in turn create an opening into the etheric realms, which we are calling a portal or stargate.

The change in the EM field polarity can be measured with your scientific equipment. Fluctuations in the strength of Earth's polarized field have already been detected, but so far they have only been of superficial concern for your engineers and telecommunications operators. Nevertheless, many are warning of a potential large-scale outage when EM pulses hit your satellites and other communications devices as a result of solar flares and solar storms.

Your world is heavily dependent on telecommunications, more so than at any other time in history. A communications blackout lasting three days would have catastrophic effects on many of your systems of government and finance. The pundits issuing the warning are a lot like the boy who cried wolf. Because nothing much happened during your Y2K event, and subsequent "end of the world" scenarios have not manifested, many are discounting the effects of the coming partial polarity collapse. We anticipate major disruptions during the three portal openings, and periodic minor disruptions throughout the peak of the Galactic Shift (2015-2035).

The magnitude of the fluctuations in the polarized field during the portal openings will be quite significant, and these changes will be augmented by the Galactic Shift. From now until about 2025, the overall polarization of the EM field will be decreasing. Within that general decrease will be sharp spikes as the precessional alignment of 2012, comet flyby of 2017 and flyby of Nibiru in 2030 are added to the mix.

When the polarized field partially collapses and the scalar electromagnetic impulses take over, the lack of polarity with increased scalar energy opens a partial "zero-point" field within all EM systems that are in the path of the event. This zero-point field acts much like a tunneling device or wormhole, allowing energy to flow much more easily than before between the levels and densities adjacent to the Earth's normal composite vibration.

In essence, the portal (or stargate) opens in a manner similar to that of a tunneling device that allows electrons to move across a previously impenetrable barrier. In spiritual terms, humanity is thus opened (has access to) the etheric realms, or you could say that the veils between the etheric and physical dimensions are greatly lessened for a time.

During each spike in the intensity of the EM field (such as during the portal openings), cells are mutated in the physical life forms residing on Earth. From a biological perspective, these mutations involve responses from the DNA designed to enable the organism to adapt to the new frequencies. If the organism is unable to adapt, the mutation triggers immune system failure and eventually death.

The strongest members of humanity will not only survive, but will thrive during the Earth changes. Keep in mind, dear students, that our use of the word "strong" here does not mean physical strength, but refers to a level of consciousness that includes the ability to be flexible and bend with the changes. So, in essence, the Darwinian viewpoint does have some relevancy, since most species mutations in the past have resulted in a dying off of the weakest members of the species and a transformation of the strongest members into new life forms.

This is the "separating the wheat from the chaff" that you hear about in your religious circles, although most theologians do not fully understand what is taking place. They mistakenly attribute this "natural selection" process to judgment from God, when in fact, both the ascending and departing members of humanity are equally valid expressions of God. In other words, the Godhead, in conjunction with the individual wills of human souls, is choosing to divide humanity, without judgment, into various aspects, some of whom are ascending and some of whom are leaving Earth and reincarnating on other worlds.

In Chapter 3, we detailed the preparations necessary for souls who wish to remain with the Earth and go through ascension. Despite the opportunities presented by the zero-point openings, there is no actual deadline among currently incarnated souls for deciding which path to take, but the longer you "sit on the fence," the harder life is going to get. (Notwithstanding the above, after December 21, 2012, virtually no souls vibrating at third density will be allowed to incarnate on Earth, so in a sense you could say there is a deadline for incoming souls.)

The portal shifts act like slingshots, dramatically intensifying the effects of the choices souls are making on Earth. This often manifests as no longer being able to tolerate anything that is out of alignment with your own true path. For those who resist the lessons of the portal shifts, life on Earth will become more and more difficult.

Souls must learn to match the new frequency of Earth by tuning into her diligently and with great sincerity. Paying lip service to responsible stewardship is not enough. You must tune into your beloved Mother Earth and feel her breathing, moving and evolving as a conscious Being.

Grid Lines and Ley Lines

How do EM fluctuations come into the Earth? How are they distributed to all life forms?

Not all beings on Earth receive equal doses of EM energy from the sun and stars. Often, the location and placement of organisms is a major factor in deciding how much radiation gets absorbed. If two organisms are sunbathing, for example, and one resides on a major ley line or vortex site, and one does not, the one on the ley line or vortex will initially receive stronger and more direct EM energy fluctuations than the other organism.

All souls on Earth will go through the mutations, but the ones living on ley lines and vortices will receive the energies first and with greater magnitude than those living away from ley lines and vortices. The scalar EM pulses emanating from the sun and stars flow first into the north and south magnetic poles of the Earth and then flow across the planet from north to south, or south to north, along longitudinal meridians. These are not the perfect systematic longitude lines of your navigational charts, although the concept is similar.

These ley lines criss-cross the planet, sometimes over land and other times over sea. The grid network of ley lines intersects at various points, called vortices, or vortexes. Where the ley lines cross, the energy tends to become more concentrated.

The EM energy then moves out from the ley lines and vortices into the surrounding areas, gradually filling in the volume of the Earth's surface. Areas at high altitudes will get more direct transmissions than areas at sea level.

The fluctuations move through the atmosphere and then through the water and finally across the land. As the energy moves out from the ley lines and vortices, it does dissipate somewhat, but is still much stronger than the so-called normal background level prior to the EM pulse transmissions.

If you are an advanced soul who has cleared a lot of emotional and psychological trauma, it might be to your advantage to place yourself on a ley line or vortex during the portal shifts, or live there for a period of years during the Galactic Shift. If you are hypersensitive or have a lot of unresolved issues, it is probably best to distance yourself somewhat from the ley lines and vortices. This will give you a bit more time to process through your unresolved issues.

Cities that are located near ley lines and vortices will tend to change more quickly and often with greater volatility than cities that are away from the distribution points of EM energy. Because the energy changes are more dramatic on the ley lines and vortices, the resistance of human beings can also be greater. This can often precipitate violence and turmoil above the so-called normal levels found in most cities.

In addition, you have man-made vortices, such as places of constant religious prayer and worship. These centers act in a similar manner to natural vortices, concentrating the energy. An example of a place with both natural and man-made vortices would be Jerusalem. One would expect to find greater than normal turbulence and change occurring in such a place, which is indeed the case. (Although the religious traditions have been carried on there for thousands of years and can be considered rather stable at least as far as the ceremonies and rituals are concerned, the overall energy of the area is anything but stable.)

In summary, ley lines and vortices are areas of concentrated EM energy, which in turn create an amplification of the balance and imbalance within human consciousness. How a vortex is experienced depends a great deal on your state of consciousness. In general, your thoughts and feelings are magnified when you are on a ley line or in a vortex. Many souls who live in places like Sedona, Arizona, for example, find that hardly a day goes by without some cleansing, purification, or negative issues coming up to be healed.

For those that have worked through much of their negativity, the energies of a vortex location can amplify their good intentions and creative visualizations, augmenting their ability to manifest their desires.

The Effect of Human Consciousness on Earth's Grid System

Strictly speaking, positive and negative EM field polarities have nothing to do with good or bad, light or dark, or life-affirming or life-denying. Nevertheless, there is a correlation between the way consciousness emanates from human beings and the characteristics of EM fields. In other words, the quality of consciousness of a soul determines many of the properties of the EM energy that emanates from the physical body. This energy can be measured using EEG machines and other devices.

If a large number of souls are negatively-oriented, meaning that their dominant state of consciousness involves fear and life-denying thoughts, these thoughts, which resonate within the group and between each soul of the group according to the law of attraction principle, will tend to congregate and amplify one another until a large resonant negative field is formed in or around the area where the negative thoughts are being generated.

Chapter 4 – The Outer Changes

Areas where massacres or violent historical events have happened are prime candidates for the formation of a negative vortex. Negative manmade vortices tend to alter one's perception of time and space, just as naturally occurring negative energetic vortices do. Typically, time seems to move more slowly in a negative vortex and energy seems to drop. A feeling of tiredness or fatigue is common in such an area.

Positive vortices operate according to the same principles, but in reverse. Places where great reverence has occurred over many years, such as sacred buildings, temples, monasteries or shrines, often generate positively-oriented EM fields. Typical characteristics of positive vortices include time speeding up and a feeling of lightness and more energy.

It is possible to reverse the polarity of a negative vortex by sending positive thoughts and feelings into it repeatedly. Unfortunately, it is also possible to turn a positive vortex into a negative one in the same manner. We observe both of these conditions occurring upon your world. You have places of great conflict where large numbers of souls are praying for peace. You also have souls sending positive vibrations at a distance to places of conflict on the Earth. This peaceful energy mixes in with the negativity and in some cases is enough to transform the negative vortex into a positive one.

Conversely, we have seen negatively-oriented people sending their judgment and fear into positive vortices, thereby diluting the positive effects or in some cases turning such places into negative vortices.

At vortex sites you will often find heightened positive and negative energies since a vortex tends to magnify whatever energy is placed within it. One of the simplest of vortices is a crystal. Crystals, by themselves, do not possess any healing ability or magical properties. The consciousness placed into the crystal, however, will be magnified due to the vortex nature of the molecular structure of crystals, so the crystal acts as a talisman, increasing the energy that is placed into it.

Earth's vortex sites are the same way on a larger scale. When a place becomes recognized consciously by humans as a sacred site or vortex, it will tend to attract both positive and negative souls who wish to amplify and magnify their creative efforts. Just as performing a psychic cleaning on a crystal is a good idea, if you have a favorite vortex where you conduct ceremonies, rituals, prayer and healing, it is a good idea to clear the energy of that vortex regularly, using a standard clearing technique. You can contact the channel for more details on clearing techniques.

Negativity occurring along ley lines will tend to be transmitted from the ley lines into the entire grid network of planet Earth. Since about three-fourths of the thought forms on Earth are negative (according to our previous definition), this negativity eventually ends up being distributed worldwide along the Earth's grid system. These negative vibrations also attract negative entities or thought forms from other places.

Negativity in ley lines contributes to instability in the Earth's tectonic plates. The negative vibrations are out of phase with the Earth's natural rhythms, and she will attempt to correct this imbalance by shifting the layers of her being. She is already altering her frequency to match the incoming energy pulses from the Galactic Shift and portal openings. If the energy within her grid system is negative, this will clash with the incoming frequencies, thus often resulting in earthquakes, volcanoes and violent weather.

Beings from intermediate dimensions travel along Earth's ley lines and vortices. They use the EM grid system of Earth to navigate and propel their spacecraft. If the energy of a specific area of the grid is predominantly positive, the more enlightened beings will travel along that section. If the energy is predominantly negative, you will get the darker ET races to navigate there.

The Arcturians are the primary volunteers for clearing the grid system, ley lines and vortices of planet Earth. This is a huge undertaking and they are kept quite busy, due to the tremendous amount of negativity that finds its way into Earth's EM field. In addition to the Arcturians, various Pleiadean and Sirian factions are also assisting, though they are supervised by the Arcturians. Balancing the grid system of Earth is not easy. It requires diligence, patience, and an understanding of human free will. It is not as simple as just beaming positive energy into a negative place, because changing the energy of a vortex or ley line must be done in such a way as to not violate the free will of the human souls who are sending energy into that place.

Generally, grid work intervention is carried out when it has been determined that leaving humanity to its own devices would result in catastrophic earthquakes, volcanoes and storms capable of jeopardizing the well-being of every soul on the planet. If the state of the Earth's grid system is such that all of humanity is endangered, then the Arcturians and their assistants are authorized to use their advanced technologies to help restore balance.

The actual process of balancing the grid system is a bit like the technique of acupressure on the human body. Divine energies are beamed into problem areas using a combination of technology and consciousness.

One of the Pleiadean factions assisting with the grid work has adopted a method of helping to trigger awakening of human souls, which has been allowed by the Arcturians and councils of Light. That method is to leave behind EM field imprints in the form of sacred images and symbols, known as "crop circles" in fields of wheat and other grains. Approximately 80% of the crop circles that appear in the fields of farmers were created by the Pleiadeans. The other 20% are created by humans and other ET groups acting as copycats, imposters or hoaxers. You can determine which circles were created by the Pleiadeans because the crop will be turned and twisted in a clockwise direction if energy is being inserted into a ley line or vortex, and counterclockwise (anticlockwise) if energy is being removed from the vortex or ley line. The human "hoaxers" do not possess the technology to create these swirls in the crops in a neat and perfect manner.

The strongest ley lines and vortices are along the longitudinal lines and intersection points that roughly converge near the location where you began your time measurement system (Greenwich Mean Time in London). This is why a large number of crop circles appear in the fields of England. An additional strong ley line runs through Egypt, the Middle East and Israel. Due to the mostly desert nature of that region and often inappropriate patterns of energy for introducing symbolic communication, crop circles are rarely created along the Middle East ley line. Additional strong ley lines can be found along the "ring of fire" region (western north and south America, extreme eastern Asia, Polynesia and Indonesia, and the Aleutian region of Alaska and Siberia).

Some Details on Interventions by Various Galactic Groups

The tireless work of the Arcturians and their assistants has helped Earth avoid many of the previously prophesied cataclysms, but due to the large number of negatively-oriented souls on Earth, it is not possible to prevent all of Mother Earth's corrective actions. Our group complex, along with the Arcturians and various other councils of Light, make regular determinations as to where and when to direct our preventive energies. Often, we allow earthquakes and volcanoes to occur. Sometimes we are able to redirect earthquakes farther out to sea away from populated areas, or reduce the magnitude of large earthquakes, or even-out the pressure inside the Earth's crust to prevent certain volcanoes from erupting.

Our intention is to keep earthquakes in populated regions of the world below 8.0 on your Richter scale. So far, most of the larger earthquakes have been successfully moved off shore. In 2011, an earthquake and tsunami caused the destruction of some of your nuclear facilities in the country of Japan. This was allowed to happen because the radiation levels released were not sufficient to endanger all life forms on Earth, and our various groups determined that allowing this cataclysm might send a strong message to those in the nuclear industry that it was time to develop safer ways of producing and delivering energy. Since the destruction of the nuclear plants, we note that a few souls employed in that industry have heeded the warning, while the majority has not.

It is important to note that none of us in the higher realms ever intentionally cause a disaster on your Earth. In addition, we regularly intervene in the affairs of negative ETs when their actions threaten the entire life cycle on Earth.

As stated previously, we keep our intervention to minimal levels and rarely prevent man-made disasters, even when it is obvious to our detection systems that a disaster is about to occur. In a few rare cases, we will warn you prior to the event, but for the most part, you are allowed to continue messing up your planet as long as there are still safe places for the Lightworkers.

The Galactic Confederation (aka Galactic Federation), a group of souls from over 1,000 star systems, is the primary group in charge of neutralizing your nuclear, chemical and electromagnetic weapons systems whenever it is determined that the use of such devices could endanger the entire Earth. They have already intervened on five different occasions when it appeared likely that you would destroy yourselves with nuclear weapons. They have also prevented large-scale use of certain EM weapons when their deployment would have threatened to destabilize the Earth's grid system beyond the point of recovery.

There have been a couple of interventions in your weather modification programs when the methods being employed threatened the stability of your atmosphere. Contrary to popular belief, however, chemtrails (aerosol spraying of chemicals into your atmosphere to control weather) generally do not significantly impact areas thousands of miles away from the area of application. Chemtrails for purposes of warfare or biological population control are not perfected to the point where large-scale intervention is necessary. The vast majority of the trails seen in your skies involve ordinary condensation from airplane exhaust.

We have contemplated intervention in your genetically modified organisms program and have considered cleaning up some of the pollution from your natural gas wells, but so far these issues have not compromised the Earth sufficiently to warrant completely stopping these programs. Also, it would be difficult to intervene in your biological experimentation without making ourselves obvious to your scientists.

We wish to reiterate that we have no intention of revealing ourselves to large numbers of humanity. Only a tiny percentage of souls on Earth are open and receptive to our messages and even fewer are ready to have spacecraft landing in their front yards. Besides, our group complex has evolved beyond the need for mechanical transport devices.

Another reason we are not intervening in more programs is because large numbers of souls on Earth are becoming aware of the inherent dangers in many of your genetic and biological endeavors and especially, genetically modified organisms. This means you may be able to reverse some of the more destructive programs without our direct help.

We note that the use of genetically modified crops, and the large amount of pesticides sprayed on those crops, has endangered your honeybees and other insects. If the bee levels drop below a certain point, a small amount of intervention may be undertaken to ensure that vital crops continue to get pollinated. We also assure you that some non-GMO seeds will be kept safe from cross-pollination.

Electromagnetic Pollution

The use of telecommunications devices, including mobile phone towers and other systems, has created fluctuations in Earth's EM field. These human-caused EM field fluctuations often interfere with your natural EM rhythms and the base rhythms of the Earth. Concentrated use of mobile phone towers and radio/TV transmitters also interferes with the navigational abilities of birds and insects.

The effect on humans is cumulative and will contribute to the decline of the immune system in a large segment of the population. The effect is most notable in your cities. The use of mobile phones for more than 30 minutes per day (depending on the specific device and any shielding being employed) can create a significant residual vibration in your EM field. There are various shielding mechanisms and exercises you can undertake to minimize EM pollution. Because it is often difficult to tell how effective a particular shielding device is, the best policy is to spend a lot of time away from crowded, polluted cities. We realize this is not easy, but living in large cities compromises your immune system unless you are already vibrating at fifth density.

Even if the city you live in is not considered likely to undergo coastal flooding or major earthquakes, you might consider moving to a less populated area in order to get away from EM pollution. (We will discuss later another important reason to get away from cities – the economic instability that is increasing almost daily.)

Changes to Your Climate

Earth's climate is a complex system that is influenced by and from many sources. This includes mountain ranges, oceans and ocean currents, solar flares, positive ions generated by large cities, high and low pressure systems, jet streams and prevailing wind patterns (warm, cold, occluded and stationary fronts) and the overall effect of the Earth's rotation, as well as the tilt of the axis (the seasons). While the effect of EM fields on weather is generally not obvious, there is, nevertheless, a relationship between the two.

To go into detail on the relationship between electromagnetism and weather would require a highly technical and extensive discussion, so we will attempt to keep it simple.

The Earth is an electromagnetic Being of Light, existing on seven levels. The various levels interact with one another, often in harmony and sometimes not. Although weather exists in fourth and fifth densities, it general falls into the third density category. Human consciousness is fourth density and electromagnetism, fifth density. It is common knowledge in the higher realms that human consciousness affects the weather and vice versa.

The influence of negativity from the mass consciousness of humanity on the EM systems of Earth was detailed in our previous section. The influence of negative consciousness on the weather of Earth will be discussed now. Basically, the EM field of Earth exists on all three primary density levels: third, fourth and fifth. The level most relevant to our discussion is fourth density because that is the realm of mind over matter.

While most individual souls on Earth have not perfected the art of psychokinetics (the ability to convert the energy of consciousness into a tangible mechanical force in order to move objects by thought, etc.), when a large number of souls all think and feel the same way (or at least in a similar way), it can cause temporary positive or negative vortices to form that cross over from purely electromagnetic into the geophysical realm. If the predominant consciousness is negative, these vortices will be negative. Usually such negative energy fields interact with weather phenomenon that is already in a state of great fluctuation (such as intense low pressure systems, hurricanes, cyclones and tornadoes). The imbalances created within the negative vortices of human thought can interact with these weather patterns, enhancing their destructiveness.

It is also possible for the collective thoughts of humanity to change the direction of storms (alter the storm track). For example, a few souls praying that a tornado spare their village rarely generate enough energy to make much of a difference. (This is due to the unconscious belief in powerlessness underlying prayer in most souls. If a group of highly enlightened souls uses concentrated prayer, the effects can be much more significant.)

If you are a Lightworker and you live in a sparsely populated area, you will have a greater positive influence on the weather around you than if you live in a city because in a crowded place your thoughts can become "diluted" by the prevalent consciousness of the area.

As an aside, there are world-renowned psychics who cannot successfully influence slot machines at crowded casinos or win lotteries due to interference from the thought forms of others. In the case of lotteries, the problem is quite obvious. You may have millions of souls all trying to influence the little colored balls in the tumbler, and all that psychokinetic energy bounces off itself. Nevertheless, there have been a couple of cases where lotteries have been won through psychic means.

Returning to our main discussion, while it is not a good idea to assume you can influence the weather directly at your level of evolvement, it is also important not to discount your powerful, spiritual nature. We suggest you go ahead and attempt to influence the weather, but do it carefully. Preface your prayers and meditation with a statement such as, *"If it be for the highest and best soul growth, happiness and well-being of the people of this community, I ask that this storm (or earthquake, or volcano) be stopped or steered away from here. Thank you, beloved Mother Earth, for answering my prayer."*

Know that there are many cases where the souls in an area affected by disaster have a collective agreement to go through that event. One such example was the tsunami of Indonesia in late 2004 that killed over 200,000 people. Most of the souls in that region lived in dire poverty and a large percentage had basically given up hope of living a meaningful life and fulfilling their soul purpose. Some had come in specifically to learn what it feels like to live in dire poverty and they had learned all they desired from that experience. Others came in to teach love and compassion to those of greater affluence.

This disaster was allowed to happen because of the collective soul agreement (though mostly unconscious) of the people living in that area. For enlightened souls going through that experience, they were either there to assist in the rescue efforts, or they received guidance to move prior to the event. A few souls who were partially awakened may have needed to clear some karma or heal some unresolved emotions and needed an event such as that to help trigger their healing process.

Regardless of the reason for experiencing a weather-related disaster, the role of human consciousness in weather needs to be understood. Humanity in general has not evolved sufficiently to greatly affect natural events, but a collective effort does make some difference. A unified humanity is capable of altering the trajectory of celestial objects, for example. Conversely, an area with a lot of negativity can bring undesired weather conditions.

To review, it is pretty much agreed that weather can affect human moods, but not very many souls are aware that it can go the other direction as well. An area with a lot of suppressed anger, for example, can attract to itself violent storms. While it is overly simplistic (and not very compassionate) to state that people bring natural disasters upon themselves because of their unresolved emotions, there are, nevertheless, many situations in which this has played itself out in Earth's history.

Regardless of how much of a role humanity plays in attracting or repelling weather-related calamities, it is possible to tune into the "moods" of planet Earth and anticipate where violent weather will strike and how you can be safe from extreme storms.

To do this, the first step is tuning in to the natural world. This may seem obvious, but a lot of souls get so caught up in their daily lives that they barely take time out to gaze up at the sky and notice the types and direction of clouds. You can determine the level of barometric pressure even if you do not have any instrumentation, by becoming aware of the subtle changes in your body and that of animals and plants. An area can communicate to you its general feelings about the coming seasons. Even if the trees do not drop their leaves early, you can often sense when it is going to be a hard winter.

After each section below, we will give our perception of the places most likely to be relatively unaffected by severe cataclysms, such as violent storms and earthquakes. Due to free will, these "safe" places can shift over time, so take this only as a guide and not as gospel

Violent Storms, Cyclones and Tornadoes

Over the next 20 years, the number and intensity of extreme storms is likely to increase dramatically. The year 2011, for instance, was one of the most active ever recorded for tornadoes in the USA. Many of the largest rivers in that country have had historic floods. Severe flooding has also occurred in China. Cyclones have become erratic, sometimes occurring out of season, and moving in more unpredictable ways. A number of major cities are predicted to be in the path of severe storms as the Earth changes continue to accelerate.

The areas most likely to see violent weather in the years to come are essentially the same places that are already experiencing these conditions, including parts of the Caribbean, ring of fire in eastern Asia (Japan and Indonesia) and northern Australia (Queensland).

Cities in the path of severe weather may include Miami, Florida, Houston, Texas, New Orleans, Louisiana, Tokyo, Japan, Brisbane and Cairns, Australia, and many places in Asia (populated areas there are too numerous to mention individually).

Interestingly, one of the biggest problems facing cities is not severe weather, but drought. This is due to two factors. First, pollution emitted from cities tends to form positive ions, which inhibit the formation of storms. You might note that large, general storms still hit cities regularly, but in areas or at times of the year when storms are more localized, they will often circumvent large cities due to the blocking ridge of positive ions. Second, a lot of souls love warm, sunny weather, regardless of whether or not they live in a sunny climate zone. The combined thought forms of "Rain, rain, go away, come again another day," can influence the formation and path of storms. We will talk more about drought in the next section.

Best Places to Avoid Severe Weather

Almost every area of the planet experiences some severe weather at different times of the year. By listening to your inner guidance, you can receive instructions as to when to plant crops, protect property, seek shelter, etc.

There will be a few places that normally do not get cyclones (hurricanes, typhoons, and windstorms), tornadoes or large hail, that will start experiencing these conditions more often. However, for the most part, the areas currently favored by these events will simply receive more of them, with greater intensity. If you live in a heavily forested mountain area, you will tend to get more erratic winter snowstorms (some years with heavy snowfall, others with almost none at all).

In general, there will be a greater variance than usual in the temperate zones, but you will likely not experience many severe outbreaks during the warmer seasons if you live in the northern forests of North America, Scandinavia and Siberia, or the southern areas of South America and New Zealand. Keep in mind that the areas mentioned below include the places least likely to be in the path of hail and windstorms, but do not include places safe from drought and floods, which will be covered next.

Table 4 – Best Places to Avoid Severe Weather

<u>North America</u>: Southwest Canada, Northwest USA

<u>South America</u>: Parts of Argentina, Brazil and Uruguay

<u>Europe</u>: Southern France, Northern Italy, Greece

<u>Middle East</u>: Most areas

<u>Asia</u>: Ural Mountains, Mongolia, northwest China

<u>Africa</u>: South Africa

<u>Australia</u>: North New South Wales, South Queensland

Droughts and Floods

Although there are many parts of the world that will likely be free of violent storms, almost every part of the Earth will experience more erratic climate conditions. This means more floods and droughts, and the problems that result from these imbalances; namely, fires, mudslides, ruined crops, pestilence, starvation and lack of fresh water. Indirectly, this means more disease and pollution as well, not to mention disrupted economies, unemployment, and massive debt as governments attempt to financially bail out stricken areas.

Your insurance companies will eventually be unable to pay for all the repairs and replacements needed after the escalating disasters.

Millions of people will become displaced from their homes and businesses. Some will have the means to easily relocate, but the vast majority will become homeless and may end up wandering from place to place looking for fresh food and water.

As mentioned in our previous work, the increased solar storms associated with the EM null zone (Galactic Shift) will tend to warm up and dry out many regions of the Earth. This, coupled with deforestation in some parts of the world, and your continuing emissions of greenhouse gases, will cause an overall rise in temperature. This rise will not be uniform throughout the world, but will tend to exacerbate areas that are already hot. The biggest difference, for those of you taking note of specifics, will be higher nighttime temperatures. In addition to the heat generated by cities, the radiation of heat leaving the surface of Earth after a sunny day will tend to become more and more trapped as a result of greenhouse gases.

We remind you that the Galactic Shift is responsible for about 90 percent of Earth's warming. Only about 10 percent is attributable to the burning of fossil fuels. Even if you were to immediately stop all greenhouse gas emissions (something we do not believe will happen), the warming and drying out of Earth would continue.

This is not to suggest that the entire world will turn into a desert, but we do see deserts expanding 10 to 20 percent between now and 2030. Unless you make enlightened agricultural practices a high priority, it is unlikely that food production will keep up with demand, since as of the time of this transmission, your population was still increasing, while available tillable land was decreasing.

Although overall levels of precipitation will decrease, storms will become more stagnant due to a weakening of the jet stream and trade winds in some areas. This will cause many storms to last longer and, in the tropics where there is a lot of moisture to work with, will cause heavier rainfall in localized areas.

The Prospects for Another Ice Age

Some of you have received predictions of another ice age. Paradoxically, the warming and drying of the Earth actually supports unusual cooling in specific areas. There are two main factors determining the harshness of winters in your temperate, populated zones. One is the ocean currents, and two is the position of high pressure zones in the sub-arctic regions. We anticipate moderate to severe changes in currents such as the Gulf Stream, and unusual behavior in your northern Canadian high pressure zones, which will cause countries and provinces bordering the North Atlantic Ocean to have wild fluctuations in temperatures from year to year.

Already this is occurring in Great Britain, with generally warmer summers and colder winters in recent years. The complexities of ocean currents and high pressure systems are too great to detail, but you can expect more extremes in the years to come.

Let us repeat our prediction regarding a coming ice age. There are several prophecies that predict a mini or complete ice age within the next several years.

We do not see this happening right away, but we do see colder winters in some parts of the Earth due to alteration of ocean currents. Most notably, the Gulf Stream, which keeps the U.K. moderate in winter, will likely weaken and move, causing much harsher winters in that area.

The next significant ice age is likely to be about 500 years from now.

The Rainfall "Haves" and "Have-Nots"

Returning to the subject of flooding, we see major problems with your rivers, dikes, levees, bridges and surrounding farmland in many countries.

During the spring and summer of 2011, we noted major flooding of your Mississippi and Missouri Rivers in the USA, while only 300km away in the state of Texas, one of the worst droughts in your recorded history was underway. By the end of summer 2011, the heat and drought in the middle of the USA was the worst since the dust bowl of the 1930s.

You will see more of these disparities in the years ahead. Single storms will dump as much rain as some areas usually see in an entire year. Local places will receive little or no rainfall, while barely 100km away, locations continue to be deluged.

This irregular distribution of moisture will in turn cause difficulties in water supplies. Already, much of the water supply for your major cities is polluted and this will make things worse. In some places, you have several cities relying on a single reservoir or river and these reservoirs and rivers are in danger of drying up.

We observe that in some of your existing deserts, there are lush green golf courses, water parks and artificial lakes. It seems in your desert cities that the vast majority of the population is in denial about everything that is necessary in getting water there. As long as water flows out when you turn on the tap, it's business as usual.

We note that the rivers, dams and canals that are most relied upon by large cities are increasingly becoming a source of water right disputes, particularly in the desert southwest of the USA, as well as in some of the rivers of North Africa. It is estimated by your mainstream engineers that the Colorado River basin will fail to supply the water needs of Los Angeles, Las Vegas and Phoenix by the year 2030.

With significant portions of your agricultural land under water due to flooding, and rivers and streams drying up a short distance away, your supply of high quality food and fresh water will continue to erode (pardon our pun).

Chapter 4 – The Outer Changes

How Droughts and Floods Affect Food Distribution

In your western civilizations (and some of your eastern ones as well) you are heavily dependent on factory farms that ship goods hundreds, if not thousands of kilometers away to central distribution centers. From these centers, your fossil-fuel driven trucks transport the food to supermarkets and warehouses. If floods or drought strike one of these central agricultural regions, then it will be necessary to get your food from even farther away if you have no local options established.

You have no doubt noticed the escalating cost of fossil fuels. As it gets more expensive to ship the dwindling supplies of food and water, prices will inevitably rise. The channel notes that in the year 2011, the average price of some major commodities rose between 40 and 80 percent over the previous year.

(We also note that a lot of this increase was due to commodity price speculation, a legal form of gambling that occurs in your stock and options markets. Essentially, financial traders bet that the cost of resources will go up and they trade accordingly, forcing the prices up artificially above the levels normally associated with the economic principle of supply and demand.)

To cut costs, agribusiness companies are resorting to genetically modified crops and are taking shortcuts in their inspection programs. You can couple this with the fact that a huge portion of food grown in the industrialized nations gets heavily processed with chemicals in order to keep it on store shelves longer without spoiling. Of course, there are also chemicals to make the food taste and look better, almost all of which have been determined to be unhealthy to the human body.

We do not intend to ramble on about the sorry state of your food distribution system. Certainly in fertile areas local organic farms are sprouting up (again, pardon our pun). The phrase, "Eat and shop locally," is more than just a catchy slogan. It will be a way of life in the years to come. Since only about 10 percent of the world's land surface area is considered a "fertile region," those living in desert cities and other areas with limited agriculture will experience a sharp decline in standard of living. This will cause mass migrations.

Starvation and Thirst in Humans

Many humans are currently underfed and dehydrated. This is due, in the poorest countries, to insufficient amounts of whole food and fresh water, but in the industrialized countries it is due to poor diet and the over-use of sweet and caffeinated beverages. As the economies of most countries continue into decline, many humans will cut corners to save money, opting for the brightly colored package with no nutrition inside, over the healthy product that costs much more.

As Earth approaches the year 2015, shortages of basic food products will begin to appear (or disappear) on store shelves. This will be due not only to climatic conditions, but also the escalating cost of fossil fuels and instability in governments. Many of the riots and revolts currently being experienced in the Middle East will spread to seemingly more stable countries, including the United Kingdom, USA and even China. As standard of living conditions worsen, the people will have less tolerance for continuing to live in a system of "haves" and "have-nots."

These revolts will tend to happen in the more affluent parts of the world, because in the areas already hit by scarcities of food and water, there is very little energy available to put into protests. People are more concerned with just trying to survive day to day.

As mentioned in Chapter 1, the day will come when roving bands of people in search of food and water will overrun towns and villages, plundering as they go along. Those communities vibrating at high fourth density and above will not fall victim to humans desperate for survival, because of the principle of psychological invisibility (which was discussed earlier). In some cases, the desperate humans will not even see these enlightened communities and even if they do, they will be unable to take over and control them due to the difference in vibration between their roving gangs and the Lightworkers.

Up to 10 percent of humanity might perish from droughts and floods between now and 2030, or more accurately, from the results of these conditions – pestilence, disease, and the aforementioned political and social unrest (this does not include immune system failure). The actual numbers washed away in a flood, or killed by dehydration in desert heat, will be relatively small. More likely is the scenario of illness from contaminated water (found in both floods and droughts) as well as famine from ruined crops.

In the table below, you will note that many of the areas predicted to have drought and floods are already prone to these conditions. They will simply experience greater frequency and severity of outbreaks:

Table 5 – Areas Predicted for Droughts and Floods

North America – Mississippi River Delta and New Orleans (flood), Southern Florida (drought and flood), Central California including deltas and San Joaquin/Sacramento River Valleys (flood), Southern California (flood with mudslides, especially in El Nino years), Midwestern USA (drought and flood), Central South Canada high plains (drought and flood), Central Mexico high basin lands (drought and flood), parts of Guatemala and El Salvador (flood).

South America – Upper Amazon River Basin (both drought and flood), Southeast Coast including Brazil and Argentina and the major cities of Rio de Janeiro and Buenos Aires (drought).

Europe – Southern United Kingdom (flood and drought), Northern and Central France (flood and drought), parts of Belgium and the Netherlands (flood), Southern Spain (drought), Northern Italy below Milan (flood), parts of Greece and Turkey (drought), parts of Yugoslavia and western Russia (drought and flood).

Africa – Northern countries (flood), East Central countries (flood), West Central areas (drought)

Asia – Northern and Central Russia (drought), Northern China (flood), Southern China (drought), Malaysia (flood), southern Japan (drought), Central India (drought and excessive heat), southern India (flood).

Australia – Southern and Western Victoria (drought), Northern Queensland (flood)

The Best Places to Avoid Floods and Droughts

In determining our criteria for the best places to live, we are taking into account many factors besides climate, including assessing the infrastructure already in place to consume locally produced food, as well as water tables and level of pollution. For example, the San Joaquin valley of California in the western USA may produce a lot of food (until the sea levels flood the levees in a few years), but the quality of the food is generally very poor, with high levels of pesticides in most crops and depleted soil from over-use. This region currently grows almost one-fourth of the produce distributed in the USA. Therefore, the inland valleys of California are not on the recommended safe list. Generally all the areas listed below need to be at least six meters above sea level to be considered safe. Here is the list:

Table 6 – Best Places to Avoid Drought and Flood

Southwestern and Southeastern Canada

Northwestern and Northeastern USA

Portions of inland Southeastern USA

Costa Rica and portions of Central America

Uruguay and parts of Argentina

Southern France and Northern Spain

Parts of the Ural Mountains in Southern Russia

Portions of Western China and Southern Siberia

Portions of Central and Southern Africa

Portions of Northern New South Wales, Australia

Note: You can also see that the United Kingdom is not on the list. This is due in part to the anticipation that the summers will become hotter and winters colder due to disruption of the Gulf Stream. It is also due to soil depletion and over-grazing in some areas of that region.

Earthquakes and Volcanoes

We mentioned during our discussion of the balancing of negativity in the Earth's grid system that the various groups working with the Earth will do their best to prevent any major earthquakes from occurring in or around major cities.

That said, in this section we will discuss the likelihood of major quakes and where to anticipate them. We will then detail the places least likely to experience earthquakes.

A certain number of quakes are a normal, natural part of the process of Earth's evolution and can be witnessed as the gradual shifting of the tectonic plates. However, you also have destabilizing effects caused by human and negative ET souls. These include: (1) negative energy being generated by large numbers of humans (and negative ETs), especially those living on or near ley lines and vortices; (2) the effects of hydraulic fracturing of shale in order to extract natural gas (a practice often known as "fracking"); (3) underground tests of nuclear devices, a practice that has declined in recent years, but still occurs in some countries; (4) the surge in volcanic activity in certain portions of the "ring of fire" that triggers earthquakes and tsunamis in some cases; (5) a small number of quakes induced electromagnetically by humans (and negative ETs) tinkering with the upper atmosphere in projects such as HAARP; and (6) intentional manipulation of the Earth's magnetic field by negative ET groups.

(Please remember that the activities of negative ET groups are being closely monitored by many positive ET groups and in any cases where the activities of the negative ETs are endangering the entire Earth, they are being neutralized by the positive ET groups.)

The prophecies that state that major portions of land masses will disappear under the sea, or new land masses will rise thousands of meters into the air, are either erroneous, or are based on a very large time frame (relative to human generations). In other words, this channel has correctly stated that it would take 9.0 magnitude earthquakes occurring every day for about 30 years to cause 4,000-meter tall mountains to sink beneath the sea, or new mountains to rise out of the sea to that altitude.

During the increasing intensity of the Galactic Shift (up until about 2025), the frequency and magnitude of earthquakes will continue increasing, but not to the extent described in many of the "doom and gloom" prophecies. Many of the doomsday prophecies were given as warnings to humanity that this is what can happen if humanity does not make major changes. We see, however, less than a 0.1% likelihood of cataclysmic earthquakes during the portal shifts.

Essentially, without any intervention in humanity's affairs, the Earth changes would indeed be much more severe than they are currently. This is because the negativity generated along the ley lines and vortices would have triggered a great many 9.0 plus earthquakes by this time. In addition, as stated numerous times before, you would likely have annihilated yourselves with nuclear weapons on at least five occasions.

Without Divine intervention in the form of positively-oriented beings from higher dimensions, the negative ETs would have successfully taken over your planet, either directly, or through interbreeding. Some of these groups would have found a way of destroying all life forms on the planet except those that are appropriate to their own selfish ends.

The very fact that you are here reading these words is attributable to the various Divine Dispensations that have been granted to ensure that there are always safe places for the Lightworkers.

Let us now take a look at the most and least likely places to see earthquakes and volcanoes in the years to come on Earth.

Notwithstanding the Divine Dispensation information given above, here are the latest predictions of where earthquakes and volcanoes will occur and locations of safe places where there is little or no chance of earthquakes and volcanoes.

The Where and When of Earthquakes and Volcanoes

First of all, let us respond to a few recent prophecies given by others before we give our own.

We do *not* anticipate an eruption of the super-caldera, Yellowstone Lake at Yellowstone National Park, for about 10,000 years. Such an eruption would make most of the southern part of Canada and northern part of the USA uninhabitable for years.

We do *not* anticipate volcanoes going off to such an extent around the world that it would cause three days of darkness; i.e., a nuclear winter syndrome.

At this point, there is less than a 50 percent chance that Mount Shasta in Northern California will erupt in the next 30 years.

Chapter 4 – The Outer Changes

Mount Rainier in Washington State has about a 50-50 chance of erupting in the next 30 years. Various ET groups are monitoring the situation to see if intervention is appropriate.

There are two volcanoes in northwest Canada and two more in southern Alaska that may erupt, as well as two farther out in the Aleutian Island chain. There are three volcanoes in the Asian region of the "ring of fire" that may erupt. There are two mountains in Indonesia and two in the Philippines that could erupt. These are in addition to the ones that are currently active. If you wish more details, such as the names of each individual volcano and its likelihood of eruption, please furnish the channel with geological maps. Keep in mind that the activities of the Arcturians are influencing the likelihood of these eruptions.

As for earthquakes, we anticipate several moderate ones in the region known as southern California, between 6.0 and 7.0 on your Richter scale, within the next few years, but the only one we see above 8.0 would occur about 200 miles off the coast of Eureka, California. We see a moderate tsunami being generated from that quake. The anticipated window for this quake is spring to summer of 2012.

About 300 miles west of the Olympic peninsula, we see an earthquake occurring between 7.0 and 8.0. We see a minor tsunami being generated. This quake is most likely to occur in the fall of 2012.

South of the Aleutian chain, we see several earthquakes in the 7.0 to 7.5 range, generating small tsunamis. These quakes will likely continue through 2012 and 2013.

In Japan, we see two additional earthquakes in the 7.0 to 8.0 range, generating small tsunamis, probably aftershocks of the one that occurred in early 2011 that had a magnitude of 9.0. By the time this book goes to print, these aftershocks will likely have already occurred. The window is late 2011 or early 2012.

We see two new quakes not related to the one in 2011, one north of Japan and one south, in the 6.0 to 7.0 range, during 2012 and 2013.

We see two quakes in the Indonesia area between 7.0 and 7.5. At this time, we do not anticipate major tsunami activity from these events. Damage will be relatively minor. The most likely time window for these quakes is near the end of 2012 (around the time of the portal opening).

We see one quake in Chile, South America, at about 7.5. We are working with the Arcturians to help move this quake farther out to sea. Nevertheless, we anticipate some damage and casualties. The timetable for this quake is uncertain. Originally it was anticipated for late 2011, but the Arcturians are attempting to push it into 2013.

We see a quake off the west coast of Africa at about 6.5. There is no window of time calculated at this point.

We see a quake in central Turkey at about 6.5. We have some channels in the area that will hopefully alert the people of Turkey beforehand. This is not a particularly strong quake, but substandard construction in that area can cause major damage during quakes above 6.0. The window on this quake is mid-2012 to mid-2013, which gives the people time to shore up their buildings somewhat.

We see two quakes in central China in the 6.5 to 7.0 range, mostly in relatively unpopulated areas, in 2012 and 2013.

We see several quakes in the Madrid fault of central USA in the 6.0 to 6.5 range. We see possible levee breaches along major rivers in the area as a result. Your engineers are attempting to shore up the levees after historical flooding during the spring and summer of 2011 in the areas near the Madrid fault. By the time this book goes to print, several smaller quakes will likely have occurred (late 2011), which are precursors to larger ones in 2012 and 2013.

We see several smaller quakes in the Middle East region. No time windows are given.

We see two quakes in Mexico in the 6.5 to 7.0 range. These will likely occur in the high mountains south and east of Mexico City, causing only minor damage. The Arcturians are attempting to move smaller temblors in the 5.5 to 6.0 range away from Mexico City, since there are millions of inhabitants of that city that live in substandard dwellings capable of being completely destroyed in quakes above 5.5.

Table 7 - The Safest Places to Be During Earthquakes and Volcanoes

Eastern Canada and Eastern USA
Western Gulf of Mexico
United Kingdom and Scandinavia
Central Europe
Northern Siberia
Eastern South America
Eastern and Central Africa
Western Australia

Changes to Your Coastlines

Most of the changes that will likely occur along your coastlines are what you would expect when a large body of water rises as much as several meters over a period of 10, 20 or 30 years. This would include gradual erosion of beaches and inundation of fresh water estuaries with salt water, incursion of salt water into levees holding back rivers during flood season, reclaiming of marshland by the sea, etc.

The gradual rising of the oceans will not cause immediate wide-scale destruction. It is the combination of rising sea levels with violent storms, and the resulting storm surge, that will wreak havoc with coastal properties and communities.

For example, if a windstorm, such as a hurricane, were to move into the east coast of the USA at high tide, you would have the rise in sea level, coupled with the tide, added to the storm surge. Due to the counterclockwise (anticlockwise) circulation of such storms in the northern hemisphere, if you live north of the center of the storm as it hits the coast, you have the onshore wind, plus the direction of the storm, added to the storm surge.

Some coastal cities are certainly better prepared for things like this than others. However, we have observed that in most of your cities, profit taking (making money) has a higher priority than safety in architecture. Even if you use conservative estimates, sooner or later that beach condominium is going to experience unusually high wave action.

You have heard the expression, "If you build your house on sand…" In other words, do not get attached to your coastal real estate, and have a back-up plan to be somewhere else.

Migration from Coastal Cities

As the climate grows more variable and the sea levels rise, a greater number of people will become displaced who live in coastal cities. This, coupled with increasing economic instability in most countries, will force a lot of souls to migrate away from their current residences. If they can afford to buy a house in the country, they will do so, but the vast majority will either not have that option, or will not have the insight to know how to exercise that option. This mass exodus will likely be slow at first and then pick up speed as the escalating disasters continue to unfold.

Due to the law of attraction, souls will tend to migrate to places that match their level of vibration. In some cases, the karmic issues of souls will lead them to areas where they are to teach or learn specific lessons, so it is not entirely correct to say, "The fearful will go to places where others live in fear and the loving will go to places where others live in love." You might have a soul assignment to be a loving and compassionate presence and go where others are in fear in order to be a demonstration of another way of life. Those in fear might be attracted to a loving place because their souls are ready to learn about love.

Generally speaking, if you have a loving and wise consciousness, you will be attracted to a safe place. You will likely receive some sort of warning before a disaster is to strike and the warning will prompt you to take action before it is too late. The guidance may be overt, as in a spirit guide coming in a vision and telling you to move, or it may be more covert, such as losing a job and receiving a new job offer in a safer location.

The souls receiving the migrants who take part in these "Divine appointments," may or may not know why they are hiring the recently laid off worker, or taking a fearful person into their home despite the objection of their egos.

No matter how clairvoyant or intuitive you are, you will not be able to see every detail of the upcoming Earth changes. Not even our group complex (the Founders) can know everything that is going to happen. That is the beauty (and curse) of free will. The best you can do is ask your God Presence within to guide you as you determine the safest and best place to live. The ideal location will be one that stimulates your soul growth, as well as bringing a sense of well-being. However, it will not be without its challenges. A path of rapid soul growth is almost never easy. But you have what it takes to meet those challenges.

The Psychological Impact of Rising Sea Levels

Your mainstream scientists have admitted that many of your coastlines will be altered in the years to come. The main disagreements are about how long it will take to inundate the major cities. The more conservative pundits are saying it might be 100 years before Miami and Fort Lauderdale disappear beneath the sea, while a few are saying it could happen in 10 to 20 years. Our assessment is similar to the small minority that expects the process of coastal flooding to increase quickly within a short time period. This is because we are expecting the effects of the Galactic Shift to compound the other factors involved. One major factor (discussed earlier) is the rise in sea surface temperatures and resulting increase in violent storms.

A big problem humanity has involves overdevelopment of sensitive land areas, such as marshes, wetlands and deltas. Although the rising sea levels will have a major impact on everyone living close by at altitudes of less than six meters, those who are proactive and take the necessary steps can minimize their chances of wave and erosion damage.

If you simply must have a house on the beach, at least raise it up on solid columns or beams capable of withstanding hurricane force winds and waves 10 meters high. Otherwise, you should consider selling your beachfront home and moving inland at least 20 to 30 miles, to an altitude of at least 30 meters (to be completely safe), or at least 10 meters (to be safe in the short term).

Many people who live in cities do not believe they can afford to move because their employment is there, or they do not have the funds to rent or buy a house inland at higher altitudes. However, if you are a Lightworker, then you know that you have the power to change your life and it is just a matter of applying the higher principles of creativity that you have already been taught.

It will be necessary to release your belief in lack and limitation. Do your emotional clearing work. Get in touch with the fearful self and give it some healing and therapy. While you are still living in harm's way, bless the coastline and the surf. Bless each storm as it passes by. Ask your God Presence within to show you the specific steps you need to take to get yourselves to safety.

Some of those steps may not appeal to your ego. For example, if you have been putting off healing your relationship with your parents, going to stay with them until you have the resources to find your own place might seem like the farthest thing from your mind, yet it might be exactly what your soul needs to finish unlearned lessons. Your soul might gently nudge you by allowing you to lose your job in the city just as dear old Mom and Dad invite you back to their farmhouse in the country.

As you know, a willingness to let go of materiality is essential to your well-being in the years to come. This is not the same as sacrifice. The idea of sacrifice implies that what you are giving up has tremendous value, but must be released in order to get something of even greater value. Yet value is often in the eyes of the beholder, and what is best for your soul growth has far greater value than many of the things your ego might hold dear. Often these are the things that hold you back on your path, regardless of how many dollars something appears to be worth.

You may have family members that do not want to leave the coastal city and move inland. They might believe you have gone "off your rocker" with the doomsday scenarios. This is not doomsday, but common sense and it is based not only on our prophecies, but on the predictions of mainstream science.

A few of you may be called to remain in the cities to offer assistance to those who are suffering. If you feel a strong sense of needing to remain, just know that you will be safe through the floods.

Pay close attention to the subtle (and obvious) signals coming from your higher self. Notice how your body feels as you contemplate each decision.

As you grow and evolve, you will feel a great deal of peace and confidence that you will be in the right place at the right time.

We have not included any tables detailing places to avoid danger or find safety regarding rising sea levels, since there are hundreds of major cities located at sea level that will not be safe in the years to come. Safe places will be inland and well above six meters in altitude.

Changes to Animals and Plants

We often get asked about household pets and other animals that may be near and dear to you. Specifically, you want to know how many of these creatures will be making the transition along with the Earth.

All plants and animals (and minerals, for that matter) that make the shift will undergo a change in their DNA structure. Although it is often stated that first density is the realm of minerals, second density the realm of plants, and third density the realm of animals and animalistic humans, that is not exactly the case because minerals, plants and animals also evolve along with humans and the Earth herself. It may seem strange, but a first density mineral, or second density plant, can evolve and remain with Mother Earth all the way through fourth density. Let us turn our attention specifically to animals.

Animals generally do not make sudden shifts. In fact, many species will continue incarnating over and over again as the same sub-species with similar lessons, perhaps hundreds of times, before taking a new path, so the transformation is usually not as dramatic as with humans. For example, a border collie breed of dog may keep coming back as a border collie hundreds of times before moving on to, perhaps, a great dane. (We are not implying that danes are higher in vibration than collies.)

That said, we anticipate about one-fourth of the existing species of plants and animals surviving the Earth changes. In addition, we see new species being introduced to the Earth that are already more aligned with fourth density than many of the existing life forms.

From a nonlinear perspective, all these higher dimensional forms already exist. You simply cannot see them until you raise your frequency to match theirs.

From a linear perspective, the DNA of existing species will mutate to form new species.

Your household pets, including dogs, cats, horses, etc., will mostly survive, but a lot of the animals currently used for food, such as cows, pigs, sheep, etc., may not make the transition. Some of these creatures contracted to be used as food for humans, while others desire to evolve on planets where they will no longer be used for food. A few of them who really want to stay on Earth might make it into the Golden Age where humans no longer kill them for food, or they may evolve into new forms more aligned with fourth density. The remainder of these species will likely contract contagious diseases as a means of exit from the Earth plane.

The more evolved animal species on your world, including dolphins and whales, will continue into the New Earth, although their numbers and sub-species may change. Many of the dolphins have been dying for various reasons, but they have assured us they do not plan on going extinct, as they are eagerly anticipating the New Earth. Some are leaving for the same reasons that many fourth density human souls are – because they want to reincarnate in a more positive environment after things settle down, having determined they are not ready to ride through the most turbulent of waters over the next ten years or so.

You will find that certain plants and animals thrive in the New Earth that did not do well in the old world, and vice versa.

As you grow in consciousness, you will see it tangibly demonstrated that your state of being affects the life forms around you. Some of you will become highly telepathic with both plants and animals, and perhaps you will be able to grow exotic fruits and vegetables in hostile climatic zones by providing the right level of consciousness to the plants. Speaking of agriculture, that brings us to our next segment.

Agricultural Adjustments in the New Earth

Over the next few years, there will be two highly disparate agricultural practices. Both will rise in popularity and both will claim to be the answer to feeding the world's increasingly hungry masses. However, one will be the path of the enlightened and one the path of the deluded.

These two methods are as follows: (1) genetically modified organism (GMO) crops, technologically perfected and mass produced in most countries of the world; and (2) local, organic farms practicing permaculture, hydroponics, greenhousing, and other environmentally friendly technologies.

Many will opt for GMO crops because of the lower initial cost. As economic conditions worsen for most souls, saving money will become a bigger and bigger issue. When GMO grains and meats sell for half the price of organic grains and meats, the choice will be obvious to those on a limited income who do not see the hidden costs to health and the environment inherent within GMO crops.

The problem with many GMO crops is twofold: (1) the molecular rearrangement of the food causes the body's biological mechanism to fail to understand how to properly assimilate, digest and metabolize the altered grain (or vegetable or meat). This causes a lot of excess waste and improper conversion to useful energies in the body, meaning malnourishment; and (2) GMO crops use more pesticides than ordinary commercial farming methods. That is one of their primary purposes. They are designed so that the pesticides kill everything but the crop (all insects, fungi, mold, etc.), thereby increasing the yield and reducing the overall cost. However, all that extra pesticide has to go somewhere and it does, back into the soil and water. In addition, no matter how well the crop is cleaned and packaged, some of the pesticide invariably finds its way into the food product itself and, therefore, into the human body.

We have repeatedly said that if you have the means, move to a place that has relatively fertile soil and begin growing organic fruits and vegetables. Although most of the soil on Earth is partially or totally depleted of nutrients due to over-farming and pollution, there are still some areas where the soil is pretty good.

There are programs underway to re-mineralize soil by mixing mined supplemental materials directly into it. (Picture large bags of pulverized minerals distilled from volcanic lava, undersea sand, or the bottom of lake beds, not to mention gravel quarries.) While these programs are expensive and time-consuming, they can make a difference in the quality and nutrition of plants. Many species grown this way have far superior levels of nutrients to those grown in conventional soil.

Specific Steps to Take with Agriculture

We hope the following suggestions will assist you in weaning yourselves from the global distribution system:

- If money is no concern, buy a piece of land mid-way between the flood plain and the mountains, import several tons of minerals, add these and a lot of compost to the soil, and begin planting. Focus on variety, for two reasons: (1) your body will get a variety of nutrients; and (2) if some of the crops fail due to erratic weather patterns or unforeseen pests, others will thrive.

- Since many areas of the planet are getting warmer, buy your land in a temperate zone (away from the tropics) and then add some subtropical or tropical items to your temperate crops. You might be surprised, for example, that avocados, citrus, figs and mangoes might just make it north of southern California and Florida.

- Use the latest greenhouse and hydroponics technologies. Read all about permaculture.

- Learn how to properly store foods during inclement years. Do research on which storage materials are best. Make sure you select containers that do not release toxic chemicals during extreme heat or cold.

- Practice living in harmony with beneficial and harmful insects, including parasites. Bless the creatures that prey on your crops and visualize golden light protecting your land and keeping it safe from predators.

- Support your local heirloom seed bank. As GMO crops continue to proliferate, it will become harder to find uncontaminated seeds (due to cross-pollination).

- Know your local farmer, or be your local farmer. If you know the farmers in a 100km radius to your own land, you can trade, barter, volunteer and get involved in each other's farming projects. If you get wiped out by hail, probably others will have crops that survive and you can assist the farmers who have the good yields and be rewarded with their surplus. If you are the fortunate one, be willing to feed those whose crops get ruined. Maybe one year the hailstorm will hit your field and everyone helps you, and the next year it will hit your neighbor's field and you can return the favor.

- If some of your neighbors are not informed about the hazards of GMO crops, do your best to educate them. There are volumes of literature detailing the problems with such crops. If one of your neighbors insists on continuing the GMO practice, you will need to cover or otherwise protect your crops from cross-pollination.

- Use prayer, meditation and higher consciousness techniques to raise the yield and quality of your produce. The Findhorn community in Scotland is a prime example of this. For years, they have had the best produce in Europe, even though their soil and water are just average. This has been attributed to prayer and mindfulness, as well as harmonious and joyful living.

- If you can, talk to the plants. Commune with them. Learn to telepath. It might be easier than you think.

- Although you will not grow enough to feed the entire world, learn to be generous with your neighbors. Use protection to keep thieves at bay. Send love and compassion to those in the cities that are having trouble finding food, but set your intention to become psychologically invisible to anyone who would steal your crops or farm equipment. Erect an etheric dome of golden, loving light around your farm and those of your neighbors.

- Have regular community meetings with everyone in the area. Propose a purpose of the meetings, such as, "We have gathered together to assist each other in a bountiful harvest, and to share ideas and insights on how to grow better crops."

- Talk to the nature spirits. They will often know what kind of winter is coming, or whether a particularly exotic fruit will flourish or die in your temperate climate. Devote small portions of your farm to crops that your intellect might say you are crazy to plant, but for which your inner guidance says go ahead.

- Balance your time between farming, family and spiritual practice. This is not easy, since farming can be quite labor intensive. Share your talents and abilities in a balanced way with others. You might not be the farmer, but you might have the money to buy the property. That might be your primary contribution to the community. Everyone has unique sets of talents and abilities. Encourage souls to express their latent, as well as obvious, abilities. Ask for what you truly need.

- Visualize a community that has a balance of talents and abilities, so that you attract one person who is good at plumbing, another who has an electrical wiring background, another who can purchase and install solar panels, etc., instead of attracting 100 plumbers and no electricians.

You want a balance between highly grounded souls who work with their hands and the Earth, and those who are more visionary and mental. Both are needed for a successful enlightened farming community. You will need some administrators and those who are natural leaders, but you do not want everyone trying to be the boss. We will discuss more on the structure of intentional communities in a later chapter.

Outer Reality Changes – Concluding Remarks

In this chapter, we have focused primarily on the natural disasters and anomalies likely to occur in the coming years, whether caused strictly by nature or with a contribution by humans. In our next chapter, we will focus on those human-created constructs that are not part of the natural world, including systems of finance, government, and social systems.

Once you have achieved a balance with nature and can be flexible during her tempests and tantrums, it will be easier to deal with the man-made realities, knowing that you are no longer wholly dependent on your outer authorities and the security network set up to protect you from yourselves.

Being a free soul means having both inner and outer freedom, and that means having the ability to think critically, without blindly believing any of the man-made belief systems or constructs that surround and influence humanity every day (unless you live in a cave high in the mountains).

We, the Founders, and the higher self of this channel, are dedicated to assisting you in your quest for inner and outer freedom.

CHAPTER 5
Popular Conspiracies – Fact or Fiction?

Because this channel gets a lot of questions about the conspiracies, we decided to include a special section in this book. From our observation point outside the frequency fence of Earth, we are able to see a lot of the things going on within certain factions of humanity. We observe your media systems and the highly distorted nature of your news programs. We see that material gain often seems to triumph over common sense and the well-being of humanity. We also observe how many of you exaggerate or distort what is taking place, and how some are quite gullible and will believe just about anything they are told.

Below, we have listed some of the more well-circulated conspiracy theories, along with our comments. Please use critical thinking every time someone offers a conspiracy theory or explanation for something that seems difficult to comprehend. In many cases, there may be some truth to what is being offered, but it could be colored by fear, judgment and limited belief systems. You will find that is the case with many of the following theories.

Conspiracy Theory #1 – The attacks on the world trade center and pentagon in the United States in September of 2001 were the result of a conspiracy.

Our observation: This is true. Both the official government story and the stories of so-called "truthers" bear this out. The word "conspire" means to breathe together. Taken in a political context, "conspiracy" means "two or more individuals coming together and planning to overthrow, destabilize, or cause change within an existing structure in order to advance their hidden or overt agenda."

Even if you believe that a terrorist group called "Al Qaeda" was the sole instigator behind the attacks, this would, by definition, be a conspiracy. You could not execute the steps that were taken on September 11, 2001, without a lot of minds conspiring to make it happen.

However, there is a lot more to the story than the official account. Often the "party line" or government position on events is partially true, but carefully orchestrated to reveal only what those who believe they are in charge want the people to know, or feel the people will be satisfied in knowing so that they will not inquire further.

This channel asked his spirit guides immediately following this event to give him the full story. We will not go into great detail here due to the need for brevity. We will, however, state a few obvious facts, at least obvious if one uses critical thinking and examines with attention and awareness what is taking place.

The attacks were carried out by a consortium of anti-Arab and anti-Muslim groups. The plan was engineered by Israel's Mossad, or secret intelligence agency, in collaboration with a group of individuals called by some, "Al Qaeda." The purpose of the attacks was to foment antagonism between the American people and the Arab states in order to destabilize the governments in the region so that the United States and Israel could gain control of oil fields and key military posts in the Middle East.

Explosives were planted in the buildings prior to the airplane attacks to make sure the destruction would have a great enough magnitude to effectively sway the United States to go to war with the Arab states. The attackers knew that airplane fuel alone would not cause more than the destruction of a few floors that were impacted directly or nearly by the planes, so the plane attacks were a cover to take people's minds off the real cause of the destruction. The attackers correctly surmised that most people in the United States would not be aware of the fact that high-rise buildings are designed to prevent complete collapse and structural failure in the event of impact by aircraft or fires in their upper floors.

The collapse of the number seven building at the world trade center was due to explosives because that building contained extensive evidence of the strategies and materials employed in the attacks.

There were a few souls within the United States government that were a part of the conspiracy. This did not include the senior administration officials who were supposedly in charge of the executive branch at that time. They were briefed by various military commanders who were in turn briefed by National Security Agency personnel, who were in turn told what to say by a select group of individuals who were in touch with the organizers of the event. This method of communication is known as "compartmentalization" and is used quite effectively to keep one or more branches of a government from knowing what is going on within other branches of the same government.

The agenda behind the attacks was quite successful in that it led to the destabilization of Iraq, Afghanistan, and to some extent Iran and Pakistan, thus allowing American and British contractors an opportunity to increase their war profits and gain a foothold in the oil industry of the region.

This brings us to the next conspiracy theory.

Chapter 5 – Popular Conspiracies – Fact or Fiction?

<u>Conspiracy Theory #2</u> – There are plans for a third world war beginning in the Middle East.

<u>Our perception</u>: This is true. Those who believe they are in charge (mostly the dark Illuminati) keep their illusion of power through the "divide and conquer" mentality. If they can keep countries at war, then the inherent divisiveness of war keeps souls from gathering enough energy and fortitude to make real and lasting positive change. Also, war is extremely profitable for the elite and their military contractors. A large percentage of the profits from war get diverted into the hands of the banking cartels and their dark lords and masters.

What the dark Illuminati do not yet realize is that the impending immune system failure in third density souls, along with the general unwillingness of the populace to tolerate any more wars, will bring the third world war to a quick conclusion. Some Illuminati operatives are aware that the Galactic Confederation will not allow nuclear weapons to be used. That means the dark lords will need to rely on conventional weapons, including their limited number of fighter aircraft and munitions.

As aircraft get depleted, the warmongers will need to rely on ground troops (soldiers) to do their fighting and this is where the problem looms. There are not enough willing soldiers to do much more than fight regional battles. Many will defect while others will simply throw down their weapons and refuse to fight. Enacting mandatory enlistment will not work either because the general populace of the countries involved will simply refuse to register, and most of the governments do not have the enforcement structure in place to prosecute millions of draft resistors.

It is a common practice among the major industrialized nations to present themselves as stronger than they actually are militarily. Although some countries, such as the USA, boast a lot of weapons of various types, the personnel in the military are already stretched quite thin. There are only about half a million souls actively engaged in the military of that country, about one for every 600 citizens. If half of these are opposed to war, imagine one soldier for every 1200 people that are not in opposition to the war and who could, potentially, try to enforce enlistment.

There are many references throughout this book to the third world war, as well as discussions in "*Earth Changes and 2012*," so we will leave you to do further research on the topic. We will now move on to the next conspiracy.

Conspiracy Theory #3 – There will be three days of darkness. The Earth will stop rotating on its axis. Days and nights will change radically.

Our perception: This one is entirely FALSE. We are not sure how this prophecy got started, but we do know that it arises from a misinterpretation of a translated ancient prophecy that pertains to the partial collapse of the electromagnetic polarities at the poles of Earth.

First of all, this prophecy violates the laws of physics. In the lower four dimensions, the Newtonian laws are quite real and have an overriding impact on physical objects, including all rotational and revolving motion of planets and stars within the lower four dimensions of the galaxy. Even in the higher dimensions, Newtonian laws have influence, but in the case of the higher levels, there are other laws that often supersede the basic Newtonian laws of mass and motion.

That said, the only way the Earth would experience three days of darkness would be if any of the following occurred:

One, a nuclear war breaks out and the detonation of thousands of weapons causes a nuclear winter syndrome that blocks sunlight from reaching the Earth. Due to Divine Dispensation, this is not going to happen, for the reasons discussed earlier in this book. At any rate, this would barely change the rotation of the Earth (possibly by a few milliseconds at most).

Two, virtually all of the volcanoes along the ring of fire erupt simultaneously, causing a nuclear winter syndrome that blocks sunlight from reaching the Earth. The Arcturians are working day and night to prevent this from happening and the likelihood of such a scenario is essentially zero. Again, this would alter the Earth's rotation by a few milliseconds at most.

Three, the Earth collides with a very large object moving through space. This would indeed change the rotation of Earth and the dust from the impact would likely cause a nuclear winter syndrome, blocking sunlight from reaching the surface, or what's left of the surface of Earth. We assure you there are no significant collisions with large comets, asteroids, planetoids or rogue planets expected within the next one billion years. Only small objects (less than a few miles in diameter) are likely to impact the Earth in your meaningful future.

The erroneous translation that gave rise to this prophecy goes something like this. In the original Sumerian text (and also in the Mayan writings) there is reference to a three-day period on the Earth that is like "neither night nor day." The prophets are referring to the electromagnetic null zone and the partial collapse of the polarities of the EM field on Earth during the portal shift of 2012. A situation of neutral polarity opens up a portal or stargate into the etheric realms and creates a tunneling effect for energy to cascade down from the etheric into the physical, causing a major shift in all life forms on Earth. This is the first wave of ascension, December 20 – 22, 2012.

The partial polarity collapse (about 40% from our estimates) will cause major disruption of the telecommunications devices your society relies on so heavily, and it will cause mutations in the cells of most life forms, as discussed extensively in this book and *"Earth Changes and 2012."*

This state of decreased polarity will indeed seem like a new state on Earth, hence the phrase "neither day nor night" which is properly translated as "neither positive nor negative polarity."

Once again, dear students, the north and south magnetic poles are very different from the geophysical north and south poles. Although the polarity of Earth's EM field does affect Earth's rotation and inclination of axis to a tiny degree, it is not enough for the average human to notice.

We are disappointed that so many souls are blindly believing prophecies that defy common sense. That is one of the reasons we have included this section on conspiracies.

Conspiracy Theory #4 – Malevolent forces are spraying "chemtrails" into the atmosphere of the planet in order to control or eliminate most of the population.

Our perception: This is mostly false, but a few elements of it are true. There are chemicals being sprayed into certain areas in order to alter the weather, or to serve as biological weapons during wartime. However, these are exceptions and not the rule. You must understand, dear Creators, that a little critical thinking and common sense would tell you that there are trillions of cubic meters of atmosphere around the Earth, even though the majority of it lies within 200km of the surface of Earth. Do your math. There are not enough chemical manufacturing plants, nor aircraft, nor money available, to spray all the Earth's atmosphere with enough biological agents to significantly impact the population at large.

This is not to say that there are not specifically targeted areas where biological weapons have been and are being used. Nor does this dismiss the negative effects of attempting to control the weather. While most of the weather modification experiments are designed to restore desert areas to agricultural production, a few malevolent souls are attempting to divert beneficial moisture from countries they oppose. In a few rare cases, such souls may succeed in enhancing tornadoes, hurricanes and other weather anomalies, but for the most part, global warming caused by the Galactic Shift and the burning of fossil fuels has a lot more to do with erratic weather than any weather modification experiments that have gotten out of control.

Unless you live in a crowded city within a warfare zone, you are unlikely to be sprayed deliberately with toxic chemicals. In fact, toxic additives in processed food are more likely to harm you than chemtrails.

Conspiracy Theory #5 – There is a plan to poison the population through adulteration of vaccines and other medicines.

Our perception: It is strange how fear can blow so many things out of proportion. Unfortunately, it also gives psychopathic individuals ideas on how to inflict pain on others. Such is the case with adulteration of vaccines, or medicine, or water supplies, or food. A few malevolent individuals have indeed plotted to poison certain items intended for ingestion by humans, but in most cases, they have been stopped before they could do much damage. Twice, vaccines were intentionally adulterated and twice, they were intercepted and destroyed before a single dose was administered.

A far bigger threat to the well-being of humanity involves toxic metals used in the processing of vaccines, such as mercury, and the side-effects of many medications. Add to this, genetically modified crops and excessive use of pesticides. Then throw in the constant barrage of chemicals being added to processed food and you do have a large percentage of the population being poisoned. In most cases, this is not intentional, but is due to ignorance and obsession with making a profit. The CEO of Monsanto Corporation, for example, actually believes he is helping the planet by providing genetically modified products.

The problem with chemicals added to food, as well as genetically modified ingredients, is that the human body does not know what to do with them. It will try to eliminate these toxins, but once they build up in the body beyond a certain point, the liver begins to fail and thus, the entire body.

We do not anticipate a large number of humans dying directly as a result of ingesting processed food or genetically modified ingredients, but such items contribute significantly to the decline of the immune system, which we do see as a major source of population decline.

Fluoridated water is another example where a toxin gradually builds up in the body until it adversely impacts the internal organs. Other examples include aspartame, monosodium glutamate and toxic metals found in most seafood. While these toxins cannot be completely avoided, you can minimize exposure by eliminating artificial sweeteners, flavor enhancers and farm-raised seafood from your diet (unless you know the farm and feel confident their seafood is not contaminated). Wild-caught fish can be hit or miss on contamination, so do some research.

Getting back to the question of whether or not you should be immunized against certain viruses and bacteria, we suggest you go deep within and contact your God Presence for the answer. In general, if you are healthy physically, emotionally, mentally and spiritually, you have no need of vaccines, as your immune system will already be strong enough to repel most negatively-polarized invaders.

Once again, we remind you that we cannot legally give medical advice, but we do encourage you to find a doctor who is holistically oriented and understands the human immune system. Since certain vaccines can have harmful side effects, we do not believe your so-called authorities should force anyone to be vaccinated. All such mandatory laws are based in the fear that someone will infect the general populace. You will find, in the years subsequent to 2012, that most of your vaccines will no longer work anyway because there will be other factors adversely affecting the immune systems of the majority of humanity, as discussed earlier.

Regarding autism from mercury in vaccines, there have been cases where this poison has been ingested in sufficient quantity during vaccination of young children to cause an autistic response. Some reports state that 1 in 50 children contract vaccine-induced autism. We put the numbers at around 1 in 3,500. This is still a significant number and doctors and nurses who administer vaccines should be aware of the dangers of vaccines preserved with mercury.

Conspiracy Theory #6 – There is an evil alien race controlling humanity from behind the scenes.

Our perception: If you are a fear-based human being, then this conspiracy theory is true. However, if you are evolving into greater levels of love and compassion, then you really do not need to worry about this at all.

We have gone into great depth on the ET races affecting humanity in our previous writings, so we will be brief here. The dark Dracos, Sirians, Zetas and Orions are allowed to influence humanity up to a point, but they are not allowed to completely take over the planet. After the portal shift of 2012, many of these races will be unable to maintain their presence in the astral planes around Earth. Some will be unable to maintain a physical presence in spacecraft.

As for shapeshifting aliens appearing as your human leaders, this is false. Shapeshifting is a highly advanced psychic skill employed by souls vibrating at ninth density and above. (Others in levels four through eight can employ a holographic projection technique that mimics shapeshifting.) Those who attempt to influence your planet from the astral realms are not sufficiently evolved to shapeshift.

Some clairvoyants see reptilian beings overshadowing certain world leaders. Unlike your science fiction show, "*Invasion of the Body Snatchers*," these human beings are normal flesh and blood people. The reptilian images are holographically projected from the astral realms as a means of mind-controlling world leaders. In other words, these people are possessed by astral entities.

Why? The reason is simple. Negative ETs feed off fear, anger and the desire to be in control, and many world leaders emanate these qualities to the satisfaction of the reptilians and other races. For various reasons, these negative ETs cannot beam themselves directly onto the Earth, so they settle for astrally merging a part of their being with power-hungry, bloodthirsty individuals in order to get their "high" of lust, revenge, rage, and other negative feelings and qualities.

Our advice to you is, heal your fear and negative emotions. Do whatever is necessary to process and integrate your negative belief systems, especially the belief that another entity or group of entities can control you against your will.

You are powerful beyond belief. It is time to rise up and claim your sovereignty and take your power back from the reptilians or whomever you think is in control of this planet. These entities feed on fear. They depend on you not noticing them. They are counting on you to stay in blissful ignorance. You are not ignorant any more and you no longer fear that which you have kept hidden in your subconscious. All your skeletons are clanking and clinking as you pull them out of your closet and hold them up to the light of day. With the high-powered Light of Truth penetrating their illusion of substance, they are revealed as having no power because you are now withdrawing your belief and energy from them.

We suggest you send love and compassion to all dark forces, dark lords, negative ET races, Illuminati members, and anyone else that you are tempted to believe can control you. The law of attraction states that love and compassion will be returned to you, if not by these entities, then by your loving guides and teachers. Your love and compassion might bring a few of these dark beings to the Light. The rest will be leaving the Earth plane very soon, if they have not already left by the time this is published. Give thanks for the negative reflection these beings have given you. They have helped you see where your soul is not yet integrated. Be grateful that they have held up a mirror so you can see the places within yourselves that still need Light.

Chapter 5 – Popular Conspiracies – Fact or Fiction?

Conspiracy Theory #7 – There is a plan to force all souls to carry an embedded chip in their skin to monitor their every movement. Without the chip, they cannot buy, sell or trade goods and services.

Our perception: This is the "mark of the beast" spoken of in your scriptures. Again, there are a small group of souls that are hell-bent (pun intended) on implementing something of this sort, because they are control freaks. They desperately seek to control everyone and everything on Earth in order to satisfy the incessant cravings of their egos.

The solution to this conspiracy is simple. Grow your own food or know your local organic farmer, buy land, install wind, hydro and solar power on your land, come together with your neighbors and pool your skills and resources.

If you do not depend on the global distribution system and are willing to live without credit cards, then you can refuse to be part of a system such as RFID or electronic implants, and you will do just fine. It is those souls who value security above freedom, and ignorance above enlightenment that can fall prey to such a scheme.

The souls that are trying to stay in control are desperate because their time is drawing to a close on Earth. In their last gasps of illusory power, they are pulling out all the stops, and so it is very likely they will create an artificial catastrophe of some sort in order to get their plan in action. The idea is to create an emergency, suspend normal citizen rights, invoke martial law, and then force the implanted chip upon the general populace.

We, the Founders, send love and compassion to these deluded souls and hope they eventually find their way to the Light. In the meantime, continue to do your spiritual practice and work on yourselves. Know that everything you truly need is within you and resolve to be free of all negative implants, whether electronic or otherwise.

There is great power in numbers. As millions of you refuse to continue being a part of the global distribution system, you will have no need of the things the system says you need in order to be safe and secure. There will inevitably be a few souls arrested and incarcerated for resisting the "establishment" and its edicts, but the vast majority of humanity will be left alone, due to the relatively small number of enforcers of these draconian policies.

Conspiracy Theory #8 – The Galactic Federation is going to come in a fleet of motherships and lift the Lightworkers off the planet and ferry them to safety while the rest of the planet is cleansed (destroyed).

Our perception: This is perhaps the most dangerous of the conspiracy theories going around, because even the Lightworkers of Earth can be fooled into accepting so-called "help" from well-meaning, but ignorant ET races.

The background on this one was given in "*Earth Changes and 2012*," but we will repeat the highlights here. The fourth density Sirians were heavily involved in the downfall of civilizations on Earth in the past and, determined to atone for their perceived "sins," many of them are now on a "Messiah" trip, intending to rescue humanity from itself.

The 4D Sirians (and several other ET races) do not fully understand human free will. They do not realize that you, the Lightworkers of Earth, volunteered to come to Earth during the great transition and to be beacons of Light during the more difficult times. You who volunteered to be here during the shift would have your mission cut short and your souls' desires unfulfilled if you were to accept the free pass offered by the Sirians.

The Sirians are not being allowed to carry out their perceived assignment because it would violate too many free wills on Earth. This does not prevent their channels from going on and on about how great it will be when the spaceships come. Like the fundamentalist preachers who are constantly predicting the end of the world, the mouthpieces for the Sirians continue to postpone the date of the beam-up, always coming up with some excuse or another as to why the space brothers have not yet arrived.

Humanity is not ready for a mass-landing of any type of ET race, benevolent or otherwise. There will come a time when visitors from the stars will walk openly among you, but that time has not yet arrived. Rather than trying to escape your hardships on Earth, we advise rolling up your sleeves and getting to work to heal yourselves and your planet. We know it is hard work and we have compassion for your suffering. But you must pull yourselves out of the quicksand, with our help and the help of thousands of other benevolent star races. However, these beings will not do your work for you. They will encourage and suggest actions, but that is all. Stop waiting for the spaceships now, today, and tune in to your soul mission on Earth.

We hope this section on conspiracies has been helpful to you, dear Creators. We will now continue our discussion by looking at the economic situation on your planet.

CHAPTER 6
Economic Realities

The Economics of Duality

By the time you read this book, it will already be quite evident that your financial structure is collapsing. No, it will not happen all at once. There are a lot of built-in safeguards to prevent that. But no matter how much rhetoric is bandied about, the expression, "The Emperor has no clothes on," applies quite well to your situation.

As we have stated previously, your economic system is not only out of balance with the energies of the ascending Earth, but its principles are almost diametrically opposed to the paradigms of the New Earth. The new fourth density human beings are concerned for the welfare of all citizens. The opposite of this is having a small, elite group who live high on the hog while everyone else lives under control and manipulation (read slavery).

The belief in the "haves" and "have-nots" stems from identifying with the material world and forgetting your spiritual nature. As materialistic souls witness the laws of entropy that rule the lower worlds, they become fearful that they, too, will wither and die, becoming powerless in the face of nature. Therefore, out of this deep sense of powerlessness, they erect all sorts of fanciful structures in order to have some sense of control.

The egos of the dark ones sincerely believe they are the "chosen people" and deserve special status. Their attitudes toward others may vary from having pity and a false sense of compassion toward the downtrodden, to feelings of outright disgust and disdain for the "lower class."

Understanding the illusions suffered by the so-called elite will help you, the Lightworkers, have true love and compassion for these deluded souls.

The systems of the lower worlds were not designed to last forever. They are the "scratch pads" of Creation, a temporary playground for gods in training, similar to a movie set. Once production is finished, the movie set is taken down. Once soul lessons are learned, there is no longer a need for a stage, or costumes, where players can act out the oppressor or oppressed, victim or victimizer, good guy or bad guy, etc.

As the soul lessons change, new sets are constructed appropriate to the learning environment required. In the case of the more violent outer worlds, perhaps they remain long enough to entertain new groups of young souls who wish to go through the ordeals of war, poverty, misery, suffering and the like. Such worlds will be receiving the warmongers who leave Earth during the Galactic Shift.

Of course, the lower worlds also contain a great deal of beauty and that is certainly an inherent part of the soul lessons of many – to recognize not only the outer beauty but the beauty within. So for a time, the world plays host to souls who are learning love and compassion, as well as those who are suffering from identification with the ego.

A central soul lesson on Earth is that you can create Heaven or hell, depending on the state of your individual and collective consciousness.

The Root Cause of Control and Oppression

Identification with the mortal third density self inevitably breeds attachment to the ego, because the ego is synonymous with identification and attachment to materiality (specifically, within the entropic worlds of the lower four dimensions). The ego is a self-construct designed specifically to overcome the soul's perception of powerlessness and helplessness in the face of unknown dangers lurking within an uncaring, hostile Universe.

This feeling of littleness stems from the Original Cause issues the soul took on when descending into the lower worlds (a topic we have visited repeatedly). The experience of physicality, starting with the birth process, was so intense that the soul forgot he was connected to an all-powerful Source.

The ego became an ally of the intellectual mind, the part of the self that continually tries to explain the how and why of Creation. The intellect, being aligned with the science of the lower worlds, cannot perceive the higher realms and so all it sees is a brief period of life followed by an inevitable death. Unable to see the eternal nature of the soul, the ego lives in constant fear of the body's death, and hence, its own end.

The ego, being identified with form, will do whatever it takes to maintain itself in its vain attempt to remain secure (based on its definition of security) or beautiful (as it defines beauty). Meanwhile, it lives in constant fear that wrinkles will replace its body's smooth supple skin, and the ravages of aging will claim its trusted friend, the intellectual mind.

Being attached to materiality, one becomes addicted to acquiring more and more "stuff". You even have a slogan, "The one with the most toys wins." Your self-worth becomes tied up in your "net worth." Instead of seeing money as simply a medium of exchange, something to make the trading of goods and services more convenient and efficient, money becomes a symbol of power and status.

Even those of you who think you have evolved beyond this idea probably still have some etheric imprints from past lifetimes regarding the "haves" and "have-nots." After all, most of you have lived "like a pauper and a king," to quote the lyrics of one of your popular songs. So deep within the recesses of the subconscious mind, materiality still has control in most people of Earth.

The Problem with Renunciation of Materiality

Religions have gone too far in the opposite direction, branding materiality to be evil and urging humanity to suppress its desires for wealth, pleasure and comfort. Some of you have had many lifetimes in a monastery, convent, or temple where you renounced everything and became the ascetic. While this may have had some temporary value in helping extricate you from your attachment to materiality, most likely the materialistic part of you was simply suppressed, locked down and out of sight from the conscious mind. A few enlightened souls have managed to free themselves from the ego's sense of deprivation and loss that usually accompanies renunciation, but the vast majority of souls have simply pushed their desires underground.

Most of you are caught between trying to attain material wealth and trying to resist it. This brings to mind another of your favorite expressions, "What you resist persists." Until you completely love and accept all aspects of yourselves, there will be an internal battle between the part of you that wants material comforts and the part that feels it should do without them because of their perceived corruptible nature.

Or you rationalize that you are beyond the need for material wealth, and then curse the world when it reflects back to you an inner perception of lack. You might try to be a good and charitable person. The key word here is "trying." Any time you try to be something, it means that you either believe you cannot obtain it and are somehow vainly attempting to have what you cannot, or you are failing to accept yourself as you are.

Charity comes about naturally when there is true love and compassion in your heart. It does not need to be cultivated or preserved. Of course, you will need to look at the places where you are holding on to what you have out of a fear of losing it, but you also need to see if your giving is genuine and coming out of a consciousness of overflowing abundance, or whether you are trying to prove something to yourselves or others.

So how does a soul move out of this seesaw between worldliness and other-worldliness? How do you deal with the insatiable ego self that always wants more? (More stuff, more enlightenment, always more, more, more.)

You can start by simply having awareness of the "needy little me," to quote one teacher. Simply observe how this little self tries to overcome its own perceived shortcomings by painting pictures of who it thinks you are, or should be. Just watch the way it weaves illusions out of the deeper feeling of emptiness that drives it insane.

A great way of overcoming the attachment to materiality is by appreciating and being grateful for what you already have. Money is neutral. It takes on the meaning you assign to it. If you truly believe you are wealthy, it matters not the size of your bank account, for you will always have everything you truly need. You can create great beauty in and around you simply by feeling gratitude.

Creating beauty, prosperity and harmony around you is normal and natural. It is part of your Beingness. You do not have to try and create beauty. You just naturally let it express itself, perhaps through art, music, writing, teaching, or whatever moves you.

The idea that you must battle to overcome entropy, mortality, and death, implies that there is a formidable force to be overcome, subdued and destroyed. You have, therefore, created a split between you and the thing to be overcome. Of course, the only thing that truly needs to be overcome is the attachment to overcoming, and for that, pure awareness must come into being.

Becoming aware of all the ways you are attached to materiality, without judging, condemning or avoiding it, is the key.

We are not going to go through a long list of the consequences of becoming attached to materiality. You can see that by looking at the world. Rather, our aim is to teach you that you are vast, creative, spiritual beings, and that you do not need to rely on outer authorities of any kind whatsoever in order to create the kind of world your souls wish to experience.

To sum up, there is ultimately nothing wrong with materiality. It is the identification with and attachment to it that is the problem. We have said this before and we will likely say it again.

Now that we have taken a brief look at the causes of the disparities existing in the world between the "haves" and "have-nots", let us make a few predictions about your economic future.

The Collapse of the Western Nations

The western economy is collapsing, not because anyone is being punished by God, or because any of you are bad or wrong. None of you need suffer as a result of the collapse of the old world. In fact, it is a cause for rejoicing because it affords you the opportunity to create a New Earth economy based on true spiritual principles.

The more attached you are to the present system, the harder it will be for you to embrace the New Earth because you will be mourning the loss of the things you are attached to, such as bank accounts, houses, cars, expensive clothes, and the illusion of power and control that these things seem to offer you.

Things, in and of themselves, are neutral. They take on the attributes of those that use them. A perfect example is physical energy. It can be used to create or destroy, depending on the consciousness that is using it.

Being in gratitude for what you have, and learning how to make do with less materially, are great qualities to embrace. This is not the same as sacrifice, because you are not really giving up something of great and lasting value in order to have peace of mind. You are merely giving up your attachment to the outer world.

The things of this world can be useful tools for fulfilling your mission and purpose for being here. We are in no way implying that you must do without basic necessities. In fact, as you realize that you are inwardly prosperous beyond measure, then you become a wise steward, or vehicle, for the use of the tools of materiality. As Lord Sananda once said, "*Seek ye first the Kingdom of God and all things shall be added unto thee*." This means having your priorities straight. You are here to help awaken humanity and bring them into the New Earth. Whatever outer levels of materiality you need to accomplish this purpose will be given you by your own soul in collaboration with your spirit guides, ascended masters and the Godhead.

You might not understand how you come to acquire what you need, but you do acquire it. You will be guided as to what you truly need and what you need to let go of.

The western economy is collapsing because it has become grossly out of balance with the emerging New Earth. This is a wonderful thing, but it will not seem wonderful to those who still believe their happiness comes from their income, bank account or credit card. It will seem like cruel and unusual punishment to those who have invested their whole lives in a system that is based on power and control rather than love and cooperation.

Specifics of the Collapse

You are probably aware that the economies of the western world are based on what is commonly called "fiat currency" or legal tender, money printed and given an arbitrary value by a central bank. If traders agree to the arbitrary value, then the currency keeps the economy afloat – in theory.

However, due to compound interest and fractional reserve banking, schemes set up to enrich the banking elite at the expense of the working class, the system eventually implodes due to runaway debt induced by these schemes.

The problem is not loans in general, but the way they are structured. If someone with money were to loan it to someone else with the expectation of getting repaid, and charged a small fee for the service, such as simple interest of 10%, there would be no problem. Mr. Jones would borrow $1,000 and at the end of a period of time, pay back $1,100. Or, to put it in current real estate figures, he buys a house for $200,000 and pays back $220,000. That's doable for a lot of people.

But with compound interest, the longer Mr. Jones waits to pay back his loan, the more interest he accrues. After 10 to 15 years, the interest on his $200,000 debt becomes almost as much as the original debt, meaning that very shortly he will owe $400,000 on his original loan (less his payments already made).

Compound interest applies to countries, as well as people and institutions. Many countries currently owe money to other countries that will never be paid back due to the cascading effect of compound interest.

But wait, it gets worse. Now let us introduce fractional reserve banking. This means that banks are allowed to loan money based on a tiny fraction of what they have received from depositors (and borrowers who are repaying their loans). So let's say that Mr. Jones puts $10,000 in a savings account. If the bank is given a 10% fractional reserve base, that means it can make loans up to $100,000 based on the $10,000 it has in hard assets.

Where does this money come from? In essence, it is created on a computer ledger or, to put it more bluntly, it comes out of thin air. Effectively, this introduces more money into circulation, which might seem like a good thing, except that no real service has been provided with this money (other than perhaps hiring an accountant to keep track of it all). Sure, it fulfills a temporary purpose, allowing someone else to borrow even more, which in turn can be fractionalized again into an even larger sum of money, which can then be lent out yet again.

If you perceive that this is like some sort of pyramid scheme, you are absolutely right. Theoretically, you could keep on printing money forever (as long as you have ink to run the printing presses), but a curious thing happens.

Chapter 6 – Economic Realities

The amount of services that have real value eventually become far less than the amount of money in circulation, thus creating inflation, a situation where a given amount of money, over time, buys less and less products and services that have real value.

Real wealth consists of products and services that have tangible value, such as food, clothing, durable goods, etc. It also includes services, such as teaching people a skill, counseling, and the arts – music, poetry, prose, etc. In an economy that has runaway inflation, you will inevitably also have runaway debt, as the interest continues to accrue and more and more money must be paid back, and that is what has been happening in the western world the past few decades.

This combination of debt and inflation means a lowering of the standard of living for more and more people over time, while the bankers and a few shrewd investors get richer. Eventually, the value of the currency can no longer be propped up by those who want to keep the system going, and it comes crashing down in one of two scenarios: (1) hyperinflation, or (2) depression.

In hyperinflation, money keeps getting printed to cover the mounting debts owed to a central bank, such as the Federal Reserve Bank of the United States, or the Bank of England. The country that owes money keeps printing more to satisfy the debt, thus devaluing the currency. This devaluation occurs because there is now more currency in circulation without any additional products and services of real value being added.

In an economic depression, controls are implemented to limit the amount of currency being printed, thus drying up the money supply. In such a scenario, businesses and individuals can no longer borrow money and therefore are unable to invest in new products and services, which in turn causes massive layoffs of employees and a high unemployment rate.

At the present time, the western countries (USA and UK especially) have about 20 trillion dollars (15 trillion pounds) in outstanding debt. The EU is facing a similar situation and several countries within the European cartel are on the verge of dropping out of the system and starting their own currencies. At the time of this writing, Greece and Iceland were essentially insolvent and were relying on assistance from the EU and other banking authorities. Many people in those countries are urging their governments to default on their payment to the EU and to print independent currencies.

In addition to mounting debt caused by compound interest and fractional reserve banking, many countries have speculative investments, called by various names, including derivatives, options, etc. The value (on paper) of these securities amounted to over 600 trillion dollars (450 trillion pounds) as of mid-2011. If only 10 percent of the investors were to call their trades (cash in on their investments) all at once, the system would bankrupt quickly, since 60 trillion is more than the combined gross domestic product of the developing world. No banks have actual cash-on-hand anywhere near that amount, due to the fractional reserve system.

We are not going to give you a detailed lesson in economics, but we wanted to point out a few principles of the decaying present system to show you why it is dying. The real reason, once again, is that it is not based on the principles of a fourth density Earth, and that is the current vibration of Earth as she moves through the portals.

The law of attraction implies that the enlightened souls who inherit the Earth will create (or attract) an enlightened economic system, one that serves everyone and not just the elite bankers. You can do your part by visualizing and knowing that you live in an abundant, unlimited free Universe that truly has your own best interests at heart (despite what the present system has taught you).

The Collapse of the Eastern Economy

The eastern world, and primarily China, has a role to play in the dissolution of the old world economy and emergence of an enlightened New World. In some ways, the economies of the east and west are similar, but in other ways they are quite different.

The manufacturing process, which used to exist primarily in the west, has been transferred to the east. This is due to many factors, including cheaper labor and a stronger work ethic in the east, but it creates an interesting scenario, because the eastern countries, being manufacturing centers, depend on the western countries to purchase their products.

When the western countries go bankrupt (as they are now doing), they will no longer have the money necessary to continue purchasing the goods manufactured by the eastern countries. Thus, the manufacturing plants will begin closing due to lack of demand, sending millions of workers home. This is particularly devastating in the east, where the work ethic is so strong.

While ultimately, this is a good thing because it will force souls to rethink the true meaning of productivity, in the short term it will be quite traumatic. An additional silver lining in the ending of the manufacturing boom in China (and other eastern countries) is that it will finally put a lid on the high levels of pollution being experienced there. As of this writing, Beijing in China is the most polluted city in the world.

The currencies of the eastern countries are closely tied to the currencies of the western world. If the east were to divorce itself from the west and divest itself of western currencies, this would exacerbate the problem by sharply devaluing the currencies of the west and thus throwing the western countries into more severe hyperinflation, or deeper depression (depending on how the western governments and banks respond to the crisis), thus drying up the demand for eastern goods even more.

Timetable for the Collapse

Due to free will, it is difficult to predict exactly when certain economic events will occur. Many souls are continuously clinging to the old system and to a limited extent, this draws out the process of change, pushing back the anticipated ending dates of the present economy. The portal shifts will act as major catalysts here. It is our understanding that the American and European currencies will likely decline dramatically between 2012 and 2015, resulting in severe hyperinflation or depression, depending on how the central banks respond to the deepening crisis. At the same time, the value of real goods (including gold, silver and agricultural commodities) will rise significantly.

Real estate was hyper-inflated for many years due to speculation. In 2006 the bubble burst and it has been declining ever since. We anticipate that it will continue to drop for a while and then stabilize and eventually climb, since land and buildings are real assets. However, it is likely that by the time it appreciates significantly in value, housing and land will only be available to those who have gold, silver and precious metals as collateral.

A few wealthy individuals may be able to pay cash for their real estate (using inflated currency), but the vast majority will need to rely on bank loans, which will simply be unavailable.

It is recommended that you prepare for the collapse by prioritizing your investments as follows: (1) buy land and grow your own food while you still can; (2) buy gold, silver and other precious metals (have the metal on hand in a safe place); (3) keep cash on hand rather than deposited in the bank; (4) keep liquid assets, such as checking accounts and credit/debit cards; and finally, (5) invest in forward-thinking companies that have excellent management and are contributing to the well-being of the world (such as alternative energy and environmental cleanup companies).

Remember, this is in order of priority. If you only have enough money for some of these, make sure items (1) and (2) are handled first.

Solutions Offered by the Power Elite

Most of the bankers and extremely wealthy individuals are not stupid. They know they cannot keep their pyramid scheme going forever. Sooner or later they will run out of resources to buy and sell, or the debt will become so burdensome that their customers (borrowers) will be unable to pay back their loans. Therefore, they are already dreaming up new ways of retaining their illusion of power.

One of their favorite tactics is to introduce new currencies that are shared by several countries in a geographical area. The Euro is an example of this strategy. The idea is to have more control over more countries by enacting a central bank to handle the new currency, thus replacing the individual banks of the member countries.

A similar strategy is planned for North America, with a new currency called the "Amero." This currency would replace the Canadian and United States dollars, and the Mexican peso. A central North American Bank would be created to manage these assets (and of course, print them out of thin air).

The elite will likely attempt to convince the people that creating a common currency would unite them and make it easier to travel. While this would be true on one level, it would not be the primary motivation for having a regional currency. The real reason would be to dissolve trade barriers and make it easier to corner the market on various commodities. A new trade agreement called the North American Union (NAU), that goes well beyond the boundaries of NAFTA), would be drafted to go along with the Amero. There is already a Free Trade Area of the Americas (FTAA) in its infancy stages.

One of the benefits to the elite of such a structure would be that this dissolving of boundaries between countries would normalize wages (making them considerably lower for Canada and the USA, while raising them a little for Mexico). The end result would be cheaper labor and greater profits for the global corporations as well as the banking cartels.

Enlightened Solutions to the Collapse of the Economy

In a perfect world, the solution would be to eliminate all the jobs that do not produce a product or service of real value (such as most of the activities of Wall Street), and replace them with companies and organizations that are making the world a better place (such as groups tasked to clean up the environment or distribute food to the hungry). The idea here is to get everyone to contribute to the well-being of everyone else. However, this does not just happen as if by magic, particularly when people are attached to power, prestige and the illusion of security.

The solution is not some sort of socialistic utopia where everyone has the same assets and opportunities. True, the "have-nots" must be given the means of ending their poverty and suffering, but it is not as simple as just giving them money or jobs.

There must be a fundamental change in consciousness among all groups of souls on Earth. As long as souls are identifying with the ego (body/mind/personality complex), there will be a perception of lack and the resulting hoarding and greed that go along with that perception.

As consciousness shifts, so do the priorities of the society. Instead of spending endless billions on military defenses and bailouts to bankers, the focus would be on education and the empowerment of the people. That includes taking care of planet Earth and restoring her to health.

We are talking about real education, not just memorization of those facts that the elite want you to know, at the exclusion of the facts that are less convenient to the agendas of those in power. Real education attempts to answer questions such as, "What does it mean to be a human being?" and "What is enlightenment?" and "How do we create a society where all souls are valued and respected?"

We in the heavens have worked with countless planets such as yours, and while every one of them is different and unique, there are a few common denominators that are worth mentioning.

First, let's give a little praise. As one of your teachers recently said, "Never in the history of this galaxy has a planet that has fallen so far been lifted to a higher frequency so quickly."

Your planet is one of the most interesting, and challenging, of the worlds we have worked with. That said, those worlds that have placed education at the top of the priority list are the ones that have awakened most easily and quickly.

Although young souls desire to learn about suffering in all its many forms, older souls have learned all they need to about misery and poverty and they are ready to move on.

It is rare for a planet to accommodate both old and young souls at the same time and it presents very unique challenges.

Without transferring the younger souls to a planet more suited to their level of evolution, it would be next to impossible to bring humanity up to the next level. Mother Earth, in her nearly infinite patience, has reached the point where her very survival is threatened, and for that reason she has been working with the Godhead to arrive at a solution that ultimately serves all souls.

A time will come on Earth when the enlightened souls who remain with her will no longer require any kind of formal economy. However, there needs to be a transition period, so the following sections are devoted toward the exploration of various new economic paradigms. Some of these will be implemented before the existing old world system has completely crumbled.

A few so-called "solutions" are already being offered by the souls that brought you the problems to begin with. Although these "solutions" are irrelevant because their instigators will soon be gone from the Earth, we have included them below in order to provide contrast.

Let us start with some of the more popular ideas for either "fixing" the existing economy or creating a new economy. This is not an exhaustive list and we encourage you to come up with new ideas of your own.

Precious Metals and Bringing Back the Gold Standard

This is a temporary fix only and, if not done properly, will serve to prolong the old world economy rather than help humanity make the transition into enlightenment. Nevertheless, it can alleviate some suffering and will help redistribute economic power back to the people and away from the banking cartels.

Precious metals (gold, silver, platinum, etc.) do have some real value as industrial components, and as art and jewelry. By tying paper currency to precious metals, this gives it a base value or benchmark. Such a system is more stable than fiat-based money creation.

Governments would be required to hold hard assets (precious metals) in their storehouses to back up the value of their printed money. They would issue gold and silver certificates, representing gold and silver and being exchangeable for actual metal upon request. In other words, everybody would agree that gold and silver would have the actual value, and that the paper certificates would simply represent gold and silver, making trading much easier (gold and silver are very heavy and hard to carry around).

Abolishment of the Fractional Reserve and Compound Interest Banking Systems

The souls that believe themselves to be in power (and those that give them that power) would never willingly agree to abolish the fractional reserve system or compound interest, but hand-in-hand with bringing back the gold standard, such a move would quickly restore balance.

The idea is as follows: Banks could lend money, at simple interest not to exceed 10% of the principal amount, and must have 100% of their assets on the books at all times. In other words, if you deposit $1,000, the bank holds that money (in gold or silver certificates) until you make a withdrawal. Loans must be made out of the original principal investment of the bank. If the bank borrows money from another lender, the same rules apply to that transaction and the other lender. No exceptions.

So if someone creates a bank with $100,000, he can choose to make ten $10,000 loans with that money, thereby collecting $110,000 in payments (at 10% simple interest). He can then re-loan that money, which is then worth $121,000 in payments (10% of $110,000).

The bank is free to offer interest to depositors at a rate less than the loan rate. That's how the bank makes money. So if ten depositors get a 5% return, the bank's profit is 5% if the loan rate is 10%. It's pretty simple. (This system would put a lot of accountants out of work.) So now the soul who started the above bank has made $10,500 (half of the $21,000 made on loans was paid to depositors). That's a nice little salary for the small inconvenience of filling out some paperwork and cutting some checks.

Land (Real Estate)

Land is the most valuable commodity on Earth, because if the land is in the right place, you can grow food on it and collect water as well. Land is worth more than gold and silver because you can eat the food grown on the land, and you cannot eat gold and silver.

If you have the means to buy land that has fertile soil and fresh water, now is the time to do so. We recommend that you buy a parcel that has both open space and forest. If you do not have any forest, then set aside up to half of your land to plant trees. The other half of your land should include fruit trees, a vegetable garden and, or course, dwellings for living and working.

You will want to set up your homestead and workplace as close together as possible to minimize the use of transportation devices that burn fossil fuels. As long as you have satellite technology and the Internet, it is recommended that you do as much of your business as possible online so that you do not need to travel to and from work every day. Eventually, this will be irrelevant because you will develop new transportation methods using electromagnetic propulsion devices, but for now, you are looking for ways of "reducing your carbon footprint" and being less subject to the extreme fluctuations expected in the energy markets in the years to come.

The energy to run your homestead (or intentional community as the case may be) should be from hydro, solar and/or wind power, so you will want to select a location that has, hopefully, at least two of these in abundance. A desert location will have sun and wind. A mountain location will have water and wind. We will have more to say about buying land in our section on intentional communities.

Let us now take a look at the idea of creating new currencies at the "grassroots" level, meaning within individual communities and local groups.

New Currencies

The purpose of money is to make the trading of goods and services more convenient. That's all, folks. There's really nothing more to it than that. Instead of hauling a truckload of apples to exchange for a truckload of oranges (when you get tired of eating apples), all you need is a piece of paper (or coins). That way, you can wait until the oranges get ripe (usually three months after the apples do) and redeem your paper (or coins) at that time. Both farmers will like that, because the apples will not go rotten waiting for the oranges to get ripe and the orange farmer will not have to pick his oranges while they are green.

This may seem like an absurd example, but that's really the purpose of money. You humans have given it far more importance than it actually has. You tie your self-worth to it. You live in constant fear of being without it. You hire millions of people to count it, insure it, store it, trade it, invest it, etc. A tremendous percentage of your energy as a species goes into spending, saving, investing and protecting your money.

All new currencies need to be based on the one principle given above – to make life easier. Such currencies should be based solely on the real value of products or services offered. We realize some things are not easily assigned a value, and that is why extensive council meetings will be required by those towns, villages, provinces and countries who wish to introduce new currencies.

For example, you might determine that someone who bakes bread has a lower net worth than someone who builds a house. In the beginning of the new currency, there will be unavoidable inequities. Some professions are currently overpriced to the extreme, such as medical and legal. Others are grossly undervalued, such as teachers.

There will be various interpretations as to what constitutes real value. After all, one counselor may help her clients tremendously, while another does not. Should they both charge and receive the same amount?

The law of supply and demand will partially correct this imbalance (if it is allowed to run its course without interference). For example, the counselor who is very effective will have a lot of clients willing to trade their currency for her services, while the one who is not effective will have very little business.

There are some currencies already in operation in various cities around the world. Some of them consider all work to have the same value, so an hour of legal consultation is worth the same as an hour of teaching about how to bake bread.

As souls evolve, the real value of goods and services will be recognized and rewarded amiably. In order to help bring everyone into an enlightened state, certain services should be provided free of charge, including basic health and education. Rather than impose income or property taxes, a city or province and its citizens could agree to donate a certain percentage of their earnings to health and academic educators on a regular basis. Although this would, in essence, accomplish the same thing as taxes (and could be construed as a voluntary tax), without compound interest virtually all of the money raised in this manner would go to actually funding education, rather than the majority of it going to pay the interest on the principal amount of a loan.

We recommend you do some research and visit one of the cities using alternative currency to see how it is working and the challenges involved.

A Word about Secession

In some countries, states or provinces have a constitutional right to secede from the central government. The biggest challenge in doing this is generating enough labor and resources to be self-sufficient. The citizens of many "developed" countries are heavily dependent on their governments for welfare, social programs, interstate commerce, etc., and in order for a region, state or province to secede, this dependency must cease.

In countries composed of states or provinces, and even in countries with just a few counties or shires, it may be possible to introduce currencies and trade programs that apply just to those regions. The idea here is not to exclude anyone or become isolationist, but to focus on growing, producing and manufacturing goods locally. This is, in a way, an extension of the ideas put forth in the upcoming chapter on intentional communities.

If you want to describe the three parallel Earths in terms of economics, you could say that the fourth density souls are seceding from the third density world and are setting up a new society with new currencies and trade practices that support their value system. The fifth density souls will have little need for economics since almost all their needs are provided internally.

We have included a few additional ideas about your future economies.

Enlightened Economics

As long as fourth density souls on Earth require basic resources, there will be some need for an economic system. It could be simply trade and barter, as it was in many times past, or it could be a sophisticated system of currencies and accounting, as it is today, or perhaps somewhere in-between.

The fundamental difference between an enlightened economy and one that is based on greed, lack, scarcity and selfishness, is that the primary and most important goal of an enlightened economy is the well-being of its entire citizenry.

Unlike socialistic systems where the value of individuality is squelched, and unlike capitalistic systems where the value of the corporation becomes more important than its members, an enlightened system is based on intelligent, wise decisions usually made by a council of elected elders who have demonstrated a great deal of knowledge of economic matters; i.e., what people truly need to be prosperous and happy in the outer world.

An enlightened economy begins within, by recognizing that all souls live in an infinitely abundant Universe that is based on love and cooperation. It has been scientifically proven that there is an almost infinite amount of energy in the vacuum of space (which is really anything but a vacuum), so in essence, an enlightened economy is simply an outer expression of an inner truth, the truth that you are free, unlimited and very prosperous.

The first tasks of the new economy are to: (1) educate people about the prosperous nature of the Universe; and (2) develop ways of harnessing this abundant energy and making it tangible and productive in the everyday lives of souls on Earth.

We have observed that if the money spent bailing out your banks and supporting your militaries were instead spent on the two items listed above, within a few short years you would have programs in place to ensure that all human beings are living happily and abundantly, with no physical lack whatsoever.

Even with your existing technology, you have the means of taking care of everyone many times over, yet because of economic and political iniquities, and the belief in lack and scarcity, almost two-thirds of the world is malnourished or starving.

As the fourth density communities of Light become more established, many of our groups in the higher realms will be able to interact with you and share our advanced technologies and science. Many ET groups would love to do this now, but the situation on Earth is far too unstable to permit this without upsetting the balance of free will.

Chapter 6 – Economic Realities

In an enlightened economy, everyone contributes according to those avenues of expression that most satisfy the inner yearning of each soul. In other words, a successful society makes education top priority, and within that educational process, encourages souls to discover their true meaning and purpose in life. If every soul were to contribute and work in jobs that were truly fulfilling, an amazing thing would result. There would be a perfect balance of skills, talents and professions. You would not have a million Reiki healers and no psychotherapists, or a million hairdressers and no electricians. Every need would be filled because every soul would see the bigger picture and how he or she fits into it. The God Presence of each soul would show him the most joyful and creative ways to express and contribute to the needs of the community at large. In other words, each soul would see the Oneness between himself and the whole and respond accordingly.

Just as honeybees, ants and other creatures work together to create magnificent structures within their world, so do enlightened humans, but with one important distinction: Humans are not colonies of workers. They are creative individuals working to simultaneously fulfill the needs of self and the community.

When a member of an enlightened economic system falls on hard times, for whatever reason, the community becomes a support system to help that individual get back on his feet. Each member recognizes the Oneness that exists spiritually within the group and so in a sense, if one person is unfulfilled, the whole group is unfulfilled. Your visionary Gandhi said, "As long as one child is starving in the world somewhere, we are not free."

In summary, an enlightened economy is based on the premise that there is more than enough for everyone, and focuses on the science of harnessing, producing and distributing the prosperity and abundance that is already present within the etheric realms.

We in the higher realms long ago learned how to tap the etheric realms to revitalize and regenerate the lower worlds. While we cannot give you every detail of the process whereby this is accomplished (or this book would be too large and specialized), we can point you in the right direction and communicate with your inventors and scientists to the extent they will listen to us.

As we stated previously, advances made in science and technology between 2012 and 2015 will allow electromagnetic energy devices (often called zero-point or free energy systems) to begin proliferating on Earth. This will essentially prove that there is more than enough for everyone. Such systems will cause the old third density economic system to complete its collapse so that the economic phoenix of the New Earth can rise from the ashes.

Suggestions for Responding to the Economic Collapse

Before the new economy is firmly developed, there will be a transition time, and things will likely be quite messy for a while.

As the old world system comes to an end, so will the global distribution system. We have already painted a sober picture (from the perspective of third density) based on dwindling fossil fuel reserves, increasing pollution, runaway debt, and the failing immune systems of humans. When the cost of fuel becomes too high, planes, ships, trains, trucks and other methods of transport begin to break down.

Since many of your governments are already bankrupt, you cannot count on them to step in and keep things going. Perhaps you have seen the government's response to some of your natural disasters. Did the USA respond appropriately to the disaster in New Orleans? Did the Japanese government handle the earthquake and tsunami adequately, especially at the nuclear reactors?

Inwardly, the best response to the economic realities of the next few years is to take responsibility for yourselves and each other, growing food and trading locally, developing alternative energy, and asking yourselves the question, "How do I meet my basic needs if the global distribution system breaks down? What do I truly need?"

Most humans in the developed world consume far more than they actually need. By relying more on your inner Source and less on outer materiality, balance can be restored. Tune into Mother Earth. Listen to her rhythms. Hear her words. Respond accordingly.

That said, we will give a list of the places most and least likely to handle the transitioning economic structure gracefully.

Places to Avoid During the Economic Transition

Before we list the safest places, let us remind you that the worst places to be are in large cities that are located in arid regions, or at sea level. Large numbers of people living hundreds or thousands of kilometers from agricultural regions will have a very difficult time in the years ahead.

Also on the list of places to avoid are those cities and regions that rely heavily on fossil fuel transport systems, where there is little or no public transportation or community gardening.

Unless you know how to grow food at high altitudes, it is a good idea to avoid places higher than 2,000 meters above sea level, or that have long harsh winters or extended hot summers.

You want to stay away from monoculture-oriented communities that place "all their eggs in one basket." Seek instead a place where there is diversity, both socially and agriculturally. Select a place that has a highly developed transportation system, as well as a lot of services for the elderly, incapacitated, and minority groups.

Safest Places to Be Economically During the Transition

Table 8 – Best Places to Be from an Economic Standpoint

--Any place with fertile farmland and a minimum of people

--Portions of the northwestern USA / southwestern Canada

--Portions of Argentina and Uruguay

--A few places in Central America

--Western and southern Russia, near the Ural mountains

--Portions of eastern Europe, Armenia, Yugoslavia

--Southern France and northern Spain

--Extreme northern Italy and southern Switzerland

--Inland eastern Australia

--Portions of central Africa

CHAPTER 7
Political Structures

As most of you know, the major political systems on your world have been designed to keep in power the souls who believe they are in control. It matters not what they call their system, or which "ism" has been assigned to label it. All of your "isms" have some beneficial qualities as well as built-in limitations.

You cannot make a blanket statement and say, for example, "The Illuminati are all bad," or "The problem is the Aussie government," or "The Mossad of Israel is evil."

Some of the so-called controllers of your world are Lightworkers who have gone undercover, for two reasons: (1) to learn exactly how the so-called "dark" side works; and (2) to spread light covertly throughout the hallowed halls of darkness.

In your Illuminati, which were founded by Light beings, you have 10 to 20 percent who have not been corrupted by the ego and its insane desire for control over others.

In many of your secret societies, including the Freemasons, who founded the United States, you have had Light beings involved. The constitution of the United States was designed mostly by Lightworkers, although many of them were not aware of their higher spiritual nature at the time it was crafted.

Due to interbreeding with various light and dark races, and the many twists and turns in the saga of free will, the constitution of the United States has not been able to do what it was intended to do – keep checks and balances on abuse of power.

The situation in the United States is not unique. The United Kingdom, Germany, France, Spain and many other European countries are struggling with many of the same issues.

Almost all of the developed nations of your world have central banks that form a network, or cartel, controlled by the Illuminati. Because up to 90% of the Illuminati are aligned with the ego (dark forces), the policies made by these central banks almost always benefit the elite group that controls most of the wealth and resources of the world.

This wealth and power game has been going on for thousands of years, or actually, millions of years if you take into account players from other worlds. (In *Earth Changes and 2012*," we went into great detail on the major influences from other star systems and their historical impact on humanity.)

The souls who believe in domination and control maintain their illusion of such by convincing the masses that they are weak, helpless and powerless to make any real changes in the world. The financial and social systems designed by the bankers are intended to keep them in power and the masses powerless.

We have already taken a brief look at economic manipulation, including the major weapons of the elite, fractional reserve banking and compound interest. Now it is time to look at another of their weapons – the business of weaponry.

The Last Great War

The so-called "powers that be" go to war for two main reasons: (1) to fulfill their "divide and conquer" agenda by pitting various forces against one another in order to prevent any one force from amassing enough power to defeat them; and (2) to profit enormously from the manufacture, sale and distribution of weapons of war and all the accoutrements that go with these weapons.

The dark Illuminati are not concerned about taking sides in these wars. In fact, a careful review of history will reveal that the same few individuals and corporations have financed both sides in most major wars.

Virtually all of the wars that have occurred on Earth were orchestrated (engineered) by the dark Illuminati (or their precursors) for the above reasons. The standard modus operandi is to start with a real cause, such as border disputes, lack of resources, religious conflict, etc., and then foment the conflicts using media propaganda, economic manipulation, ideological tenets, and in some cases, planting "terrorists" and dissidents amidst the populace.

Many of your authors have exposed this latter method of fomenting conflict, by outlining the various steps used to control the populace through warfare. The idea is quite simple: (1) create an "enemy" or opposing force; (2) offer a solution that involves consolidating power and control; and (3) convince the people that they are better off under the new system.

An example of this involved the "terrorist" attacks on the trade center in New York and Pentagon in Washington, DC. The co-conspirators in this attack (members of an anti-Arab group commonly called "Al-Qaeda" and a faction of the secret Israeli police commonly called "Mossad") came up with a plan to get the United States to see the Arab countries as "enemies" of freedom.

In order to go after the enemies, certain resolutions were passed by the United States Congress that effectively took away rights of the people (mainly through the so-called "Patriot" act).

In the minds of the dark Illuminati, this accomplished three things: (1) it helped to divide the American people and instill fear in them; (2) it made it easier to control them by taking away many of their rights; and (3) it boosted profits by allowing the dark Illuminati to manufacture additional weapons to wage war in various countries in the Middle East, thereby acquiring valuable resources in the process (such as oil).

Since that event, war contractors have made hundreds of billions of dollars in military contracts. Some of these contractors were hired to build the weapons of war and assist the military in using them (often on innocent civilians), and then the same contractors were awarded contracts to rebuild the destroyed countries. Many a corporate executive "sold" his soul for these double profits.

If you are not a citizen of the United States, you might think this form of corruption does not apply to you, but unfortunately, you would be mistaken. With very few exceptions, if you live in a country with an organized military, similar deals and contracts are going on without your knowledge.

The endgame in this plan of tyranny is to host a third world war, pitting the major developed countries against themselves in support of a few "pawns" in the Middle East. Israel (backed by the United States), Iran (possibly backed by China and Russia) and a few other countries, are likely to escalate their conflicts to the point of involving soldiers from all of the major countries. Despite the possibility of a Russia/China alliance, it is fairly certain that the dark Illuminati will also find a way of pitting these two countries against each other at some point.

The east/west conflict used to involve the "evils" of capitalism and communism, but since China has embraced a form of capitalism, such a strategy no longer works. Many of these countries depend on each other for trade, so new "enemies" must be manufactured to keep these countries divided and at war.

Most likely, new "terrorist" attacks will be manufactured to get the world war started. In fact, attempts have already been made that failed due to intervention by the Galactic Confederation. A few years ago, in 2005, some secret alliances in Iran attempted to launch a nuclear device into Iraq in order to enlarge the conflict between those two countries. The goal was to get the United States to go to war with Iran and then get Russia and China involved.

When the warhead failed to make it out of the silo intact, the manipulators knew they would need a new tactic. They then changed gears and started working on a way for Iran to attack Israel. Twice now, those plans have failed, due to exposure of the plot by covert Lightworkers in the Illuminati.

We in the heavens have been giving the likelihood of a third world war at about 60 percent. However, we have also said that such a war would be short-lived. More and more souls in the developed nations are awakening to higher truths and no longer want to be part of a global conflict. In addition, the economic collapse that is already underway is making it harder and harder for countries to spend money on military adventures.

This means the covert (secret black operations) factions must fund these wars. Despite their nearly unlimited funding (due to profits from drugs and weapons on the black market and kickbacks from the banking cartel), more and more people are going to become disenchanted with war and will simply refuse to support the military.

In addition, between 2012 and 2015, the increasing frequencies on Earth will start impacting the immune systems of more and more humans, especially those locked into a lower vibrational pattern. This means illness, disease and disharmony will ensue among the military leaders, which will cause an inability to fight effectively within the ranks of soldiers.

So you have those who simply refuse to fight because they no longer require that soul lesson, combined with those who are too sick to fight, combined with depleted funding, and then you have fewer souls needing to learn lessons about war, which means fewer recruits to replace injured or killed soldiers and, therefore, fewer soldiers overall to keep the wars going.

As we have mentioned numerous times, only conventional warfare is allowed to continue on Earth, so this means eventually exhausting the supply of warplanes and ammunition, even with geared up manufacturing plants for these items. That means more and more ground forces, which require a lot of soldiers.

One by one, the major countries involved in this conflict will simply quit, realizing that the war is destroying their own economies and well-being.

As the year 2015 approaches (and the world's population begins to level off somewhere below eight billion), it will become evident that the ever-escalating medical crisis demands the attention of the world's governments more so than war

Exposing the Tyrants

Throughout the next several years, there are a number of factors that will contribute to the demise of the old world system and its leaders.

A major aspect of the awakening process on Earth involves the exposing of darkness in all of its many forms. Before illusion can be dispelled, it must be seen clearly in the bright light of awareness. This is why attempting to deny the darkness or pretending it does not exist, only serves to strengthen its sense of reality. Ultimately, illusions are only as real as the energy given to them. When you deny something, you are still giving it energy in the form of subconscious patterns of repression. When you fight it, you are coming from the belief that it is potentially as powerful as you.

Do you not see, beloved Creators, you are so powerful that you can create unlike the naturally harmonious structure of the Universe? The more you give your belief to the things of third density, the more real they will seem to you and the harder it will be to truly transcend them.

Transcend means to go beyond. It does not mean to circumvent, deny, or rationalize. To transcend darkness, you merely expand your consciousness to include more and more of who you truly are – an amazingly powerful, creative Divine Being.

As Mother Earth ascends in vibration, all who have been hiding in darkness will be forced to crawl out of their hiding places and face the truth of their Being, which is also your Being. Your Light is affecting them now. By making a commitment to your awakening and choosing to ascend with Mother Earth, you are coaxing the dark ones out of their caves, nooks and crannies. They might resist and, because of free will, they have a right to resist if they so choose. But free will is no longer the dominant force when it comes to oppressing and controlling the Lightworkers on Earth.

Through Divine Dispensation, Earth is becoming a fourth density planet. That means there are certain laws and principles that are beyond the scope of free will. It also means lower-vibrational souls will no longer be able to maintain their grip on this world.

Those dark ones who attempt to dig a deeper hole to get farther away from the Light will be digging their own graves. Their immune systems will feel the vibration of Earth as she ascends and attempt to get away from her. The only way they can do that is to leave their bodies, or in some cases, leave on a spacecraft. Either way, it is only a matter of a very short time before they will be gone from the Earth.

In the meantime, they are being shown the Light and the way out of their self-created hell. The numerous "outings" of souls who have committed fraud, deceit, and various crimes will continue. A large number of souls will be shocked at some of the revelations that will be forthcoming in the next several years. The people will rightfully feel betrayed by their own governments and leaders. Then they will need to move beyond their anger and into forgiveness, not only for their betrayers, but for themselves for allowing the betrayers to seduce them with empty promises and rhetoric.

It matters not what political party the dark ones belong to, or what country they seek to have dominion over. All lust for power is the same, though the form may vary greatly. One by one the people of the world will demand the truth from their leaders and when their leaders are unable to comply, there will be revolution.

It is taking place now in many countries, and more will follow. Sometimes it will take great hardship before the people revolt; other times a well-placed Internet blog or scandal exposing the leaders will do the trick.

The central soul lesson behind the exposing of the tyrants is straightforward and obvious. You are to rely on your own God Presence and not the so-called wisdom of those who appear to be in power. An enlightened society would elect leaders that reflect the enlightened values of the people. They would be a mirror for the consciousness of the people. Now that the people are becoming more enlightened on Earth, the leaders will need to reflect that enlightenment.

According to the law of attraction, the betrayers will likely relocate to a world where souls are still learning about betrayal, or they will evolve beyond the desire to betray others. A few may see the Light and move out of the consciousness of oppressor and become part of the New Earth. In old fashioned religious terms, this is known as "atoning for your sins."

Understand, dear Creators, that there is no judgment in any of the above explanations. It is not wrong for a soul to betray or be betrayed, at least not from a higher perspective (nor is it right). The souls who manipulate and con their way into high offices and use their power to abuse others are operating from a frightened ego that believes the only way to survive is to dominate others.

These souls derive their power from convincing others of their need for outer security. Some of your more awakened leaders in the past have uttered statements such as "Those who seek security over freedom deserve neither." We would not agree, because all of you deserve freedom no matter what you have done. But we do understand the consequences of believing that someone outside of yourselves is going to save you. The only savior is your own God Presence, that part of you that is directly connected to the Godhead, the Source of All That Is. No ETs, enlightened or otherwise, are coming to your rescue, at least not in the sense of saviors.

This does not mean you do not have help. In fact, you have an incredible array of helpers from all levels and dimensions working to assist you in awakening. But they cannot and will not do your soul work for you. All they can do is show by example, and send you lots of love and compassion.

Do not rely totally on us, dear Creators. We, the Founders, are here to serve and assist you in any way possible, but it is up to you to drive the demons from your midst and return to the sanity and true security of your God Presence. We can only point the way, suggest actions and provide inspiration.

Chapter 7 – Political Structures

Going Beyond "isms"

In our chapter on intentional communities, we will outline some structures of government that will likely serve you in the years to come on Earth. Some of the methods employed in these structures will take the very best of your various "isms" and synthesize them into a new order.

It bears repeating that the quality of your outer political structure is a reflection of the quality of your consciousness. Until you heal your negative emotional issues and core negative belief systems, you will continue to have leaders that reflect the portions of your consciousness that are unhealed. This is intentional, as it is the fastest way for souls to grow and evolve at this time.

An example would be the president of the United States from 2000 to 2008, Mr. George Bush, Jr. Although he is most likely not conscious of the role he agreed to play on a soul level prior to coming to Earth, he did, nevertheless, do a great job of fulfilling his role. His role was to be so polarized and aligned with the elite and so oppressive of the masses that they could not ignore him. If he had been merely a mediocre president who did not accomplish much, most people of the United States would have remained asleep. However, the polarization was so obvious that it woke up a lot of people to the need for major change.

The next president, Mr. Obama, was a step in the right direction, but unfortunately, he had not cleared enough of his own negative issues prior to being elected to be able to actually shift the consciousness. Mr. Obama is reflecting that part of the soul's consciousness that still abdicates responsibility to others rather than facing issues directly.

This is not to say that most of your leaders have no sincerity. Mr. Obama truly wants to do what is right, but he is simply incapable of doing so at his present level of consciousness. To his credit, he has a higher level of awareness than his predecessor but he is still subject to the beings that pull the strings from the shadows.

As you know, the president (or prime minister, depending on the country) is not the one in charge. The banking cartels, along with the high councils of the Illuminati, are the ones calling the shots politically at the national and international levels. The presidents and prime ministers are in power solely because a majority of the souls within their range of influence have agreed that they have power. The people may have become convinced that this leader or that one will make good on their promises of greater prosperity and security.

Of course, you all have power, but most of you have not yet learned how to use it effectively. As you come into your true power, most of what your elected and appointed leaders do will become irrelevant. You will not need them. That means you will not resist or fight them, but simply live your life while having respect for the rights of others.

In prior discussions, we mentioned that most of your world leaders are partially or totally possessed by astral entities, such as the dark Dracos. In addition to the astral entities, there are physical ETs in spacecraft attempting to manipulate your world leaders. This is allowed as long as it does not result in total domination of humanity by a particular ET race.

These dark ETs feed off the anger and fear lurking within the subconscious minds of the elected and appointed officials. As world leaders clear their negative emotions and belief systems, they will no longer be the target of negative astral beings and ETs in spacecraft.

A Word about Personal Power

There is nothing inherently bad or evil about power. Like most things in life, it is neutral until imbued with consciousness.

When you look out at the world and see your leaders misusing their power (using it to benefit themselves at the expense of the people), it is understandable that you would not want to embrace your own powerful self. As you continue to clear your consciousness of all that does not serve you, power will no longer seem fearful and you will no longer avoid coming into your own magnificence.

It is necessary to forgive those souls who have misused their power, and forgive yourselves for those lifetimes in which you abused yours. That might include earlier in your current lifetime.

Power, simply defined, means the ability to get work done. Some of the most powerful souls on your planet are not in positions of authority, nor are they in the public eye at all. They are the ones quietly working behind the scenes to bring about change. They are the ones who have learned to love and accept themselves, including their egos. Now their egos are their humble servants as they go about fulfilling their purpose and mission.

The Prospects for Peaceful and Violent Revolutions

At the time of this writing, there were almost a dozen countries in various stages of revolution, some peaceful and some not. As expected, the majority of the issues giving rise to revolts center around the well-being of souls living in those countries. Places where the citizenry is subject to so-called austerity measures, or where rights are blatantly taken away, usually see uprisings almost immediately.

The so-called powers that be recognize this and attempt to introduce new measures of control and oppression gradually enough to keep the "boiling frog syndrome" intact. By gradually reducing freedoms, or increasing prices, or withdrawing the supply of certain goods and services, people living under such regimes do not see the contrast quite as sharply and it is therefore easier for them to get used to the changes.

Nevertheless, the higher frequencies coming into planet Earth are stirring up the emotional and psychological issues of virtually every human being, and a significant number of souls, when stirred, tend to react assertively or aggressively.

For example, if you are a citizen of a country with some degree of oppression from its leaders (that would be about 90% of the countries on Earth), and you have a dream one night in which you receive visions of a world living in complete freedom and cooperation, you will likely awaken the next day with a whole different perspective on the society in which you live.

As the energies continue to increase, more and more souls will have these "satori" experiences where they are clearly shown, from higher dimensions, the fact that things do not need to be the way they are on Earth. Couple this with the seventh increase in the price of bread within one year, and you have a formula for revolution.

The question of whether such a revolution will be peaceful or violent depends on many factors, including: (1) How long has the will of the people been suppressed? (2) How severe is the oppression? (3) How deep are the austerity measures? (4) What type of media propaganda does the country have? (5) What are the likely responses of police and military to open protests? (6) What are the demographics of the areas most prone to conflict? (7) What is the history of conflict in that country? (8) How much fear do the citizens have? (9) What are the prevalent religious beliefs in the area and what do the religious tenets say about violence?

The bottom line is this: How desperate are the people of that country? If they are merely dissatisfied with their way of life and see a peaceful protest as bringing attention to their plight, then the revolution will likely remain relatively quiet, but if they have been driven to despair through no availability of work, shortages of food and water, yet having ready access to the Internet where they can witness other countries living high on the hog, then the chances of violent revolution are much greater.

The powers that be in the more volatile countries are depending on depleted energy from the protesters. After all, they could be weak from not eating or drinking properly, or they might not have enough money to purchase weapons, either legally or on the black market.

On the other hand, many of the downtrodden feel they have nothing left to lose, so why not revolt? In a few cases, something will snap inside emotionally and all the rage and suppressed anger will come pouring out. It might be channeled through marching in the streets and shouting slogans, or it might come out more erratically in looting and rioting.

One thing is for sure. As souls awaken, they will be less and less willing to put up with control and oppression, whether overt or covert. It is predicted by our group and this channel that virtually every major country will go through some sort of revolution during the next 30 years.

In this channel's country (the USA), at least 30 to 40 million souls are extremely dissatisfied with their government. As stated previously, you only have a few hundred thousand people working for the government in the USA and there is no way they can put down an uprising of 30 million marching on their capital. In the U.K., the ratio of government employees to those who are fed up with their leaders is similar. As the fear and intimidation tactics by the government begin to unravel and the citizens realize that as a group they are more powerful than the police and military, they will be more willing to take to the streets.

The uprisings in Tiananmen Square in China in the 1980s failed because there was still too much fear among the general populace to take on their government. Control and oppression in that country has been elevated to a fine art form over many decades. Now they are attempting to restrict their Internet to keep young Chinese from receiving information being transmitted by radical groups around the world. However, they cannot restrict what is being transmitted from higher dimensions, and many Chinese are open and receptive to higher truths. It is only a matter of time before revolution will be successful in that country.

A lot of affluent souls in first world countries are afraid of losing their jobs or prestige if they take part in a revolt. However, with rising unemployment and deteriorating quality of life in many of these so-called technologically advanced places, even the well-off among you are ready for a change.

After a revolution, what comes next? If there is not a realistic and easy to implement plan of action, there exists the possibility that a regime change will not improve life significantly.

Every few years in the channel's country, they elect a new president, congress and senate. For the most part, the members of his government belong to two political parties, the democrats and the republicans. Yet both parties are largely mouthpieces for the status quo.

This channel has a favorite expression: "Changing political parties in the United States is a lot like rearranging the deck chairs on the Titanic." No amount of reforms, promises, or cosmetic improvements is going to change the fundamental fact that the present economic and political system in almost every country in the world is based on old third density principles of win-lose, haves and have-nots, controller and controlled, oppressor and oppressed, rich and poor, etc.

As the Earth ascends, revolutions will be born and many will successfully propel the world in the direction of a new way of thinking and acting that is more in harmony with the higher principles of love and compassion.

The New Enlightened Leadership

In the years to come on Earth, there will be less emphasis on single individuals, and more emphasis on group councils to provide effective leadership. There are beneficial elements in the system you call "representative democracy" in the sense that each section of a community can elect a person to represent a certain group of individuals. In other words, each member of the council would be tasked to carry out the desires of his or her specific group of souls, similar to the way your state and federal representatives work in theory.

As the consciousness of humanity expands and ascends, the representatives, or elected council members, will reflect that higher state. There will be less interference from the darker elements, currently manifesting as corporate lobbyists, black ops funding sources, negative ETs, etc. As each elected council member goes within to the Source of his or her being and truly listens to the souls in the community, intelligent decisions can and will be made.

We, the Founders, humbly suggest the following priority list for newly elected council members, whether they are part of an intentional community, small town, county, shire, province, state or country:

First, quality education would be provided for every citizen. That means that however funds are raised for community projects, the highest amount goes to educational facilities and teachers. The curriculum would be based on learning what it means to be a human being, or rather, a spiritual being living in a human body/world. Courses taught would include how to develop creativity, what it means to clear the psychological and emotional self, how to be in relationship with others, what steps must be taken to ensure basic needs are met for all souls in physical embodiment, the study of different soul paths for the purpose of understanding the viewpoints and perceptions of each group, etc.

Second, resources would be devoted to scientific research and application. Specifically, funding would be allocated for alternative energy projects, agricultural advances, transportation systems, cleanup of the environment, and exploration of the cosmos.

Third, emphasis would be placed on cultural advancement, including creative architecture, community gardens, cooperative building and re-building projects, implementation of new economic paradigms including enlightened currencies, and providing of the latest technological systems in every household that desires them (but not necessarily with emphasis on the latest gadgets for hours of mind-numbing entertainment). The priority here is to enable more efficient communication and awareness of world events for all souls. Also, it is important to be sure and include entertainment and down time.

Fourth, opportunities would be provided to help individuals express their spiritual freedom. Encouragement and support will be given for souls to build churches, mosques, temples, synagogues, monasteries, healing retreat centers, therapy and holistic bodywork facilities, and more. The truth may be within, but it is helpful to have an outer environment that reflects the inner truth.

In this enlightened community structure, those who commit injustices against souls, individually or collectively, would be brought before the councils and provided with counseling, therapy, healing, and as a last resort would be temporarily removed from the community at large until stability is restored.

Your present society lacks the understanding and know-how to adequately address the cause of criminal behavior and how to prevent it. It is far easier to simply toss someone in prison and throw away the key rather than devote the necessary time and attention to true rehabilitation. We know there are some fine programs headed by compassionate people seeking to reverse the old model of crime and punishment, but they are still very much in the minority.

When it comes to providing for the well-being of the citizens, instead of a military, such an enlightened system would have a group of souls responsible for ensuring the safety of all members, with emphasis on each member creating inner peace and security, rather than relying on others to provide safety and protection. There will come a time on Earth when all that is necessary is to visualize a golden field of light around a community and the community will be protected from all outer forms of negativity.

We have given several glimpses into the new enlightened society and, in fact, we will be going even deeper into ways of governing yourselves during our discussion of intentional communities.

As we continue to focus on solutions to your present situation, it is vitally important to face the darkest places within yourselves and your world in order to start them vibrating and moving into the Light. Remember, dear Creators, to shine your Loving Light into all facets of Creation, including the parts we are about to focus on next.

Update on the Illuminati's New World Order

We would like to take some time now to talk about the plans the dark Illuminati has for the Earth and how those plans are about to come unraveled.

The future of third density Earth lies in the willingness of humanity to wake up and face the issues, both within and without, that need healing. We have already indicated that it is our perception that about 75% of humanity will not make the shift into fourth density. That number can still change, but the variance at this point is quite small. A liberal margin of error would indicate the departure from Earth of between 70 and 80 percent of humanity.

The dark Illuminati, seeing the likelihood of a mass exodus, would like to make sure that those who leave are the ones likely to cause them the most trouble in their plans for total world dominance.

A few fringe members of the dark sects have engineered plans to control the world's population through various means. This select group of psychopaths would like to wipe out 90% of humanity, leaving about 10% that can be easily controlled and manipulated into doing their bidding.

We would like to point out that this is a minority of a minority, a small group of souls who belong to the so-called dark forces, which are comprised of about 20% of the extraterrestrials who have influenced humanity since the beginning of civilized Earth. However, several of these misguided souls wield a lot of Earthly power, in terms of wealth and influence.

From a fourth density point of view (and higher), this power is an illusion, and that is precisely why this group would like to eliminate the souls who pose the greatest threat to their plans. This dark sect feels threatened by anyone who would expose their inner and outer workings.

It is this small group that opposes advancement in the sciences and medicine, by pushing drugs and food additives that are known to be dangerous.

It is this small group that has already attempted to adulterate vaccines in order to make people sterile, or to destroy their immune systems.

It is this group that is experimenting with biological weapons of mass destruction, even though deployment of such weapons would be immediately blocked by the Galactic Confederation.

Some of these dark Illuminati members are controlled by astral influences, as well as dark Orions, Dracos and Sirians. Others are merely caught in the net of their own egos, driven insane by their desire to control everyone and everything.

A somewhat larger group of dark Illuminati are not hell-bent on destroying 90% of humanity, but do desire to retain what power they seem to already possess, and want to increase this power exponentially by creating a one world government under the control of a one world banking system.

These are the people behind the North American Union and the Amero, as well as further consolidation of power in the European Union and soon to be Asian Union.

These souls are behind the consolidation of the major media outlets and the drumming up of mass hysteria regarding terrorists. They want to keep the masses in fear and confusion.

These souls are attempting to control the weather, both for profit and to potentially harm their perceived enemies.

Outside this circle of dark Illuminati souls is an even larger group of third density power brokers, who do not understand the forces at work behind the scenes, but nevertheless do their bidding because they have been brainwashed into believing that their egotistical efforts are somehow making the world a better and safer place. Meanwhile, they amass great physical wealth and donate a portion to charity in order to feel good about their disproportionate share.

These are the stockbrokers, bankers, lawyers, judges, and corporate executives who have been programmed to succeed at all costs, even if it means stepping on the toes of others along the way.

Some of the more visionary members of the elite are idolized in modern economic textbooks. They are constantly spouting theories and are teaching various get-rich-quick schemes. They are combining success motivation, creative visualization, and self-confidence building techniques. Many expound upon the virtues of creating your reality by changing your thinking. This would be beneficial except that such activities always have, at their base, the goal of helping others fit into the status quo. They frequently engage themselves in multilevel marketing and network marketing companies that are based on a win-win model of success.

Again, this would be great if it were tempered by true love and compassion, but most of the time the motivation behind helping others is to increase one's own wealth. There is still an emphasis on coming out on top of the existing financial pyramid. There is no fundamental shift in consciousness in the vast majority of souls teaching success motivation and network marketing.

Along with these power brokers are the aspects of the general populace who are security minded. These are the citizens that support embedded microchips in place of plastic credit cards. They believe such an ID chip would make it easier to track people in case of emergencies such as medical crises or missing persons, etc. Of course, they are quick to point out how wonderful such devices would be for law enforcement, reminding their faithful family and friends that law abiding citizens have nothing to fear.

These souls naively believe that if everyone stays neatly tucked in their little boxes of "normalcy" then everything will be alright. They consider those who refuse to accept the "Mark of the Beast" (as it is called in your scriptures) to be wackos, weirdos, or lunatics.

These are the souls that still believe big daddy government is somehow going to save them if there is a real disaster, despite what happened during the Japan earthquake, Katrina hurricane, Gulf oil spill, etc. They only see what they want to see, and when the government asks for their help to implement a national ID program in the U.K. or U.S.A., they are all too willing to play their part to "make the world safer."

They might perhaps shrug their shoulders when they hear about record oil company profits, or fat cat military contractors profiting from sales of weapons to *both* sides of a conflict, and then dismiss this as an aberration. "Of course there are a few bad applies in the bunch, but overall, these electronic chips will make us safer. After all, if we get lost, someone will be able to find us because our chip will be transmitting."

The New (But Really Old) World Order

The old world order, masquerading as the new world order, will never come to fruition because too many souls are waking up to the fact that the only real security comes from within. Although some are discouraged and feel like simply giving up and going along with the herd, a large number of souls are "mad as hell and will not take it anymore."

While we in the heavens do not condone acting from anger, we do observe that those souls who are angry with the way things are going in the world have more aliveness than those who simply change the channel and pop open another beer when something too disturbing attracts their attention.

The energies of the cosmos, as well as the opening of the portals on Earth, are causing everything to rise to the surface of consciousness to be healed. This means all the lies, cover-ups, deceit, and covert strategies are being exposed, either by whistleblowers, investigators, or through some seeming chance discovery. One of your songwriters called this, "Instant karma."

This is the reason the Illuminati's new world order will never succeed. There are just too many souls with what you call "BS detectors." In other words, they intuitively feel something is not right whenever the Illuminati come up with another scheme to enslave the populace, no matter how many pretty words are used in the presentation.

There has been talk among humans of a staged religious event, some sort of angelic being coming out of the clouds with a promise to save mankind. This scenario would be complete with holographic projectors and images beamed from lasers through the sky to make it believable. Yet what the group of deluded souls behind this project fails to see is that they cannot counterfeit energy itself. A beautiful being shimmering in the skies that has no real higher energy would instantly be recognized as a fake by those who have partially or totally awakened.

Stopping the Dark Illuminati

There are many programs and projects underway to help the dark ones fulfill their agendas. We in the higher realms are not allowed to "spill the beans" about specific operations in a general release to the public unless the entire Earth is being jeopardized by such operations. Yes, we can alert our channels and students about potentially hazardous situations. We can even, on occasion, intervene to prevent disaster.

We are aware of the dark Illuminati and their plans to enslave the entire human population. Our first bit of advice to you is to stay in love and compassion. Do not allow fear to enter. It is fear itself that attracts negativity. It is fear that attracts systems of government that look like they are offering security, when in fact they are playing on your fear, increasing it and feeding off it like vampires.

Do not give them the pleasure of feeding off your fears. Instead, shine your Light of compassion deep into the center of each fear, allowing it to rise to the surface and be dispelled. Face your fears directly and completely from the vantage point of your God Presence. Invoke your God Presence as often as you can remember to do so and direct it to shine brilliant truth and wisdom into every dark corner of your psyche.

As each place within you is brought to the Light, darkness has no where to turn and so it disappears into the nothingness it has always been. The dark lords, having no foothold, lose their grip on humanity and fall quickly out of the picture. Without a fear-based populace to feed on, their time on Earth is over.

Chapter 7 – Political Structures

Beloved Creators, you are already far stronger than the most formidable of the dark lords. Keep beaming your pure, unconditionally loving Light into the midst of the dark Illuminati, with no investment in the outcome. They will either accept your gift of Light or dismiss it with a sneer. "Another deluded soul thinks he can take us on," they chortle, but deep inside there is uneasiness. Their illusion of control is rotting away at the foundation and some part of them knows it.

Having their pride and arrogance, they dig their heels in deeper and go back to the strategy board looking for a way to speed up their conquest and amass even more power. Desperate, they pull out all their big cards, or throw all their chips on the table, in the fervent hope that the latest ploy will forever ensnare their opponents (which are everywhere).

Even within their ranks, they know there are souls working for the Light. They hate the Light. They hate God. They blame God for every pain they have ever felt. These pains go so far back in time that they cannot remember how it all began. If they could, they would realize there is nobody and nothing to fight, and the game would be over. But they have not evolved that far yet. For them, the costumed character they are playing on the stage of life is the truth, and they fight with honor and dignity lest someone, somewhere, see them as weak.

In our previous writings, we have given the story of Lucifer. We defined Luciferians as those who would deny the emotional body in favor of the supreme intellect. The Luciferians continue to hold on to their supreme intellects, as they spend more and more energy trying to suppress the emotions roiling below the surface. Their credo is to stay focused on the intellect and do not be distracted by the "weakness" of emotion. Stand to attention, push down the feelings, and be a "man." Be a strong and proud soldier, never showing anyone your weakness.

The Luciferian branch of the Illuminati is always strategizing new and better ways to control themselves and others. If only there were enough control, those emotions would be banished forever.

Meanwhile, their souls continue to fragment and split, growing weaker with each passing moment, until the day comes when their immune systems call it quits. Then it's "exit, stage right," and off they go to find another world to try and conquer. Until the day they wake up and stop this silly game.

We, the Founders, encourage all of you reading this to embrace your own emotional bodies. Love and accept ALL parts of yourselves, especially the little ego and its weaknesses. Give it your most tender love and compassion. Let it know that Spirit is in charge, now and forevermore. Amen.

CHAPTER 8
Social Systems

In order to build an enlightened world, it is necessary to have an infrastructure that supports souls in going within to explore the nature of the self and then to encourage them to express that inner beauty and harmony among each other.

Below, we have outlined a few aspects of this new social structure, alongside a review of what needs to be released in order to allow the new structures to take root.

You have no doubt noticed by now that we are creating a blend of illustrating what is out of balance with offering of possible solutions. This is because it is important to focus on all aspects of what is taking place, without downplaying the negative or obsessing on it. The problem and solution are both contained in human consciousness and that is the primary purpose of going back and forth between problems and solutions. Let us now take a look at the present state of your social systems and offer some solutions.

The End of Consumerism

Your present society arises from a profoundly deep and intense inner perception of lack and scarcity. While some of this is founded in previous generations where it may have been necessary to work from sunup until sundown in the fields just to harvest enough food to keep the family alive, a lot of this goes back much farther in time. In fact, the belief in lack/scarcity goes back to the fall, Original Cause, the decision of souls to enter into the lower worlds and thereby forget their Divine nature.

As the ego self became more entrenched in the lower densities, its consciousness turned to identification with material form. Materiality became the dominant religion of the times. Believing that you are a body/mind/personality causes you to perceive the world as outside yourself, disconnected and uncaring. Your Newtonian physics augments this perception by painting the Universe as a place of randomness, chance and impersonal design.

If you believe your Creator does not care about you, or that you are insignificant in the scheme of things, then naturally you will do everything within your power to overcome that deep feeling of inadequacy.

The first place you start is with the physical body. It appears to be flawed, weak and easily assaulted by a variety of outer occurrences, from cold and hot, to attacks from other bodies. While it certainly makes sense to clothe the body properly in extreme environments and provide for its nutritional needs, the deep sense of inadequacy arising in the ego self takes the concept of body enhancement far beyond healthy proportions.

There is nothing wrong with adorning the body and enhancing its natural beauty. The problem arises when your self worth gets tied into these enhancements.

Consumerism is a form of economics that depends on souls' addiction to improving or modifying the physical body in order to overcome the deep sense of inadequacy. There is always a need for more and more and more. Not just more, but better and better. Products are continually improved. While this might be beneficial to a certain degree, companies go far beyond merely improving their products. A device that is fully functional and serves its purpose is periodically discarded in favor of something that fits the latest trends, or is now in style (according to some arbitrary decision made in a board room somewhere).

Clothing and jewelry that may serve a useful function are suddenly outdated and a new line of fashions are now in style (according to some arbitrary decision by a fashion designer somewhere, along with a whole lot of slick, glossy advertisements in trade publications, magazines, and other media).

The basic message underneath consumerism is quite simple: You are inadequate and your life will get better if you buy the right brand of this or that, or more of these, or less of those. If you are advised to buy less of something, you can be sure that this is to create a temporary state of lack so that something else can be bought to fill the empty hole.

The only empty hole, in reality, is the one you create in your own consciousness by believing you are lacking or limited in some way. As you let go of the belief that the one with the most toys wins, and recognize your inner prosperity, fullness and completeness, you will no longer have any desire to spend endless hours shopping in malls, or browsing through online catalogues, hoping for something that will give you sex appeal or take away wrinkles.

Let us repeat this, ad nauseum: You are already beautiful, whole and complete. No clothing, jewelry, perfume, makeup, hair color, breast enhancement, or tummy tuck is going to change who you are at a fundamental level. If you want to enhance your body, fine, but do not make it into a religion.

Go within and shine your Light on the little self that believes it is not good enough. Talk to that part of you that might think popping a pill is going to make you better, or buying an expensive new piece of workout equipment will make you more competitive in the dating game, or belonging to the right gym will make you feel like you are in style.

You are not here on Earth to impress others or get them to like you. Once you unravel the approval-seeking aspect of ego and start to honor your own natural rhythms, you withdraw yourself from the merry-go-round of consumerism. The latest pop culture icon no longer holds any meaning for you. You stop spending money you do not have on things you do not need. You remove yourself from the debt merry-go-round as well, helping the old system return to the dust where it belongs, a memoir of a time when the ego ruled the roost and foxes (corporate advertisers) guarded the henhouse (the welfare of the people).

Specific Things You Can Do to Reduce Consumerism

The most important thing you can do is take stock of what you truly need versus your ego desires. We do not recommend simply "railroading" over your ego, or attempting to force it into submission. Feeling deprived will only create further conflict within the self. Nevertheless, start by seeing how efficient you can be in your overall lifestyle.

Begin with simple things like turning off light switches, installing power strips that save energy, driving a little slower and accelerating gently, reusing plastic bottles (keeping them cool to avoid chemical leaching, or better yet, using and re-using glass bottles) and reclaiming waste water. Buy as many things as you can that are gently used (pre-owned), especially clothing. Use paper made from recycled fiber. Buy energy efficient appliances. Use perishable products that are made from recycled materials.

Turn off the television set. Shop online. Go to farmers markets or grow your own produce. Cook your own food or support restaurants that buy local produce. Use debit cards instead of credit cards for most purchases, or pay off your credit cards each month. Learn to "design on a dime" when remodeling your home. Grow plants that are appropriate to your climate. Avoid lawns that require constant maintenance and mowing. Boycott any golf courses that do not use recycled water. Use composting toilets if you are in a rural area.

In our section on intentional communities, we will cover a few common sense principles for installing wind, hydro and solar power.

Most of all, spend your time wisely. Invest in your own spiritual growth. Attend workshops on personal development. Listen to beautiful, uplifting music. Meditate. Walk in nature. Do not simply fill up your time with endless activity because you are bored or want to avoid unpleasant feelings. Let go of workaholic behaviors and take some down time. Downsize both your lifestyle and your mind. Teach your children the difference between wants and needs. The only true needs human beings have, besides food, water, clothing and shelter, would be a loving environment with supportive people. Do your best to provide that to the people in your lives. Encourage them to think for themselves and to take responsibility for their emotions. Have regular get-togethers with live music, drumming, singing, dancing and potluck.

Living and eating naturally will greatly reduce the chances of contracting chronic or serious illness, which will in turn help you avoid the pitfalls described in our next section – medical care.

The Medical System

Even your most die-hard traditionalists and business as usual advocates admit that the medical system in most highly developed countries has broken down. In fact, things are going to get a lot worse in that regard. Whether you live in a private, for-profit medical system, or one that is subsidized by government, the problems are essentially the same.

The following account is especially true of medical care that exists in the private, for-profit segment of the medical profession, but many of the points are equally valid in a government-subsidized environment. Let us start with medications.

Most drugs are designed to treat symptoms, rather than causes. This is because it is often extremely difficult to understand and reverse the root cause of an illness, particularly if it is chronic, genetic, or not well understood by the medical community. Very few allopathic practitioners and drug companies understand the holistic element and the fact that you have multiple levels of being that must come into alignment and integration in order for true healing to take place.

Your drug companies exist for the purpose of enriching the pocketbooks of their owners and investors. For the most part, they do not have your best interests or your health in mind. They make money when you get sick, not when you stay well. A healthy population will not buy drugs to make themselves *feel* better, or to give themselves the illusion of *being* better.

You cannot open a magazine that accepts advertising without seeing several ads for the latest pills, potions and medical devices. We have noted that the area of the advertisement listing the side effects for each medication is often larger than the part devoted to extolling the virtues of the drug being pushed. On television commercials, more time is spent going over the side effects than describing the benefits of the drug, even though the lawyers are speaking so quickly that most consumers cannot grasp every word. In essence, they are attempting to cover their backside in the likely event that their drug causes serious problems for some who take it.

In fact, we also note that more people die from negative side effects, drug complications (adverse reactions with other medications), incorrect dosage (errors in administering drugs), etc., than from many of the diseases, syndromes, maladies and aberrations that the drugs are supposed to cure, prevent, reduce or suppress.

We are not saying there is no need for pharmaceutical drugs, but we are saying that probably 90% of them are unnecessary and even dangerous to your physical well-being.

We observe your children being given antidepressants simply because they are bored with your classroom curriculum and cannot stay focused on yet another lesson in sanitized, approved history. The children being born today are highly evolved. As soon as they enter this world, they are subjected to a barrage of stimuli designed to get them to forget who they are and become a consumer.

We realize this sounds harsh and judgmental, but it is important not to sugar-coat the negative programming souls get when they enter into the Earth plane. Not only do they get the genetics of their ancestors (many of whom were totally caught in limiting beliefs), but they pick up on the thought forms of parents, doctors, nurses, caretakers, family members, ministers, priests, and anyone else who comes into their lives at an early age. Add to this the constant assault of television and the media, and it is little wonder why they rebel, disconnect, or get confused.

Oftentimes, parents (who are already overworked and stressed out) will simply cave in to what seems like an easy solution: Give little Johnny a pill to help him concentrate, or slow him down, or speed him up, or somehow make him better.

Of course your medical system consists of more than just pills and potions. You have a wide range of health care professionals, some highly skilled and quite compassionate, and others who may have studied their textbooks, passed their exams, gotten their degrees, and done their internship, but have little understanding of what it means to be a human being.

Without a highly developed intuition and the ability to tune in and be totally present with another person, it is often very difficult to know what that person needs to regain health. Even if a technological advance temporarily reverses a serious disease, or a pill manages to ward off infection, how many health care professionals ask the obvious question, "What did this person do to get sick in the first place?"

Fortunately, we have observed a significant rise in the number of holistic practitioners and healers over the past 50 years. Many of the Lightworkers and those on the fourth and fifth density paths have gotten to where they are with the help of enlightened caregivers, therapists and teachers.

In addition to the 20 to 25 percent of humanity already on the path of awakening, an additional five percent or so of humanity is ready to wake up but does not know where to turn for help. So they reach for a pill, or call a doctor, or read a magazine offering solutions (just have your Visa or MasterCard ready). You, the Lightworkers, might be their next real step in the healing process.

We offer our support and encouragement to those of you who are building a bridge between the holistic and allopathic medical fields. We know it is not easy to get doctors and nurses to open their minds to new ways of thinking about healing, but little by little, progress is being made.

As you witness the breakdown of the current medical system, know that you are part of the solution. By demonstrating that true health comes from within and involves living your life in harmony with your inner selves and the environment, you show this five percent of the population that there is another way to achieve true and lasting health.

The Future of Medicine

What is the future of your medical system? From a third density perspective, it does not look good. Despite the rise of holistic medical practices and encouraging research in many areas, the vast majority of health care professionals are caught in a web of greed, oppression and control. Over the next several years, the problems with allopathic medicine and quality of health care will become more and more obvious. Most caregivers will feel even more overwhelmed than they already are and with good reason. We touched on some of the immune system problems in our previous dissertations, but let's look a little deeper now.

As we stated earlier, souls that are not ready to ascend with the Earth will find a way of exiting their physical bodies and reincarnating on planets better suited to their level of vibration. This process will accelerate dramatically during the portal shifts.

Because the ego is almost invariably at odds with the soul, there will be a conflict within the self between the part that wants to move on into another lifetime (the soul), and the part that wants to stay on Earth (the ego/personality).

Perhaps such a soul has attachments to family, friends, lifestyle and material things, and has a deep sense of duty and obligation to take care of others. The thought of leaving all this behind is less than appealing. So this soul will be constantly looking for ways of prolonging life on Earth even though the body continues to deteriorate. This superficial desire to resurrect the body, combined with a deeper desire to let go of it, often results in chronic, prolonged illness. As the deeper desire slowly wins out and the body gets weaker, such a person requires more and more care from others just to perform basic bodily functions.

There are only so many caretakers available and so many medical devices (wheelchairs, walkers, oxygen tanks, inhalers, braces, special beds, etc.). Sooner or later the number of souls needing such assistance will exceed the assistance available and many are left on their own or must wait for long periods to receive care.

In the years to come on Earth, hospitals will be filled to overflowing, doctors and nurses will burn out from overloaded work assignments, patients will be sent home without proper care, and diseases will spread among those whose immune systems are weakening. From a third density perspective, this is not a pretty picture. In fact, it is a formula for a return of the plagues common in Europe about 800 years ago.

We already discussed the state of your economic system. Add to this a ten-fold increase in the number of sick people requiring care, and you have complete breakdown of government-run medical care, as well as a crisis in the private sector.

The only solution to your medical crisis is to heal yourselves, by understanding the real causes of illness and opening to higher consciousness for reintegration. As Lightworkers, you will be called on to administer to the sick and dying. You will need to know how much you can do and where and when you can do it, so that you, too, do not get burned out.

Ask your God Presence to bring you just as many patients, clients or customers as you can handle. Receiving compensation for your work is secondary, but important. You will be provided for as you do your healing work. Simply be open, take care of your own physical, emotional and mental needs, and give compassionately as the need arises. Trust that you are part of a benevolent, prosperous Universe.

On the other hand, if you are guided by your higher self to devise a business plan or marketing program to make others aware of your services, then do so willingly and without judgment. There is nothing wrong with "tooting your horn" as long as the primary purpose of your business is service to others.

Let us repeat: Take time for yourselves. If you are a personal caregiver, do not accept three 12-hour back-to-back assignments if you know that you cannot be fully present for the third person.

The Dynamics of Holistic Healing and Therapy

If you are a healer, some of your clients will benefit greatly from your healing work and others will not. Give up any investment you might have in the outcome of your services. Just do your best, pray, and be compassionate. If you receive guidance to try a specific healing technique on a client, that's great. Otherwise, simply be present. In therapy, the ability to be present and truly listen to another human being is roughly 90% of the process. Technique is only about 10%.

The psychotherapist that concentrates on how to be fully present and how to listen, but forgets all the academics, is far better off than the one who studies religiously but is disconnected from his human side.

Jesus, during his time on the Earth, did not give miracle healings to everyone who came to him. In fact, only a small percentage of souls were instantly healed. Those that were healed quickly were ready for such an experience. Their souls had already completed many of the lessons necessary in order to move on from a state of sickness to a state of health. Jesus simply became the catalyst for the completion of the process.

You will not always know how your presence has affected those who come to you for help. Sometimes it will be obvious, but people are complex. You might be exactly the right person at the right time to help a soul transition out of this lifetime. Do not judge yourselves if you give someone a healing and then that person dies the next day. Give thanks that you may have been the boost needed for that soul to go on.

In the years to come on Earth, holistic healing will become more widely recognized as an answer to many of the medical problems of today. More and more doctors are turning away from strictly allopathic medicine and are embracing new ways of treating patients.

It may take dead bodies piling up in the streets, or a serious plague amidst a segment of the population, before most people break out of their limited thinking. You might be part of a group of souls that appear to be immune to everything around them. This group may inspire others to raise the question, "What is different about those people? They can walk among the dead and be unaffected. How can I learn how to do that?" And there you have an opportunity to bring another soul into the Light.

Communication in the Electronic Age

Let us change gears at this point and discuss another aspect of the social scene on Earth during the portal shifts.

Unless you have been living in a cave (or in the wilderness), you have certainly noticed the plethora of gadgets and resulting subculture that has emerged from your era of telecommunications. Despite the likely interruption of your satellites and electronics systems during the actual portal events, these devices will continue to garner a lot of attention in the years to come, especially in the younger generation.

You have your mobile telephones, hand-held computers, game consoles, navigational devices, and others, but presently, the telephone and Internet are the most popular communication mediums. You have an entire generation of young souls immersed in cyberspace. Some have nearly forgotten the art of simple verbal communication, preferring instead to text each other in a language all their own.

This virtual reality is an aspect of the fourth dimension, and certainly comes natural to souls vibrating at fourth density. Most of the children coming into the Earth now are at that level, while a few are fifth density and above.

These fourth density children pick up easily on the new electronics (much to the consternation of the older generation that might need weeks to master a simple function on a new device). Within hours of receiving a new phone or computer, they have navigated their way through a maze of instructions and code and are once again lost in cyberspace.

The cyber world that has emerged parallel to the other dimensions of space and time is so prevalent that we can accurately call it a sub-plane of the fourth dimension. The souls enmeshed in this reality are actually creating fourth dimensional constructs, and their adventures in cyberspace will significantly impact their ability to move with the New Earth.

Some will use their cyber skills to develop new technologies that benefit the fourth density souls of future Earth. Others will cycle out of this world and reincarnate on worlds that eerily match the worlds within their computers.

You might have noticed that a lot of the video games currently being marketed look like something out of the Orion wars hundreds of thousands of years ago. This is intentional. The old Orion energies still control the majority of humans on this planet. While some might argue that cyberspace gives them an opportunity to work out their aggression without actually harming real human beings, others will point out that devoting time to killing and war strategies will tend to attract those realities in the outer world sooner or later.

Regardless of the pros and cons of video game immersion, focusing constantly on anything outside of self can give rise to denial of emotions. There is also something to be said for interpersonal communication. That is the kind where people actually talk face-to-face, looking in each other's eyes, acknowledging facial expressions, observing body posture and movement, looking for nonverbal signals, and critically evaluating what is being said from a higher mind perspective. None of this is likely when texting, sending email, or otherwise avoiding real physical contact with another soul.

We ask you, how many of these young souls immersed in technology are aware of their innermost Self? How many express their feelings eloquently and succinctly? How many have quality relationships? While some obviously do, the vast majority are using technology more to escape than to face the realities confronting humankind.

Please understand. We are not judging video games, mobile telephones and so-called "geeks" and "nerds." Your society benefits greatly from technologically minded souls. Yet it is clear to us that the majority of these souls are way out of balance and are using cyberspace to avoid dealing with the unpleasantness of life on Earth.

You can see applications of cyber-mentality in the direction in which your wars have gone in recent years. Armchair strategists guiding bombs from a computer console marvel at how they can watch buildings being blown up from the comfort of their military outpost. This is a lot more palatable than being witness to arms and legs being blown off in the blast, or watching children with blood dripping down their faces as they observe mommy and daddy being carried away in body bags.

Wars continue because there is a separation between the intellect and the heart, to use a popular overly-simplified explanation. A whole human being, in touch with the deeper aspects of Self, cannot simply ignore the suffering inherent within war. Some of today's youth will learn to be compassionate and caring and will outgrow their occupation with violent video games, while others will go on to manufacture their own weapons of mass destruction – on some other planet.

In the meantime, we urge you who are reading this book to reach out to your young people and engage them in meaningful conversation. Seek to understand the part of them that hides behind the video screen. Do not condemn or judge their way of life, but let them know that theirs is a limited view of reality. Yours is not necessarily better, but it offers another perception that might be of value to them.

As your economies continue to weaken, there may not be extra money for many to buy more gadgets. Educate your children now to appreciate the things in life that do not cost big bucks. Spend time with them in nature, outside of the range of mobile transmission towers. Turn off the television set. Unplug the computer. Start with one day a week. Give them the option to come up with activities that do not depend on technology. Assign them part of your garden plot and let them do anything with it they desire. Show them your flower and vegetable seeds and give them a book on how to plant. If they want to garden with you, be available to them. Go for hiking and camping trips. Try out whitewater rafting. Take a trip to the beach. Read a book together, the old fashioned way, one with paper and binding.

Encourage them to exercise their bodies. A diet of McDonald's with Coca-Cola, gulped in-between downloads of video files, will not add to their health. If you hold the purse strings, you have a say in what they eat and what they do with their bodies. We are not suggesting a militant approach, but you *are* responsible for their safety, and it is simply not safe to allow them a sedentary lifestyle.

It is difficult for young people to understand that they are okay even if they do not have the latest game console like the neighbors. Surely, many of them can see that things are not going very smoothly in the world at large, but most have not made the connection between their way of life and the problems in the world. While on one level, they are not responsible for the way things are out there, on another level, we are all One. While they lounge in the den with their hand-held device, the child starving down the street is a part of them, whether they realize it or not. Sooner or later they must come out of denial.

We are not advocating that your children must grow up to full maturity at age 15. However, the years to come on Earth will demand a new level of awareness that very few have awakened to. The ones being born today are highly advanced, yet consumerism and electronic gadgets can veer them off their spiritual path. Whatever details embody the path of today's children, self-discovery needs to be at the top of the list. Your responsibility is to demonstrate this in your own lives and to encourage them to go deeper within.

Releasing the Work Ethic

The work ethic is drummed into every human being genetically, as well as socially. There is a great deal of collective trauma around lifetimes where souls had to do a lot of physical labor just in order to survive. From a soul perspective, this was a learning experience. "I am going to incarnate into a poverty-stricken region of Russia, during wheat crop failure and immense famine, to see what that feels like," says the adventurous soul. Remember, the soul does not evaluate and judge experiences. It just seeks to have as many as possible while embodying in the lower worlds.

Due to the severity of the experience in some lifetimes, the core negative belief, "I must struggle to survive," gets programmed deeply into the subconscious mind. Even when it becomes obvious that scientific advances, medical technologies, and new agricultural methods and distribution systems can deliver food, water and medicine to every man, woman and child on this planet, the belief in struggle invariably helps sabotage attempts to bring the world to a place of abundance and prosperity.

On the surface, it may look as though political and religious systems are preventing distribution of supplies and are keeping souls ignorant of the natural laws of nutrition and agriculture. But beneath these literal road blocks are the deeply ingrained patterns of lack and scarcity, beliefs which have been with humanity since Original Cause.

Once you identify with your little human self, life indeed seems to be a struggle. Even when you take a little down time and try to relax, pretty soon your mind is cooking up new strategies. "You must keep busy," it reminds you, "lest you forget something important."

Although there is a lot to be done in today's world, when properly guided there is also time for doing nothing, especially in the western society. Our readers vary from extremely wealthy, to possessing no money or material things (other than a borrowed computer or library book and the ability to read this). Yet without exception, every one of you can take a day off somewhere in your schedule without your world completely falling apart.

Underneath the work ethic is the fear that if you do not work hard enough, something bad will happen. In some places, the work ethic is so strong that there are actual systems set in place to punish those who do not produce fast enough, such as in the sweat shops. In this case, the fear is passed from top management all the way through the ranks, although the perspective is different depending on the level. The executive is in great fear that he will not make his quota, or profit margin, while the laborer is in fear he will be laid off if he does not move fast enough on the assembly line.

The ability to truly relax and do nothing is one of the keys to enlightenment. But to do that would mean facing the various aspects of the self involved in the obsession with busyness, as well as numerous emotions, some of which are quite uncomfortable. Notice that many of you who meditate still have moments when you feel you should be doing something else. Or you find yourselves filling up your idle time with mindless activity, lest you come face to face with the loneliness that lurks underneath your endless social engagements.

Chapter 8 – Social Systems

In the New Earth, everyone will contribute in some way, but first, all souls will become educated in exactly what is most important and why. Creating a beautiful, harmonious environment will be high on the list. That means lots of work for carpenters, plumbers, electricians, designers, engineers, etc., but it also means lots of opportunities for gardeners, artists, sculptors, painters, musicians, and entertainers.

The value of a product or service will be based on how well it contributes to the good of the community. Those elected as council members of a community will interact with the members and get their feedback. They will pose questions such as, "How do you feel about that painting?" or "What would it be like to have that building over there?"

Everyone would be given an opportunity to voice a concern or appreciation. These things would start at the "grassroots" level, perhaps initially involving only a few people in each section of the community, before gradually spreading out into the world at large. It may be too much to take on a large city with your ideas, but some of them can be managed within an extended household or neighborhood block.

Our advice is similar to what the channel often advises to his clients: Take baby steps. Do not try to save the world in one day. Work together with a few of your closest friends and family to break out of the work ethic and do what you truly love to do. Find your right place. If everyone on Earth were doing what they love to do, there would be no problem finding enough souls to perform the necessary tasks to keep a community running.

Some of you may be saying, "I do not know what I really want to be doing. I just know it is not what I am doing at present." There are various tools and techniques for discovering your passion. Ask the channel or another therapist to help you get in touch with your true desires.

In every case, the things that bring you the greatest joy in life will be connected to your soul's purpose and mission. It is important to focus on those things even if you cannot imagine a practical way of earning income or having a business in those areas.

Restructuring your lives to accommodate your true desires and joys is not easy. It requires making a commitment to doing a little bit every day to move in the direction of your dreams. Even if all you can seem to afford is a half hour every day, make and take the time. If necessary, put it into your appointment book. Block out a period to devote to doing what you love most in life. At first, do not worry about how you will turn it into a business. Just immerse yourselves in the joyful expression of your life path. Later, you can work out the details of how to manifest your dreams in ways that bring prosperity and balance.

This channel has a simple creative writing exercise to help facilitate doing what you love to do and getting well paid for it. If you are not clear on what you would like to be doing, contact him.

Enlightened Social Systems

To have an enlightened culture, you must have enlightened relationships. This means providing everyone with basic education about how to relate, something that is not taught in most schools on Earth today.

The high crime rate in many nations is due primarily to lack of love during early childhood as well as general discord in the family and relatives of evolving souls. Of course, many of you come from parents who may have said that they loved you numerous times while growing up, and we do not doubt that familial love did exist in many cases, but to love unconditionally means accepting you just the way you are, not just outwardly with periodic affection. It means caring not only for your safety, but encouraging your feelings deep inside.

This means growing up in an environment where both your humanness and spirituality are nurtured and sustained. That is not very common in most parts of the Earth.

Parents have their human weaknesses, as you well know, and there is no such thing as a perfect parent. Raising children is difficult and requires constant awareness and focus. Many parents have children before they are mature enough to provide spiritual and psychological nurturing.

This issue goes far back in your history. However, in many tribal systems of the past, there were rites of passage and special ceremonies devoted to acknowledging and supporting the various phases of growing up and maturing. Your modern society has very few of these that are still intact. Often, both parents are working, assuming they are even still together.

Children growing up in a single-parent household, or those that spend a majority of their childhood with both parents working, comprise a majority of the households in the western countries today.

In addition, your educational systems are geared toward turning out productive workers. Curriculum is designed to get you to fit into the existing society, to prepare you for the workplace.

Part of establishing an enlightened social system is in realizing that the children being born today do not have the same background as a generation ago. Many are from the stars, quite literally, and do not understand human life. They have come here to teach and heal. Recognizing this, it is your job as parents to provide them with teachers that allow both right and left brain learning, combining intuitive and logical reasoning.

As you heal your own inner child issues, it becomes easier to provide clear guidance to your children. In the meantime, your children are mirrors. They know how to push your buttons, and also how to heal, if you give them a chance. They might not know a lot intellectually, particularly if they are only a few years old, but they know intuitively. If your children seem to be clashing with you, look within and see what aspects of self are clashing with each other. What feelings are going unexpressed?

It is well known that children tend to act out the subconscious issues of their parents. In this sense, they are offering you a gift because in some cases you might not even be aware of a negative emotional pattern unless little Sally painfully points it out.

Parenting is tricky, because you need to set firm boundaries and assume responsibility for the safety of your children, while at the same time allowing them as much freedom as they need to grow and evolve with as few limiting beliefs as possible. In other words, all of you are unlimited beings living in a limited environment, for the time being. You start by learning about the limitations (boundaries) and then growing and evolving beyond the need for limitations. Eventually, you will even transcend your so-called physical limitations, but you must start with the basics.

Let us zero in now on our perceptions regarding your personal relationships.

Enlightened Relationships

Dear Creators, have you noticed how hard it is to get along with each other? As if we had to remind you. Some souls seem to do just fine with family, friends and even business associates, but when it comes to an intimate partner, all bets are off.

Most enlightened souls we have encountered during our time with Earth have learned how to find peace in virtually every situation except with a mate. With a very close person, you tend to let down your barriers because you feel safe enough to do so. Therefore, anything that is unresolved within your own being will have permission to come out and be expressed.

In addition, many couples are drawn together precisely for the purpose of working out karmic issues they might have accrued during less than enlightening past lives. Even if you are evolved to the point where you no longer have any past karma, you will likely attract a partner who will mirror those aspects of yourselves that are not yet integrated. You might not have consciously chosen each other for this reason, but on another level your souls recognized the opportunity to grow and evolve more quickly by having your partner constantly mirror the areas where you still need work.

In some cases, such couples are able to attain a level of acceptance of each other that keeps the relationship together, but often they turn their judgments and unresolved emotional issues inward on themselves. The refrain goes something like this: "I do so well when I am by myself. I seem integrated, balanced and centered. Yet when I spend time with my partner, I am constantly being shown that I do not really have it all together. I am upset at myself for not being able to stay calm and centered around my partner."

If such a soul were not in ego, there might be a great deal of gratitude toward both self and partner. After all, if it were not for the agreement of the couple to help each other heal these stubborn issues, they might go unhealed until such a time as the issues truly hindered the ascension process. A more enlightened refrain goes like this: "Thank God for my partner for showing me what I need to heal so I can get on with it. Otherwise, I might have deluded myself into thinking I had already integrated these issues."

To assist enlightened partners in truly enjoying their time together, it is important to remember that the soul in front of you is both human and Divine. Here is an opportunity to love the human side of your partner and yourself, as well as the Divine in each other.

Of course, we are assuming you already know about and are practicing good listening skills and are separating behavior from essence. Using nonviolent communication and other techniques can be helpful. The old psychological adage, "What I hear you saying is..." can be a most effective mirroring tool. Adding to this a withhold process, such as "Something I've been withholding from you is..." or "Something I've held back saying is..." will greatly assist the communication process. The object is not to confront or force confession of things, but to be truly open, with active listening on the part of the one receiving the communication.

The best communication is nonverbal. It involves giving your whole attention to the other person without rehearsing what you are going to say next. Make eye contact. Notice your body movement and posture without judging. Notice the same with your partner, again without judging. Remind yourselves that the purpose of the relationship is to assist each other in growing, learning, unfolding and rejoicing in the beauty of life. You are whole, complete souls simply desiring to share your lives with each other. You are not a half seeking the other half in order to become whole. That type of relationship is doomed to failure.

Even if you stay married for 50 years to "your other half," as long as you hold that view, there is some degree of stagnation in your growth process. You will find that no amount of mediocre time spent together will replace a few high quality years with someone that is ready to grow and evolve quickly with you.

The other person is never the source of your happiness. Your God Presence within you is. Your partner might mirror a blissful state to you, or be a catalyst for you to get through a sticky issue and into a joyful space, but you are responsible for your own state of consciousness.

The best relationships are those where the partners have a lot in common, but not so much as to take away the spice and variety of life. You want to be different, but not so different that you are incompatible. Having a variety of common interests and a lot of differences can be a wonderful thing. Sometimes you want to be complementary, meaning that the areas where you are weak are your partner's strengths and vice versa. Other times you want to co-create something that requires both of you to be strong.

If you are not in a relationship and wish to attract a partner, it is best to state clearly to your God Presence the attributes and qualities you want in a partner. These should be values such as, "a good listener, compassionate, committed, emotionally mature, etc." It is not appropriate to focus on specifics, such as body type, income, likes and dislikes, etc. A general affirmative statement with some embedded specifics, such as "I am attracting a sexually compatible and financially stable mate and we have many common interests," is okay.

Some of the bolder of you might say, "I want to attract a partner who will be a catalyst for my spiritual growth. I want someone who will challenge me and show me where my weak spots are." That's great, and most likely you will get what you ask for. Just remember to give thanks even when the mirror you receive from another feels uncomfortable.

You are living in a time when soul family members are finding each other and coming back together while in physical form. Although it is rare for twin flames to be embodied on Earth at the same time, many of what this channel calls "secondary soul family members" are likely to come into your life in the years ahead. These are soul mates, beings that you have a deep connection with from other lifetimes or dimensions. You are coming together because you are advanced souls and want to learn about co-creation, a higher way of relating than competition.

Eventually, all of you will feel a deep connection with everyone and everything, because you will learn to recognize the Oneness in all. As you grow and evolve, the quality of consciousness of those you attract will mirror your own consciousness more and more, based on the law of attraction. There will be fewer souls attracted to you as students and teachers (except in structured learning environments where this is desirable).

You are here to co-create Heaven on Earth. To do this, you need a lot of compatible souls that share your basic values and goals. You need similar levels of commitment and willingness to tell the truth, no matter what. Sometimes differences can be worked out through communication processes and structured learning. Other times the differences are just too great and it is necessary to go separate ways. Learning to recognize when it's time to roll up your sleeves and get to work on resolving a relationship issue, and when it is time to say goodbye, requires a great deal of patience, diligence and listening to your heart.

Empowering Each Other

When souls finally transcend the ego and live from the center of Being, empowerment will no longer be an issue. In the meantime, we wish to give a few pointers on what it means to be in an empowering relationship.

Even though most of you are familiar with the concept of "win-win," especially in business, you also have within your cellular structure a lot of third density patterns hardwired into the physical body relating to survival, competition, and other behaviors geared toward self-preservation. In addition, you still have some elements of societal programming that say you need this or that in order to be successful. You are taught to be in control of your environment, which includes the people around you.

The requirements for true empowerment of others are as follows: (1) You must *know*, beyond all doubt, that your well-being adds to the well-being of others, and their well-being adds to yours. When they are successful, you are genuinely happy for them, even if there is no direct benefit to you that is readily apparent. (2) You have examined and healed any and all hidden motives you may have had toward others. These motives may include seeing them as potential clients or romantic partners, wanting their love and approval, wanting agreement with your ideas and concepts, wanting to convince them of a perceived truth about some aspect of reality, or otherwise wanting to control their attitudes and behavior. (3) You are able to go beyond the words and labels regarding others. They are not simply men, women, large, small, educated or otherwise. They are powerful, vast spiritual beings. You are able to tune into them energetically and perceive the incredible beings they are beyond their physical appearance.

As you tune into others, you begin to recognize their true needs, which may be different from their human desires. You learn to communicate higher self to higher self, rather than personality to personality. You learn to telepath. There is simply a *knowing* that goes beyond all descriptions or methods. In essence, you become One with the other.

When you enter this state of Divine recognition, your actions toward others become empowering. This is not something you train to do, it flows out of you naturally because you know and love your neighbor as yourself.

The best method of empowerment is tuning in deeply to the essence of others. Ask your own God Self, "What can I do to maximize the soul growth, happiness and well-being of this person?" Then listen for the answer. Sometimes the answer will advise doing nothing, or simply being quiet and receptive. Other times you might be called to intervene in the affairs of the other person. There is no set formula for what to do; it varies from person to person depending on many factors. Do not get hung up in psychological theories or past results with clients if you are a therapist. Tune in right now to the other. Be totally present. Be actively quiet.

Simply *know* and *feel* the presence of this soul or souls in front of you. Do not put labels on what you experience. You can do this process with your significant other, best friend, any one person, or a group of persons, with or without their knowledge. You are not violating anyone's free will or intruding. You are simply *being* in the presence of another *being*. Together, you are One Being expressing through two or more bodies.

This ability to truly be One with each other will be essential in the years to come on Earth. Feeling your Oneness will make the journey into enlightened community flow more easily. The next chapter will explore some of the details of intentional communities.

As discussed in Chapter 1, it is not easy to build an intentional community, but this will be the way of the future for fourth density Earth. If you are planning to be here on Earth through the Galactic Shift, it is imperative to understand what it means to be in community. You are interdependent. That means that you are an individual, but your personal well-being is part of a collective well-being. Interdependency does not mean conformity, colony, or any form of socialism. Within the group consciousness, you have your own sovereign identity. A group that is truly interdependent does not violate the free will of its members, nor try to get them to think or feel or act a certain way. Conformity is a third density quality, while individuality is fourth density and true interdependence is fifth density.

The intentional communities described in Chapter 9 make use of this idea, which recognizes that every person's viewpoint is valid and contributes in some way to the growth and evolution of the community. Let us now explore the new social paradigm of community that is emerging and will blossom in the coming years on Earth.

CHAPTER 9
Intentional Communities

There are over 1,000 communities worldwide that fit our definition of "intentional community." We are not including cities and towns that grew up without a specific intention, but later became united or bonded through the efforts of their members. There are hundreds of thousands of tight-knit communities, but they are not set up intentionally with every member in mind. Their ability to transition into a true intentional community is there because they have the advantage of already having a degree of bonding.

We are also not counting the hundreds of thousands of extended families that share one or two houses on a small piece of property, but are not organized with regular council meetings and structured tasks and functions.

Another category we have omitted is cooperative housing, or eco-housing ("co-housing"), which is essentially a small, perhaps enlightened homeowners association or cooperative building project that may involve a single building, or dozens of buildings. In its place, we have included the "ecovillage," a step forward from co-housing that is more directly focused on community, rather than simply property sharing.

Below, we have delineated intentional communities into three major categories:

Ecovillages

The closest model for setting up an existing town or city as an intentional community is the ecovillage. The idea here is that everyone within the village participates in both individual housing and one or more community centers directly operated by the individual homeowners. Each homeowner is part of an association, but it is truly of, by and for the people, and not set up by only a portion of the community.

Every adult member of an ecovillage has an equal share in how the community is run. The village has a charter, set of goals, purposes and objectives, and lives according to ideals that must be agreed upon by its members. Some ecovillages might have as their primary focus affordable housing, or ecological sustainability. Perhaps they co-own a power generation facility, or have agreed to all install solar panels on the roofs of each building.

The advantages of the ecovillage style of intentional community is that it affords a high degree of privacy, while at the same time bringing people together of similar consciousness who want to collectively create a different lifestyle or way of living. An example of this form of community would be the Ecovillage at Ithaca, NY.

Spiritual Communities

There are two types of spiritual communities – those with a guru or central leader and those with no central person. Of those that have a leader, there are some with an active, living teacher and some based on the teachings of an enlightened saint or guru that has passed from embodiment.

The other type of spiritual community may make use of the teachings of various gurus or masters, but is not bound by any of their creeds or doctrines. Members of a specific community might model their lives after a particular saint, sage or rishi, but souls are free to explore other teachings at any time, as long as those principles are in harmony with the basic tenets of the group.

An example of the first type of spiritual community is the Ananda Village in Nevada City, California, based on the teachings of Paramahansa Yogananda, as taught by one of his students, Swami Kriyananda.

An example of the second type of spiritual community would be any one of a number of communities based around "*A Course In Miracles*," a teaching brought forth in the late 1970s by a woman channeling Lord Sananda, the oversoul of Jesus. Members of ACIM communities are typically involved in other spiritual teachings as well as those of Lord Sananda.

The advantage of spiritual communities is that they keep members focused on spiritual progress. If the leader or teacher is quite enlightened, the teachings will encourage personal empowerment and freedom, rather than strict adherence to rules and regulations. Those communities that rely too heavily on the leader and encourage members to abdicate personal responsibility are in danger of becoming a cult.

Cults are defined as religious or spiritual communities wherein most or all personal power is given to the leader, either consciously or unconsciously, overtly or covertly. The cult leader amasses personal power at the expense of the members. The core negative belief attributed to cults is the idea that someone (the leader) is more spiritual, or better, than the individual members, and that the members cannot attain enlightenment without the "grace of the master."

You can observe the workings of a community to determine whether or not power is concentrated in the leader at the center, or whether power is distributed throughout the community. Healthy spiritual communities consist of members that are free to leave, question the values of the leader, engage in dialogue with members of other communities that have different leaders, embrace multiple spiritual paths, and that are focused on self-empowerment.

Communes

To desire sexual intercourse for any thing else than bringing into embodiment another soul is not a divine desire but is a human desire, which will impede embracing one's divine nature and block ascension.

Communes are typically set up with a minimum of personal freedom and an *more* emphasis on the status of the group as a whole. Despite the low emphasis on personal freedom, some communes may appear to be based on anarchy, or people engaging in various anti-social behaviors, often with wild abandon. These are merely protests against the status quo and have little to do with real freedom.

The healthiest type of commune is really an extended family, and usually consists of amorous individuals (people with multiple sexual partners) who have simply decided to live together and pool their resources. Not all communes are sexually amorous, but the intimacy and shared nature of the community resources often arises out of some form of amorous lifestyle.

Commune members typically do not own any property, other than personal items, such as jewelry and clothing. All larger items are shared among the community members, including cars, houses, land and debt. There may be a central member who has legal custody of property, or each member's name might appear on the deeds and contracts.

The advantage of communes is that they are living examples of the Oneness of human beings. The disadvantage is that there is very little personal freedom, and usually very little privacy. The most successful communes are those run by people who have worked through their issues regarding intimate relationships, which is not a very large group of humans. Often, amorous people have simply suppressed their emotional issues and have convinced themselves that they can maintain their lifestyle without hurting themselves or others, even though they may have a lot of issues that are in denial. A few amorous individuals may have truly transcended limiting beliefs and emotions regarding intimacy, but they are in an extreme minority.

Other Community Structures

There are communities that combine some of the aspects of the ecovillage, spiritual community and commune, into a new synthesis of enlightened living. For example, some communities may have a leader or teacher that is not particularly spiritual, but has special knowledge of ecology, sustainability,

who

gardening, farming, or some other skill or discipline. While each member may have his or her own guru or religion, they share a combined interest in the skill or discipline of their leader.

With very few exceptions, anarchy has not been fully realized in any of the communities on Earth of which we are aware. There are some individuals who have co-purchased land, or who live on land trusts, and essentially do their own thing, but graciously and with a friendly attitude toward each other. They might make some decisions as a group, but generally they leave a lot up to each member, as long as he or she does not infringe on the rights of the other members.

Usually, these semi-anarchistic communities are not self-sufficient. Members work outside the community, making this arrangement little more than just co-housing.

The few communities that are close-knit and structured, but that do not have a central leader, usually consist of individuals who have done a lot of work on themselves. They are typically therapists, healers and personal growth consultants, and they are more or less experimenting with different lifestyles and living arrangements. Their success depends heavily on regular meetings where they work out their differences and come to consensus on shared goals and visions. An example of this type of community is the Hummingbird Ranch, near Mora, New Mexico, in the USA.

In order for a community to thrive without a strong leader, people need to take a lot of responsibility for their own feelings, thoughts and actions. Usually, membership in such a community is highly restricted. Members must vote unanimously, and usually after much consideration, before admitting new members. Anyone who might be overly dependent on others, or unwilling to share in the tasks and chores, or whose lifestyle is just too different, will not be admitted.

This is not a case of judging potential members, or making them wrong in some way, or being an exclusive "clique", or discriminating. It is a question of each existing member going with inner guidance and checking it out with the other members. Does it feel right to admit this potential member? Would this person truly fit into the structure of the community? Would this person have a good chance of being happy and well-adjusted in this community?

Some communities fail because they allow just about anyone in, regardless of their level of evolvement. Members of existing communities have the free will right to choose who to let in and who to refuse. Our advice in this matter is similar to our advice for your personal relationships: Send love and compassion to all souls in your own life who are not right for you, and then send them on their way in peace.

It is important to let go of any sense of obligation you might have toward your fellow human beings. You do not have to say "Yes" to everyone in order to be loving and compassionate. Sometimes it is not worth it to invest your time and energy in someone who is unwilling to grow and change in positive directions. This is what Lord Sananda meant by the phrase, "Do not cast your pearls before swine." Likewise, in communities, it is your right and responsibility to make decisions that truly benefit the members of your community and the world at large, even if it means saying "No" to prospective members.

When choosing to become a part of an existing intentional community, or when admitting new members to a community of which you are already a part, remember that a high state of consciousness attracts others who are at a similar level of vibration – most of the time. There will be exceptions, especially when there are unresolved soul lessons to be learned. For example, a discordant potential member might show up in order to teach you the soul lesson of discernment and setting firm boundaries by saying, "No." This same soul may need to learn a soul lesson around integrity, or cleaning up his own inner act before expecting to be admitted into a harmonious community.

The reverse is, of course, true as well. Souls who are existing members of a community that admit a person that is disruptive and destructive to the purposes of the community have a soul lesson to learn about setting firmer boundaries (i.e., learning to say "No.") The disruptive member who is admitted may also have a soul lesson to learn. He may have attracted loving, compassionate people into his life in order to teach him love and compassion. Once such a soul is part of a community and everyone concerned decides they will just have to make do with each other, the overriding soul lesson may be learning to accept what is, and discovering new ways of giving and receiving love and compassion between the new and old members of the community.

Certainly, it is not always necessary to know, from an intellectual standpoint, what the soul lesson is in every potential situation that may arise regarding intentional communities (or any other aspect of life for that matter). Some souls on Earth will look for a deep lesson every time the slightest imperfection, or aberration, shows up in their nearly perfect lifetime (from their perspective). For example, if you trip over a stone and bruise your foot, does it really mean you have negative karma? Perhaps the soul lesson is more simple: Watch where you are going!

How to Set Up a Community

Setting up an intentional community does involve a certain amount of trial and error. That is because you cannot know, with certainty, every free will decision that members and potential members are going to make. You can stay alert, aware and receptive to the energies of others and make some relatively wise decisions together, but there will always be unexpected twists in the ongoing saga (or drama) of living together.

In any endeavor of this type, it is important to come together with those who are co-creating community with you and concisely state the purpose of your being with each other, what you hope to accomplish, and some basic structure for doing so. We suggest you study existing communities and see what is working and what is not with each one. Ask yourselves some basic questions: "Are the people happy? Are they growing and evolving together? Do they make a positive difference in the world in some way? Are their basic physical needs met? Do they have healthy emotional expression? Are they encouraged to be human, as well as Divine? Do the members have a sense of self-empowerment (as opposed to relying heavily on their leader, if one exists)?"

Whether you are co-creating a new community or joining an existing one, ask yourself, "Is the financial and monetary structure working? Do individuals have a valid say in what goes on within committees and with leaders? What is the community's relationship with local towns, counties, shires or provinces? How do members handle conflict with each other and the world at large?"

Most "successful" communities have some sort of temporary membership provision that allows incoming souls to try out living there, and gives existing members a chance to get to know the prospective members.

Some communities have several tiers, or levels, of involvement, ranging from temporary resident, to associate partner, to permanent member, etc., with each successive level giving rise to greater responsibilities and authority.

It is important to have clear, concise agreements, written as well as oral, between members. This will minimize later surprises. For example, if the bylaws of the community state that each member must contribute at least ten hours per week of service to the community, this needs to be communicated up front with prospective new members. There will need to be a work chart or other structure in place showing the various duties and responsibilities; i.e., job slots that must be filled.

Leadership groups and councils should be flexible and reevaluate the jobs periodically to make sure priorities are in order. After all, 20 people each spending 10 hours per week in the garden during the off-season is probably not a wise allocation of human resources.

More on Community Councils

This section is not designed to be an exhaustive dissertation on how to run an intentional community. There are many good books on the subject. We suggest you peruse the Internet and do some research. Nevertheless, we will make a few brief points below.

The purpose of a community council is to facilitate the decision-making process of a group of souls. If your community consists of 12 people, you might want to have each person be a council member. Then all of you meet regularly, maybe once per week, to discuss issues common to all of you, and, just as important, to provide support to one another physically and emotionally.

You might begin your meeting with taking care of business. A ditch needs to be dug, or a well drilled, or solar panels installed. You need to decide on whether or not to admit a new member who wants to join. You need to discuss your financial balance.

Next, members will come forth with more personal needs. There could be a space provided to share spiritual insights or visions for the community, or just inner experiences that want an audience. Certain ground rules will be in effect to prevent some souls from monopolizing the energy or discussion, and to encourage the more introverted members to express and contribute.

Certain agreements are necessary to keep council meetings brief and to the point. Every person demands respect. You might use the "talking stick" approach, meaning that the person with the talking stick is allowed to talk and everyone else simply listens until a comment period starts. Most of you are quick to react to what is being said without first fully listening, with all your senses. The talking stick helps you tune in with your whole being to the person speaking.

You will need to draw up some sort of bylaws or procedures, such as whether decisions are made by consensus, majority, or some other manner. There needs to be a procedure in place for handling conflict or dissenting views. It may be basic psychology, but members need to be reminded that the behavior does not define the person. In other words, you can disagree with a member's behavior and still see that person as a beautiful, innocent child of God.

Coming Back Into Balance with Nature

Your intentional communities will consist of fourth and fifth density members. Most of you will be vibrating at fourth density, but a few of you will have crossed into a consciousness primarily dominated by fifth density vibrations. As you grow and evolve, you will come to know your Mother Earth as a vital, living Being. You will communicate deeply and intimately with her.

As you clear your emotional and psychological issues, you will have less and less in the way of hearing Mother Earth as she shares her wisdom with you. Not all of you in the community will have the same level and connection with the Earth. One of the topics that will inevitably be brought to the council involves how to treat Mother Earth with respect and how to live harmoniously with her.

We have observed ecovillages that are actually too strict when it comes to recycling, reusing, reclaiming, and respecting the Earth, to the point where the joy goes out of living. On the other hand, there are a lot of well-meaning communities that pay lip service to responsible stewardship of the Earth and her resources. Until your alternative energy transportation systems are fully in place, you may, for example, use solar, wind and hydro power to run your community, but still use fossil fuels to drive to the store 30km away. In such a case, you might have as one of your goals, to obtain a fleet of hybrid cars running on both fossil fuels and electricity.

It is important to set realistic goals and to achieve a balance point between extremes. This might include leaving the smallest carbon footprint possible, while still having a lot of fun and variety.

As you become One with all living things, these considerations will work themselves out with minimal effort. It will simply feel good to recycle, rather than forcing it on everyone. Giving up red meat will happen naturally, rather than feeling like a sacrifice. Nobody will be in judgment about these things, but they will simply emerge as common sense practices.

Over the next thirty years, new technologies will be introduced to the fourth density souls to enable them to clean up the polluted environment left behind by fossil fuels and other exploitative lifestyles. Electric cars will replace internal combustion engines. Hydrogen fuel cells will be manufactured safely and cheaply. Eventually, zero-point energy will be harnessed on a mass scale.

At some point, the fourth density souls will be ready to venture back into the third density world to restore beauty and harmony to burned-out or collapsed buildings, sewage dumps, toxic landfills, and rotting and decaying remnants of the consumerist society that will have self-destructed somewhere between now and 2030.

It will take some time before the fourth density souls will be truly ready to walk anywhere on the Earth without becoming subjected to negativity. Since the Earth's vibration will continue to rise, the process of clearing negativity will become faster and more efficient. A day will come, beloved Creators, when you will truly experience the Heaven on Earth that you have all been promised.

Living in Paradise

Paradise is a state of consciousness. It may be different for each soul. Some will consider it paradise just to be out of the city, while others may not call it paradise until their community has been stable for ten or twenty years.

A utopian world view is not what we are advocating here, but we do see a time when all human beings on Earth will evolve beyond the need to control and manipulate the world and other souls. This is a time when true cooperation reigns, when souls recognize the God in each other and walk their talk as masters on the Earth.

Your brothers and sisters from the stars will walk among you once again. They will welcome you back into the great cosmic family. The Earth will be restored to the Garden of Eden it has always been on another dimension. That level of reality will descend gently into all consciousness remaining on the Earth, and all will be One.

Until that time, there is a lot of building to be done. Below is a list of the best places to have alternative communities of Light. This is not an exhaustive list. A few communities will thrive in other areas, especially if they already have a high level of consciousness and can overcome extremes of weather or close proximity to third density cities. In some cases, oppressive governments will still make it difficult to start communities, but over time, those governments will transition into a more enlightened state.

The Best Places for Alternative Communities

Table 9 – The Best Places to Start or Join a Community

Western Canada
Northwestern USA
Southwestern USA
Southeastern USA
Southwest Mexico
Costa Rica
Western Brazil
Northern Argentina
Central Uruguay
Northern United Kingdom — WHAT ABST AVE BURY ?
Southern France
Northern Spain
Extreme southern Netherlands
Parts of Belgium
Southwestern Germany
Parts of Switzerland
Extreme northern Italy
Northwestern Romania
South central Turkey
Parts of eastern Ethiopia
Parts of Madagascar
Extreme northern South Africa
Parts of Congo
Western and central Russia in Ural Mountains
Northwestern China
Southern Siberia
Parts of Malaysia
Northwestern islands of Hawaii
Eastern Australia (southern Queensland/northern New South Wales)
Parts of the south island of New Zealand
Southwestern part of the northern island of New Zealand

CHAPTER 10
Technological Advances

One of the most important aspects of the New Earth involves the responsible use of advanced technologies. The scenarios unfolding on Earth do not involve a return to the primitive way of life that has typically preceded the dissolution or destruction of previous organized societies. (Just as a refresher, there have been four major civilizations on Earth, Pangaea, Lemuria, Atlantis and the one currently dissolving.)

After each of the previous dissolutions, life on Earth (decimated by natural and man-made disasters) resumed in a very limited state, often with basic survival skills and simple resources (such as wood fires and crude tools).

For the most part, the technological knowledge from each previous civilization was temporarily lost when things crumbled. Just a few remnants survived.

Of course the collective consciousness, in the Akashic records, contains all technological advances ever made since the beginning of Earth. As new civilizations have come and gone, the more awakened scientists have tapped into the Akashic field to rediscover the technologies of sacred geometry, crystal generators, zero-point energy, cold fusion, radionics, and more.

We have gone into the question of why civilizations fall repeatedly just when things seem to be breaking through to a new level. In every case, a few souls have managed to retain their knowledge from those times and apply it in future incarnations. Also, in most cases, a small number of souls have chosen to leave the Earth with their consciousness intact and go on to other worlds, rather than be a part of "starting over" on Earth.

The preferred way of the wise ones from civilizations past has been to remain in the higher realms and communicate with new fledgling societies through telepathic contact, channeling, and an occasional brief landing on the Earth. (The latter method, for reasons discussed previously, has been discouraged, and it is mostly the lesser-evolved ETs that interact directly with humans via spacecraft and holographic projection.)

There is a great deal of truth to the statement, made by many of your seers, that technologies were withdrawn by the wise ones to prevent misuse by the evolving humans, many of whom had forgotten their spiritual understandings when going through the destruction of previous civilizations. Due to the non-interference doctrine, many wise ones simply left the Earth plane altogether, leaving struggling humanity to make their own choices, which were often not for the benefit of maximum soul growth. This was seldom due to lack of compassion, but rather, an unwillingness on the part of the spiritually ascended to fall once again into a state of forgetfulness.

Various safeguards have been put in place to prevent the misuse of powerful technologies. The frequency fence was a collaboration of the light and dark factions of the Orion and Sirius-A star races. The dark ones wanted to trap humans on Earth and prevent them from developing psychic and intuitive powers. The light ones supported the quarantine because they did not want the negative humans on Earth to migrate to neighboring parts of the galaxy spreading their warring ways.

So there have been energetic patterns put in place on Earth to prevent the utilization of advanced technologies. Nevertheless, due to interference by the Zetas, dark Orions, light Pleiadeans and other groups, high technology was reintroduced in the 20th century in the form of integrated circuits, computers and telecommunications devices.

From a quantum physics perspective, higher technologies, such as zero-point machines, can only exist within a resonance that is supportive of superconducting fields. A predominantly negative consciousness does not create a supportive resonant field. From a metaphysical perspective, a planet that contains a large negative consciousness that believes in lack and scarcity will not attract the prosperity and abundance associated with zero-point fields.

To review, these technologies create a bridge between the etheric and physical realms, allowing the nearly infinite field of undifferentiated Source energy to flow into and regenerate the physical realm. Some scientists call this energy flow "centropy" or "charged entropy" because it is the opposite of the entropy observed in the second law of thermodynamics.

To put this in lay terms, the spiritual energy of the Source revitalizes things that have "run down" or are worn out by the ravages of third density time.

So as you can see, there are several factors that have, in the past, prevented the reintroduction of advanced technologies after a civilization has fallen.

In the present transitory state on Earth, a sufficient number of enlightened souls will survive the changes with their knowledge of higher truths intact, and this will allow them to set up resonant fields conducive to the development of higher technologies.

There will be some lag time or delay due to the likely destruction of many of the telecommunications satellites and the ground infrastructure (due to warfare, terrestrial and solar storms, etc.), but enough knowledge will remain to reconstruct and resurrect the technologies most useful (such as the Internet and telephone).

In addition, souls in fourth density will be rapidly developing their telepathic abilities, which will assist them greatly in balancing their use of technology.

Using Technology Responsibly

We wish to come back to a point made earlier regarding the need to withhold certain technologies until souls are ready to use them wisely. This can be likened to the idea of refusing to allow a toddler to play with matches.

Just as the Galactic Confederation is blocking the use of your nuclear weapons (except for a few tests here and there), they are also broadcasting frequencies to prevent the implementation of higher technologies that could conceivably be used malevolently. If an inventor is telepathically in touch with higher beings and has a sufficiently evolved consciousness, these blocking frequencies are temporarily lifted to allow the inventor to move forward with the development of the new technology.

We in the higher realms regret the need to intervene in this matter, but the state of affairs on Earth is far too delicate to simply allow unrestrained development of new energies without oversight.

After 2015, the consciousness on Earth (and the vibration of Earth herself) will be sufficient to lift the veils over the harmonious resonant fields. Once these barriers are lifted, the resonant field of Earth will allow for zero-point and other devices to function anywhere on the planet.

Consciousness and the quantum realm are intrinsically linked and must be respected. As you embrace the idea that you live in an infinitely prosperous and abundant Universe and you open to be the channels for those frequencies, you will be entrusted with the use of higher technologies.

We will give some details regarding the higher forms later in this chapter and explain how to make them work consistently one the frequency barrier is lifted.

Until that time, you will need to use non-polluting technologies that are already in place on your world. Below, we will detail our perception of how these existing technologies will be developed over the next few decades:

Existing Alternative Technologies

There are several technologies available right now to use while you are preparing to mass distribute the higher forms described earlier.

Solar Energy

Solar cells have been available for over 50 years, but the technology has been slow to progress. This is due partially to the initial cost of installation, along with the fact that solar is not completely reliable in the northern climates where it is cloudy much of the year. It is also due to intentional downplaying of its benefits by the nuclear and fossil fuel industries.

A lot of third density souls see the usefulness of solar power but are convinced that cheap fossil fuel and nuclear generated electricity will always be around, so why go through the bother of purchasing the panels, having them installed, and possibly having them "interfere" with the look and feel of the home. Yes, some souls feel the panels are ugly and detract from beauty of a home's architecture.

We anticipate some advances in the efficiency of solar cell arrays in the next few years. Since fossil fuel prices escalated sharply in 2011, there is renewed interest by some companies who now feel customers will be more willing to pay for solar systems today than they were back when fossil fuels were a lot cheaper.

Therefore, we predict there will be a two or three-fold increase in the number of residences with solar panels installed over the next five years. We realize this is still a small percentage of total households, but a lot of homeowners are feeling financially stressed and some are barely making their house payments and do not feel they can put out the money for the initial purchase.

Others will wait until there are frequent "brown-outs" and even black-outs within the existing power grid, or until the cost of coal, oil, or nuclear-based power doubles or triples.

Hydroelectric Power

There is a movement toward small hydro plants along minor streams and rivers that involve simply catching existing water flow to generate electricity for a few houses downstream. This is certainly feasible and has been used off and on for quite some time already.

Unfortunately, the vast majority of hydroelectric energy comes from large dams that flood huge land areas, often to the detriment of land and water species, as well as homeowners living upstream of the dam site. Like traditional fossil-fuel and nuclear-based plants, high tension electrical lines are installed, often across steep mountains for hundreds of miles, with thousands of trees uprooted to allow for the passage of the lines. In many areas we and this channel have observed that significant doses of pesticides are used to clear plant material from around the high tension lines. So while the initial power plant does not pollute the way coal, oil, gas and nuclear facilities do, there is still a cost to the environment.

There are low-impact hydro plants that can be installed anywhere there is ample water flow, but generally this should be considered a supplemental energy source and not the primary one, especially in heavily populated areas.

We are aware that places like Niagara Falls are able to generate a fair amount of electricity without greatly spoiling the natural landscape or significantly altering the water flow, but locations like that are an exception to the rule. Even with that water, the companies involved are heavily motivated by maximizing profits and seem to care little for the environment beyond the initial low pollution of the plants themselves.

If you have an intentional community with ample water flow, it is in your best interest to find someone who understands hydroelectricity and how to harness it without destroying the environment around the water source. With proper management of water and intelligent distribution of populations on Earth, large dams would be unnecessary. For example, over half of the fresh water in California goes to grow feed for cattle so human beings can continue eating beef.

It is not judgmental to point out that the eating of mammals takes a heavy toll on your environment. Not only would huge amounts of water be conserved by adopting a mostly vegetarian diet, but the land currently used to grow feed for cattle could be converted into fruits and vegetables for human consumption. This is not to mention the billions saved in health care costs because a diet low in red meat produces far fewer negative health effects in the average human than a typical "meat and potatoes" diet. We apologize for getting off the subject of hydro power.

Wind Power

Almost two-thirds of the Earth's surface (where temperatures are tolerable for human habitation) involve areas where the wind blows frequently. There are a few places that currently utilize wind power extensively, such as the hills of coastal California and the western plains of Texas. Again, the large commercial wind farms are primarily concerned with maximizing profit and while wind is generally non-polluting, distribution of electrical lines from wind generating stations is still disruptive to the environment.

Personal wind generators installed within intentional communities are recommended as a supplemental energy source to solar and hydro. Unless you are in a drought and the weather is cloudy and still, at least one alternative energy source is likely to be generating, and even if none of them are active, you can install battery packs to mete out the power incrementally.

Battery technology has only improved marginally in the past 50 years on Earth, but we also see some gains occurring in that department over the next few years.

All of these alternative technologies require an initial investment of money and time. Some human beings will wait until it is too late before they realize they should have had something in place. If you are used to going to the grocery store at any time of the day or night, or simply turning on the light switch to get light and it never crosses your mind that one day these conveniences might not be there, then you will be in for a rude awakening.

Now is the time to start thinking about ways to become self-sufficient as far as energy is concerned. At the same time, ask yourself, "How much energy consumption do I really need in order to be happy?" Is life really better because you have that 52-inch television? Do you need four computers all on at the same time in different parts of the house? Is it necessary to run the air conditioner the minute the temperature creeps above 21 degrees Celsius?

By reducing your consumption and installing some alternative energy generators, you can begin to wean yourselves off the big power companies.

Hydrogen Fuel Cells

This is a technology that has advanced a fair bit over the past 20 years. It is now cheaper and safer to use hydrogen directly as a fuel than it was back then, although the peripheral systems (intake, exhaust, etc.) do require some significant adjustments if you are converting from a hydrocarbon-based engine system.

Biodiesel

Biodiesel is a fuel derived from plant sources. Unlike corn ethanol, it does not require excessive energy input. It is possible to grow certain crops and process them into biodiesel without taking up large tracts of land that could be used to feed human beings. This is a stepping stone technology until more efficient hydrogen fuel cells are widely available at an affordable price.

Hybrid Vehicles and Machines

One of the current trends is to modify engines to blend fossil fuels with battery-powered electrical systems. Basically, when acceleration is needed, the car burns fossil fuels, but at the same time the battery is being charged and takes over when acceleration stops. As long as there is a balanced amount of accelerating versus coasting, braking or stopping, this technology works fine and extends fuel mileage considerably.

Best Places for Solar, Wind and Hydro Energy

The best geographical locations for existing alternative energy systems are obviously places with a lot of sunshine, wind and water. Before we give worldly locations, let us discuss micro-locations; i.e., where on a piece of land to place alternative energy generators.

Best Locations on Existing Land

Ideally, a tract of land being used as a farm and/or intentional community should be located on a gentle hillside facing the sun, with proper drainage, and only the bottom section on a floodplain so that in drier years you have access to rich soil. Houses should be placed mid-way between the top and bottom of the hill, ideally on shelves with a thin layer of soil and solid rock underneath the shallow layer. If there is not already a natural thick forest near the top of the hill, trees should be planted several layers deep across the top and on steep slopes to prevent erosion and to protect from high winds.

Wind generators should be placed near the back of open areas facing the prevailing wind direction. Hydro generators should be placed as far upstream as possible, ideally near the top of the property. Solar panels should rotate to follow the sun and be adjusted seasonally. Gardens should be spaced throughout the property wherever soil is good, both on the hillside and in the floodplain. If you are drip irrigating or running pipes from a stream, you will obviously want to make use of gravity flow whenever possible, which means some part of your garden should be below the elevation of a portion of your stream.

In the northern hemisphere, your houses should be built with east, south and west-facing windows. If octagonal, a southeast, south and southwest orientation is best. In the southern hemisphere, your windows would face northwest, north and northeast. If you are near the equator, you will probably place your solar panels directly above your house and place windows in any direction.

Keep in mind that if you live in a hot climate, you will want a way of shading your house. That usually means locating it amongst broadleaf trees. In the summer, the leaves will shield you from the sun and in the winter, the absence of leaves will allow the sun to warm your house (passive solar).

The above may be common sense and a bit elementary to those of you who are carpenters, builders, architects or alternative energy engineers or designers, but some of you who are not skilled in these areas may start your new communities before you engage the services of a professional and so the more information you have in advance, the better.

Best Planetary Locations for Alternative Energy

As for planetary locations favorable for wind, hydro and solar energies, we recommend some of the same places already mentioned in previous sections, namely, southwestern Canada, northwestern USA, southwestern USA, southeastern USA, Costa Rica, southwestern Mexico, portions of Argentina and Uruguay, southern France, northern Spain, northern Italy, northern Greece, south-central Turkey, extreme southern Russia, north-central Africa, South Africa, western China, northwest Hawaii, eastern Australia, and anywhere else where the climate is temperate (not too hot or cold and ranges from semi-arid to semi-moist).

Places to avoid would include low-lying flat plains (even though wind is often abundant), arid deserts, rain forests, and most coastlines. Also, make sure your property is not likely to be taken by eminent domain. In other words, you should not be in the path of existing power lines, or in a location directly between a large reservoir and a heavily populated area where new power lines are likely to be built.

Think ahead. Expect that the cities closest to you will be hungry, hot or cold, meaning they will want energy and food (a lot of it) in the years to come, and they may not use polite and diligent means to acquire it. Although your community might evolve quickly enough into higher densities to become psychologically invisible, do not assume that will be the case. Start your community in an area that is off the beaten path. Ask yourselves, when resources get scarce, where will nearby cities look for new resources?

Most of all, ask your own God Presence to guide you to the right piece of land. See yourselves attracting souls who are experienced with installing wind, hydro and solar generators. Set aside financial resources for purchasing these items. Expect that they will cost 50% more than you think they will, even if prices seem to be dropping on some items.

If you hire contractors, do some research. Ask others who have lived in the area for a while who they recommend. Whenever possible, inspect the work done on other properties. Talk to neighbors and neighboring communities about their projects. Do not wait until you are desperate to get up and running and then take shortcuts that you might later regret.

Coming from fear or desperation during the Earth changes will shut off your intuitive and psychic abilities and cause you to make poor decisions.

We in the higher realms are here to help you stay in your center of Being while making important choices about the future. Always go within and feel the energy of our advice as well. Learn to recognize what "highest option" energy feels like. Do you feel light and clear when selecting a garden spot? Do you feel a deep sense of peace regarding your solar panel installer? Are you feeling confident and energetic about putting together your own inverters and batteries? Do you still have money in the bank after buying all the inevitable extras that come with any project?

We hope you have enjoyed our foray into the practical details of building an alternative energy system. Know that we have included this practical advice to help round out the Earth changes information and that this is not intended to be an exhaustive dissertation on how to build your community. There are numerous books on each of the subjects we have touched on here. Go to the Internet, library, or local community business directory to find out more on these subjects.

New Technologies

Cold Fusion

Your mainstream scientists rejected cold fusion when it was first produced successfully, going to great lengths to discredit the inventors. Some countries, most notably Japan, were not so fast to write off cold fusion. Over the years, much research has come forth indicating that cold fusion is indeed real.

Cold fusion works on a principle similar to radionics (discussed next) and zero-point energy (discussed a little later). Basically, atoms in a specialized medium, such as noble gases interspersed with rare metals and other elements inserted as catalysts, will form a resonant field sufficient to change the energetic state of the medium. Unlike radionics and zero-point energy, cold fusion does not rely on centropy, or energy from the vacuum (from the etheric planes in actuality). The cold fusion process involves a release of heat as partially unstable isotopes are fused into more stable isotopes.

The process works in a similar manner to conventional fusion reactions, such as hydrogen to helium, normally occurring at very high temperatures. Because of the catalytic elements involved in cold fusion, the isotopes behave in the desired manner at temperatures barely above the average Earth environment (typically between 30 and 50 degrees Celsius). We recommend browsing the Internet and specifically, looking at Japan's cold fusion research, for more information.

Radionics

Radionic devices are constructed of somewhat ordinary materials, such as copper wire, resistors and insulators, but in such a way that they form mini-vortices capable of concentrating electromagnetic energy and directing it where it is needed. In essence, radionic devices work in a way similar to microwave technology, but utilizing a different part of the light spectrum.

Radionics differs from zero-point energy in that you are tapping into concentrated areas of electromagnetism and manipulating the flow of electrons, but not necessarily opening a wormhole into the etheric planes. You could say that radionics technology is a stepping stone between conventional electromagnetism and zero-point fields.

Pyramids, multiple-wave oscillators, Tesla coils, Van der Watt generators, and large capacitors all can be made to harness radionic EM fields. Size and dimension of these devices is critical so that you are amplifying the natural oscillations of the EM waves. (As you know, magnetic waves are 90 degrees out of phase with electric waves. By taking this into account using polar coordinates and multiple variable wave-vector equations, systems can be designed mathematically with precision.)

Gravity and Electromagnetism

One of the biggest mysteries among your physical scientists involves finding the relationship between gravity and electromagnetism. We will seek to give a partial answer to this "holy grail" of physics, omitting much of the math.

Since everything in the Universe is ultimately One, there is a relationship between every aspect of Creation, even those aspects that seem vastly different and separated by great degrees of space and time. For example, an amoeba living on an Earth-like planet in a distant galaxy 10 billion light years from your galaxy has a relationship with a human being on Earth.

Gravity is a force of affinity between life forms and also between so-called inanimate objects. Every object (including all life forms) that has mass will have some degree of gravity.

Every object (and life form) has some degree of consciousness. In fact, there is such a thing as "atomic consciousness," or the basic unit of consciousness inherent in one atom.

Without taking the time to define the constants associated with different elements, the most basic level of consciousness (level one on this channel's scale) can be quantized into a packet of energy having particle and wave-like properties, but on a much smaller scale than your quarks. We will denote these particle-waves as God Units (GUs).

The affinity principle, or gravity, in which objects are attracted to one another based on their mass and distance, we will measure in the popularly coined term, "gravitons."

If we take two hypothetical objects and measure both the electromagnetic field emanating from those objects and the gravitational field that exists between them, we can find a mathematical relationship between the two forces. This means that if we know the EM field attributes, but not the gravity, we can calculate the gravity, and if we know the gravity, but not the EM field, we can calculate the EM field. In other words, there are constants that can be determined that show how these two forces interact, effectively increasing or decreasing the EM and gravitational fields.

For example, if you increase the Love and Light consciousness between two objects, the EM field increases and so does the gravitational attraction. This runs contrary to the Newtonian postulate that assumes gravity between objects remains constant as long as the mass and distance have not changed.

The reason your scientists have not been able to measure this interrelatedness is because you are dealing with very small quantities and very large differences between the magnitudes of the forces. The actual relationship between gravity and electromagnetism can be given as follows:

GUs emanating from the first object, times a GU constant (about 6 times 10 ^-15 Joules), times Planck's constant, times the proportion of mass between the two objects, times the inverse of the distance between the objects, equals the measure of gravitons that exist between the objects. With proper substitution and differentiation of the constants and variables in this equation, gravitons can be expressed in Joules, a common unit of measure for EM fields.

We have omitted the variable definitions and resulting differential equations required to calculate these values, in the interest of our non-science readers, and because we have not been authorized to give you every detail of the relationship between electromagnetism and gravity, but there is enough here to get the serious researchers among you busy.

You will note that the equation above gives a very tiny value for gravity unless the objects are very large and close together. Your scientists already know that electromagnetism is millions of times stronger than gravity, but now you also know that the true magnitude of the difference is dependent on the level of consciousness between the objects.

A soul that focuses intently on a desired outcome, for instance, generates a larger magnitude of God Units than someone whose mind is wandering from subject to subject. Your EEG machines (and other devices) are already able to measure brain wave activity. There is a constant (derived using advanced mathematics employing multiple variable differential equations and nonlinear vectors) that describes how to calculate God Units based on the millijoules of electricity measured by brain wave devices.

Measuring Consciousness

Once your scientists calculate the value of the God Constant, they will be able to measure consciousness itself. No longer will the metaphysical and spiritual worlds of the soul be kept separate from the external world of gravity and electromagnetism.

Note: You also have the strong and weak nuclear forces, which are really one force in two different configurations. Both of these configurations also have a relationship with consciousness and, of course, with gravity. You will find that ALL forces observed in nature are directly related (through various constants and formulas). The missing ingredient in your calculations is consciousness.

Some of your scientists will attempt to simplify the mathematics involved here by giving consciousness a designation as the fifth primary force in the cosmos. Your mainstream scientists will balk at this idea because of the difficulty in measuring God Units. You do not currently have instrumentation capable of measuring Planck's constant times the consciousness constant (the power of ten here is approximately -50, or about 100 billion times smaller than one quantum packet of energy).

Others will attempt to use superstring theory and multidimensional constants to measure God Units. This will eventually look good on paper if you know the Greek alphabet, but advances in measurement technology are still a ways off for proper verification, and you will again find a lot of "creative mathematics" with this approach.

A general difficulty in measuring consciousness is that, in its pristine state, it is omnidirectional, which means you cannot simply move consciousness along a wire in one direction and expect to capture all of it at a point in space. At present, most humans, even when they focus intently on a particular object, still scatter a lot of GUs in different directions away from the intended target. This is one of the reasons only a few humans have been able to practice psychokinetics successfully (the ability to move objects that are unattached to the physical body using the psychic faculties).

One example of instrumentation that can measure the "macro" effects of consciousness is your biofeedback equipment. Note that these devices do not measure consciousness directly, but calculate the electricity generated by the mind through temperature and moisture differentials in the skin or bodily organs. Through a series of amplifiers, one can get a person to move the needle on a meter with just the power of thought.

There is a debate among parapsychologists as to whether the needle moves because the subject desires it to, or whether it is simply reacting to the subject's ability to change body temperature and moisture at the location of the electrodes. It is obvious that the mind of a subject can control his own physical body (in some cases even changing heartbeat and vital functions), but to generate enough EM field magnitude to move a distant object requires the ability to tap into the EM energy field (the etheric plane) and move it unidirectionally, rather than omnidirectionally.

Essentially, by learning to unidirect consciousness, the soul becomes a type of zero-point device, capable of giving and receiving virtually unlimited amounts of energy. We will discuss zero-point energy in the next section.

There are visualizations that involve seeing energy cascading down from the higher dimensions, entering the crown chakra and then passing through the body and out the hands. This energy can then be directed to parts of the body (of the subject or others) that are in need of healing and restoration. Basically, psychic and spiritual healing techniques are utilizing the zero-point field by opening up a resonance into the etheric planes and then "downloading" energy from those levels into the physical plane.

Zero-Point Energy

In our previous book, "*Earth Changes and 2012*," we talked briefly about zero-point fields, how they work and when to expect mass production of generators. We would like to go into more detail at this time, without losing our readers who are not scientifically oriented. It is a challenge to present this material in lay terms, but we look forward to the challenge, with the help of the channel.

The most important thing to realize about the Universe is that it is based on varying degrees of resistance. In this case, we are using the word "resistance" in both its technical and metaphysical meanings, for they are intertwined.

From a metaphysical perspective, the higher the degree of resistance, the more you are not accepting "what is" in every moment. Infinite resistance would be complete rejection of an aspect of reality, or denial. Zero resistance would be a state of complete acceptance of what is.

In electricity, infinite resistance means you have an open circuit where no current can flow, and hence, no useful electricity. If you have no resistance at all, you have infinite energy available (based on Ohm's Law).

If you use the analogy of God's Limitless Love and Compassion flowing into a human being, you can see how these two ideas intertwine. If you are resistant to the Divine, the energy cannot flow through your being and you will not receive healing. If you are in denial about some aspects of your reality, you have unrecognized resistance there. The resistance of denial is so great that almost no Divine energy can enter those places and so they wither and die. Often this shows up in the body as disease or atrophy.

The solution is to become aware of those places and send them love and compassion, along with visualizations of God's golden, radiant, loving Light.

In zero-point technology, we can apply this idea liberally as follows:

It is possible to design and construct materials that either oppose or resist incoming etheric energies, or work in harmony with these energies. Sometimes you want to block certain energies and so you design a material that effectively blocks those frequencies. The simplest example involves the element lead used to block various types of radiation.

More importantly, in zero-point technology, you create materials that produce resonance, or superconducting fields, which essentially means the atoms and molecules come together in a special pattern of resonance that allows the free flow of energy between them.

You have what are called monatomic resonant fields, or orbitally rearranged monatomic elements (ORMEs). You may start with a rare metal in its native state, where the atoms are arranged symmetrically, perhaps in rows or utilizing some basic geometry, and then by rearranging them electrically (or with the help of consciousness), they are able to align themselves into a resonant field. The popular example is the conversion of yellow metallic gold into the white powder monatomic form of gold.

When you create a resonant field within a material, there is virtually no resistance between the atoms or molecules comprising the substance. As you know from Ohm's Law, the less the resistance, the more the current (available electricity). As the resistance in a substance drops to zero, the current approaches infinity. While technically it is impossible in the lower realms to achieve complete superconductivity (zero resistance), with proper understanding you can come close to realizing this. (We know that the type of wire needed to transmit high levels of current is problematic at present, but we foresee advances in building material technology in the years to come.)

ORMEs are created chemically through proper introduction of catalysts. Zero-point technology involves inducing a superconducting resonant field through proper application of electromagnetic devices and existing DC current.

What happens when a superconducting resonant field is generated electromagnetically? To over-simplify, energy "tunnels through" from the etheric realms into the physical. These "tunnels" exist in the spaces where the polarity of the electromagnetic field of the machine is completely balanced; i.e., the point equidistant from the poles of a magnet if the poles are exactly the same magnitude of polarity.

To construct a zero-point device, you must be able to calculate how the electrons are going to move and how much resistance is in the basic building materials. In addition, you must generate electromagnetic fields at precise coordinates such that the intertwining fields match the "resonant points or vectors" of the system.

The mathematics used to construct such a device employs the use of what is commonly called "multiple variable nonlinear vector equations." The rigorous mathematics, along with the need for precise measurements of magnets, wires, insulators, coils, transmitters, resistors and capacitors, make it difficult for the average inventor to perfect a zero-point machine.

Nevertheless, crude versions can be built cheaply with everyday materials because even an approximation of the right proportions of angles, vertices, lengths, widths, etc., will generate some tunneling effect.

The relationship between consciousness and zero-point technology is not understood by most human scientists, yet this is an essential part of its development. The reason we gave the spiritual analogy of a soul completely open to the Divine is because such a consciousness in effect creates a zero-point field around it, mimicking the electromagnetic equivalent. When this consciousness field interacts with an EM field, it moves the EM field into resonance. This is a rough way of saying that an observer, who is in harmony with a zero-point device, assists the zero-point device in functioning optimally.

You may know if you have studied quantum mechanics, that you cannot achieve a quantum state that is not somewhat compromised by the presence of the observer. This is because the observer generates GUs that affect the experiment.

This is also the reason you cannot attain absolute zero temperature in a laboratory. The presence of consciousness in the laboratory generates enough energy to keep the temperature of the system a few millionths of a degree Kelvin above zero.

In fact, just thinking about the experiment is enough to generate interference within the closed quantum vacuum. (As stated in our previous section, consciousness, which consists of what physics calls "God particles", can pass through any and all known materials.)

As you grow and evolve as souls, you will learn to have a more direct influence over atoms and molecules in substances that appear to be separate from your energetic field. This is called "psychokinetics" or "telekinetics" depending on the type of influence involved. What you may not realize is that you are already psychokinetic in nature, although most of you have not learned how to direct your consciousness units in an organized way out into a seemingly separate quantum system.

Holding the intention that a zero-point device will function the way you want it to has an enormous effect on the device. Your resonant field consciousness attunes itself to the resonant field of the device, augmenting the resonance of the field that is already carefully designed using vector mathematics. If it were possible to have no influence of consciousness, then theoretically the device would work, but we know that all laboratories exist in a sea of consciousness.

The distance between an observer and the laboratory is not as crucial as the intensity of the thought forms about the experiment. If a group of one hundred scientists is on the other side of the world and is thinking negatively about an experiment, they might have enough influence to stop the desired effects, even if you are right in front of the vacuum chamber sending it positive thoughts.

The net effect of all consciousness, after taking into account the intensity of the thought fields emanating from souls, will usually determine the outcome of the experiments. This is why we have given 2015 as the year of the tipping point, when zero-point machines will finally be able to proliferate on the Earth. That is when we feel the consciousness of humanity, in collaboration with the base frequency of Earth herself, will be harmonious enough to balance out any negativity being sent to zero-point fields.

Types of Zero-Point and Over-Unity Devices

Most zero-point devices make use of circular or toroidal iron-core magnets carefully placed around coils and a DC motor. The object of the machine is to generate areas of nonpolarized EM energy, often called scalar EM fields, by passing a current through the coil while the magnet is rotating. The initial rotation would be achieved by "kick-starting" the device with a simple 12V battery (or something similar). As the magnet turns around the coil, the EM field generated along the coil interacts with and feeds back into the loop with the magnetic field of the magnet. Because electric and magnetic poles within an EM system are 90 degrees out of phase, the velocity (angular momentum) of the system will cause fluctuations within the two fields. Sometimes they will cancel each other out, and at other times the fields will combine their energy.

As the magnet rotates, you will have 0-90-180-90-0-90-180-90 etc., as your angles of incidence. As the DC current moves along the coil, the system creates a polarized field which interacts with the rotating magnet. Essentially, you will have periodic interactions of plus-plus, plus-minus, minus-minus, minus-plus, plus-plus, etc. At the midway point between the plus and minus charges of the polarized field, you cross the zero point where there is temporarily a perfectly balanced polarity (albeit lasting a few microseconds during each magnetic rotation).

Through varying the velocity of the magnet and designing it with the right geometrical precision, you can enlarge the zero-point "windows" and direct the energy that tunnels through the windows onto a collector plate. The usual configuration is to re-route the energy from the collector plate back into the system, essentially replacing the 12V battery with a "perpetual motion" machine. With proper design, the energy collected from the vacuum (really, the etheric realm) will far exceed the 12V nominal value, thus resulting in over-unity, or the ability to produce more energy out than what goes in.

Your entire physical Universe is based on polarity. In fact, you are part of the larger etheric Universe of nonpolarity and within that nonpolarized field are the variants known as positive and negative. It could be argued that the movement into polarity is what actually created the physical Universe.

Your scientists already know that there exists a nonpolarized field. They call it the Bose-Einstein condensate after two of your scientists that demonstrated it in a laboratory. They reduced the temperature of a near-vacuum until it was close to absolute zero and observed that the movement of electrons and positrons ceased sufficiently to collapse the EM field potential between the poles of the EM system. While this system approached zero-point, it was not practical because it took a lot of energy to lower the temperature and measure the results. However, it did lead scientists to realize that the static state of the Universe has superconductivity, or nearly zero resistance, and they know that the potential energy of a field of zero resistance is infinite. Thus, here is physical, scientific proof that there exists a field of infinite energy surrounding the physical Universe.

Instead of spending trillions on ways of acquiring more fossil fuels, your scientists could be using that money to develop ways of harnessing this unlimited energy. In the next section, we will look at some of the applications of zero-point technology.

Power for Homes and Business

This is the most obvious application for zero-point technology. Already, there are watered-down devices being installed in homes in Australia and New Zealand, two countries where the dark Illuminati do not have quite as much influence. Even so, the current machines are only slightly over-unity because the consciousness in these countries has not yet evolved to the point where nearly free, unlimited energy can be distributed widely.

As these devices are perfected and spread to other countries, the costs of heating, cooling, running appliances, manufacturing goods, and operating machinery will be greatly reduced. Any DC or AC motor currently being run on electricity generated by fossil fuels and/or nuclear power can be modified to run on zero-point energy.

The devices currently in production last about fifty years and, after the initial purchase, cost a few dollars a year. The initial cost of the devices runs anywhere from about $1,000 AUD to $50,000 AUD, depending on the size and application. See the channel for more information on these devices.

There are approximately six zero-point devices, manufactured by different individuals or groups around the world, that will be entering production shortly. It is estimated that by the year 2020, almost 10% of the energy generated worldwide will be through these devices.

We and this channel may be publishing a book on zero-point energy at some point in the future. In the meantime, we encourage you to surf the Internet on this topic, keeping discernment in the forefront of your mind since not all inventors have high integrity and truthfulness.

New Agricultural Systems

Now that we have introduced new energy systems, let us discuss the state of future agriculture, because this is another area in which new developments are occurring on Earth very quickly.

In addition to hydroponics, grow domes, greenhouses, permaculture practices, and other existing methods of extending growing seasons and cultivating varieties of fruits and vegetables that normally would not grow in your climatic zone, there are some new technologies emerging that promise to give you even more choices. There are service companies and individuals now offering to re-mineralize your soil so that your plants are getting all the nutrients necessary to produce healthy fruits and vegetables bursting with vitamins and minerals of their own.

There are ways of layering your plants to maximize use of space. There are hybrid species that take a fraction of the usual time to grow and produce a crop. There are new varieties of existing species that can survive in more extreme climates.

Some of these hybrid and hybridized crops are engineered in harmonious ways, while others use experimental methods and genetically modified organisms. The effects of consuming some of these crops have not been studied extensively. Although your inner guidance should be consulted before growing or consuming any experimental crop, it might be appropriate in some cases to use trial and error.

After eating some newfangled tomatoes, how do you feel? What is your energy level? Was the yield worth the extra expense? Do you think you can reproduce this new crop consistently year after year, or was this a fluke?

One of the prevalent new agricultural experiments involves different types of algae. Under the right conditions, algae can grow very quickly and produce enormous yields. It is suggested that proper growth of algae can feed all humans currently residing on Earth many times over from just a few thousand acres. To some of you, this probably sounds like something out of a fairy-tale, such as "*Jack and the Beanstalk,*" but such advances are not science fiction.

Genetic engineering has its positive side. With love and cooperation between plants and humans, the nearly infinite abundance of energy in the etheric realms can be brought into the growing and harvesting process. Despite the depletion of nearly 90% of the topsoil in the world, there is enough of everything necessary to produce healthy crops in almost every climatic zone.

As you know, coming up with enough soil, the right nutrients and adequate food production are not the main issues. Distribution problems due to unstable economic and political systems, along with the way the existing infrastructure is set up, keeps highly nutritious food from reaching a lot of those who are malnourished.

There is a great deal of misperception regarding how to feed the world's population. For example, over three-fourths of the body and blood types on the planet require an emphasis on fresh vegetables as opposed to grains, yet those in ignorance believe the answer is to grow and ship to the disadvantaged wheat, corn and soybeans (most probably genetically modified and laced with numerous pesticides).

It is true that the Asian blood types often do well with rice, for example, but not every Asian has the right body chemistry to assimilate rice, and a great deal of the rest of the world does not have the proper constitution to eat large amounts of rice.

The leaders of many of the agribusiness companies, in their deluded state, actually believe they are helping the planet by producing vast amounts of foods that the human body can barely recognize and assimilate. In addition, the monoculture practices in many countries may create an abundance of some nutrients, while at the same time creating a massive deficiency of others. (This is in addition to the obvious disadvantage of monoculture in that if the crop is wiped out due to flood or drought, there are hardly any alternatives.)

The solution to this problem (in addition to utilization of the enlightened agricultural methods outlined in this section) is for food distributors to focus on broad spectrum crops, including variety and seasonal rotation, and to realize that every human soul has a unique body chemistry.

Extensive nutritional research into ethnic groups, genetics, and adaptation in various parts of the world is necessary in order to understand which foods are appropriate in which locations.

One of the major keys to not only surviving, but thriving, in the years to come on Earth is knowing how to make gardening fun, and to enjoy eating less. If you chew slowly, but with more awareness, more of your food gets assimilated. Savoring a fresh carrot and staying in the moment with the experience may be far more satisfying than hurriedly downing a processed snack on your way to a meeting. Chewing slowly and meditatively also helps the digestion and assimilation process. You require less food before you feel full if the food is vital and fresh and you eat slowly.

We apologize for reiterating some basic topics here with which you are already familiar, but it is important to get a broad overview of the issues you are likely to be facing in the years to come. We suggest re-reading the section on diet, nutrition and addictions given earlier.

Enlightened Architecture

As near as we can tell, the main reason for square buildings is to minimize cost and time required for construction. The mathematical principles of erecting a square building are pretty straightforward and most of the raw materials can be mass produced. Yet very few designers have pondered the effects of a square building on the energy body of humans. It is true that square or rectangular buildings can assist in "grounding" souls into their physical bodies, which really means that such buildings help souls function in linear time.

However, human beings are both linear and nonlinear, and the shape of the human body, along with the auric field and developing Merkabah vehicle of Light, are definitely not square.

When designing a building, knowing how energy grids intersect and interact can be quite helpful. If you have the time and materials, you can experiment with different shapes and see how they affect your physical energy.

We in the higher realms observe that each building shape has a different effect on the body, and that circular, octagonal, hexagonal and pyramidal shapes tend to augment spiritual awareness more than squares or rectangles.

Of course, there are many other factors to consider, including the terrain, amount of light, direction of hillsides, etc. We are not going to go deeply into the subtle science of Feng Shui in this discourse, but we recommend you look into this on your own. Our main point is to urge you to pay attention to your energy body as you enter and exit various structures. There is a reason you feel right at home with some people and not others, and it is not always due to the psychological state of the people you interact with.

If you feel you cannot afford to build from scratch and have only enough funds to modify your existing structure, find out which rooms have the lightest and clearest energy. Next, observe the geometries, building materials, angles, heights, directions, and furniture of those rooms. As much as possible, modify the "heavier" or "denser" rooms to match the design of the lighter rooms.

If you are living in an older home, or have been there for a while, the heavier rooms might be the ones where souls did a lot of worrying, or performed unpleasant tasks. Doing a psychic clearing on the old energy may be necessary before making modifications.

Of course, in your enlightened design, you will want to bring aesthetics into the picture. If the first feeling, upon looking at your new dwelling, is joy and appreciation at the beauty and elegance of design, then those feelings will be magnified over time as you live there while maintaining that appreciation.

We recommend you consult with designers who are both functional and aesthetic in their approach.

Regarding buildings within an intentional community, it is important to consider how the structures reflect the overall philosophy of the community. If you are very close-knit and value intimacy, you will want to design your living quarters to be near the community gathering places. If privacy is more important, you will want to make sure you have living areas that are farther away from the community buildings.

You may want to build your dwellings in a circle, with gardens inside, and then the community buildings in the center, like spokes of a wheel. There are some communities already designed this way. Such a structure is helpful to remind members that there is no hierarchy of rule among the leaders. A founder, council president, or wealthy member will live in the same basically-designed house along the circle as a newly arrived member that has no prestige. Many enlightened leaders will, in fact, insist on living in a similar manner to the so-called "ordinary" members.

It is important to consider proper placement and type of utilities. Some people are sensitive to electrical fields and you may want to minimize their use within sleeping areas. Ideally, your community should have some buildings with electricity and some without. A meditation room, for example, may have soft music piped in to one corner, but otherwise be electrically free.

Building Materials

In some countries, it is legal to grow hemp. We recommend, if at all possible, eliminating lumber made from mature trees and replacing it with hemp-based boards and pillars. Hemp requires about six months to grow to maturity, while trees often require 30 to 40 years. We suggest combining clay, dirt, straw, and other plant-based materials for insulation and fillings. Naturally derived dyes and paints are highly preferable to synthetic compounds. This prevents buildup of formaldehyde and other chemicals in the walls of your dwelling.

If you like the look and feel of wood furniture, acquire your raw materials from recently downed trees or odds and ends from other construction projects.

Metal and crystals should be used carefully. Some people believe the more crystals, the merrier, but this is not necessarily the case. Crystals are amplifiers and you want to use them strategically in your design. Metals can also amplify both positive and negative energies and can be too harsh for some people. Do research on the effects of metallic objects on the human body, then experiment on your own body. Some souls love to sleep in copper pyramids, while others find it too energizing.

We recommend domes and pyramids for different parts of your community, depending on the specific function of each building. Domes are more relaxing than pyramids, in general, so you might want to sleep in a dome and recharge your body in a pyramid. For a meeting hall or community gathering space, you might want to combine a relaxing and energizing infrastructure.

Keep in mind that these are basic guidelines. Your budget, time constraints and available materials will impact how you design your community. If you have drawn up your purpose and goals and are clear about the intention of your community, your design will reflect this.

Cities of the Future

Later in this century, we do not predict that humanity will have highly concentrated industry and commerce centers the way you do now. First of all, as previously discussed, we anticipate a decline in your overall population. Second, the New Earth, and the souls that inhabit it, will value open space and peace a great deal. With proper construction, you can still fit a large number of people into a small space without it looking and feeling that way. You will have fewer automobiles and those you do have will use non-polluting energy sources, so there will be less need for expensive, land-consuming highways. The inner part of most communities will be free of large vehicles. If supplies must be delivered, there will be a couple of small inlets where trucks can pull up, but aside from that, walkways and bikeways will be the norm.

The largest buildings will be near the center of the cities, as they are now, but mostly for aesthetic purposes and to serve as meeting facilities, with living quarters along the periphery. Your old world cities were designed around manufacturing of raw materials and developed haphazardly out from there. The new cities will take into account the need to have gardens and open space around private dwellings. Because most resources will be acquired locally, there will be no commuter corridors with endless traffic. Any manufacturing that does occur and that requires lots of people and resources will be spaced fairly evenly throughout the city in order to prevent congestion.

The "spokes on a wheel" design for a large city is useful because, properly implemented, you are never very far away from essential services. Instead of designing your city with profit in mind, you are thinking about the needs of your people. Fourth density souls will have similar values already in place and so we anticipate that the process of coming together to design a city will be an exciting and rewarding experience.

Again, we urge you to do some research on intentional communities that have visions of growth. How are they planning for additional members? Where will they live? How will they fit into the existing infrastructure?

Our vision of your future cities entails images of great beauty and variety, without the ticky-tacky, block-style housing projects that blight many of your countries at present. A large percentage of employment will be done from home, or in small community centers placed strategically throughout the city. Factories (if needed) will also be aesthetically pleasing, as will essential services, such as libraries, medical centers, fire protection, etc.

We see a green paradise of plants, trees, flowers, lakes, streams and wildlife interspersed throughout your populated areas. We look forward to assisting you with your many building projects in the years to come.

New Transportation Devices

One of the most promising applications of new technology is in the use of propulsion systems. Clean automobiles, buses, trains, boats, airplanes and other vehicles will have zero-point devices and other alternative energy machines installed and the surrounding peripherals modified accordingly.

You have undoubtedly seen science fiction shows where airships move along corridors suspended above cities. This is one of the technologies that will be introduced in the years to come on Earth. The air highways and ships will draw on etheric energy from the ley lines of Earth, without disturbing the natural balance, and will involve force fields of energy that eliminate all accidents. Imagine floating along on a ribbon of light high above the cities and arriving at your destination half-way around the world in only 20 minutes.

As transport of goods and services becomes faster and cheaper, the cost of production will drop significantly. Visualize food being grown using new agricultural methods, then being shipped in zero-point vehicles to a distant storage location in less than an hour, then being distributed by airships to individual homes in that region. A vegetable growing in a greenhouse in Siberia could be on your table in Sydney two hours later, with almost no impact to the environment and virtually no cost to you.

Of course, this is just to illustrate a point. In reality, the new agricultural methods discussed earlier will be based on growing food more locally, but for those goods and services that are only made in one part of the world, such transport systems would be a dream come true.

One of the huge advantages of employing zero-point and other alternative energies for transport devices would be the opportunity to leave vast stretches of Earth in her pristine state. Production facilities could be concentrated in a few areas, without encroaching on sensitive wetlands, forests and deserts.

These new technologies would also be used to purify and desalinate water. In essence, water would be recycled and then processed into a product almost comparable to natural spring water. After processing, the new technology transport system would ensure that nobody on your world every goes thirsty again.

You are probably asking by now about the use of zero-point and other new technologies to travel the stars. In many fourth, fifth and sixth density worlds, zero-point spacecraft are in everyday use. As you evolve into higher densities, transport devices become responsive to consciousness itself, and so such a device will respond to your thoughts directly.

At even higher states of evolution, a transport device becomes unnecessary. All you do is think yourself to a distant star and it is so. You already do this in your dream state and many of you pretended to do this when you were children. You will see the day come when all your soul powers are restored to you, including this ability.

Time/Space Travel

This channel's guides, the Arcturians, have introduced several ideas relating to the nature of time, including past, present and future timeline healing. The ability to go forward and backward in time, and to traverse great distances in the blink of an eye, is possible due to the ever-expanding nature of timelines. As explained in an earlier dissertation, you do not violate free will or create paradoxes when time traveling. Rather, you open up new timelines and new possible and probable realities. Instead of one, fixed timeline, you have an infinite number of timelines extending and expanding outward from each aspect of the Creator.

Think of yourselves as weavers of space/time fabric. Every time you have a desire and begin moving toward that desire, you spin a thread in the fabric of time and space. You have individual threads (your own personal experience of space and time) and collective threads (ones where many souls share common areas of space and time).

For example, by collaborating with us on writing this book, the channel has opened a collective timeline. Every soul who reads this book has, as part of his or her timeline, the experiences triggered by the material herein.

The rules of time travel are simple. You cannot interfere with another soul's free will. Visiting a soul in the past or future must be done with that soul's consent (though the conscious mind of the soul may not be aware of your visit or intentions). If your visit would upset the free will choices of third party souls, then it must be modified so as not to affect those souls. For example, if this channel were to go back in time to visit one of his past selves in a former lifetime, he would most likely need to remain invisible to other souls, unless it is part of another soul's free will choice or soul lesson to have a visitation from the channel.

The mechanics of time travel (and how to avoid violating free will) are complex and beyond the scope of what can be given at this time. Basically, time and space travel is a lot like telepathic contact in that you "dial" in to the frequency of a time/space location and then create an energetic link to that location. This establishes a stargate, or portal, through which you can access the desired time and place.

In our previous work, we detailed how to access higher or lower dimensions of the Universe, using tetrahedronal grids, with ascending or descending spirals going through the capstones of each pyramid. Every spacecraft and time machine capable of traveling great distances would have a tetrahedron type of device, coupled with a zero-point generator. Such a device partially collapses the EM field along the ley lines of a particular world or area of space/time. As the EM field is altered, the spacecraft becomes relocated according to the area dialed in. In a rough way, this is a bit like folding a piece of paper to bring two dots together that are far apart when the paper is flat. In your sci-fi shows, you call this warp travel, or hyperdimensional transport.

Understanding the basic building blocks of the Universe, including 64-star tetrahedronal grids (also called the "flower of life") and spirals that ascend and descend through the capstones of the pyramids of a grid, is one of the areas of future science awaiting those fourth and fifth density souls that are planning to stay with the Earth during her transition from third to fourth density.

In this treatise, we are piquing your curiosity and triggering various insights with our words. We are not offering an exhaustive analysis of time and space, or giving you schematics of how to build a time machine. This would be counterproductive since most of you do not have the technical ability to understand such documentation. Those that do will be contacted telepathically by members of our group (and others doing similar work). It is our responsibility to determine how and when you are ready to undertake the work of building these devices, but it is your responsibility to receive the gifts of wisdom we download into your higher minds.

Due to the delicate nature of this work and the likelihood that some of the dark persuasion would manage to acquire some of these devices, we still must be careful, for a while longer, to make sure this information reaches only those souls who are ready for it. Very soon, your planet will be sufficiently ascended so as to render these safeguards unnecessary, but that time has not yet arrived. That is precisely the reason your many friends from the stars must confine their contact to telepathic communication (along with conscious and trance channeling). Only those souls who are ready to disseminate this knowledge and use it for the highest benefit of humanity will be able to contact us.

Please understand, we are not being exclusive or elitist. Our messages are free and available to anyone who can understand them. Most of humanity will glance over this book with a bit of amusement and quickly dismiss it as "too far out" or "too impractical" or downright false. That is of no concern to us. We are here for those of you that are truly ready to move out of darkness and into the new Golden Age you have been promised.

Medical Advances

Presently, your third density medical system is breaking down, for two reasons. First, it is tied to economic systems and governments that are unable to provide for the burgeoning population of aging "baby boomers" and those with immune system failure. In the "for-profit" countries, medical care is becoming too expensive for all but the very rich. In most other countries, medical care is poised to send governments into insolvency. Second, the emphasis in most medical communities has been on repairing the body, rather than in rooting out the primal causes of illness, disease, decay and death.

The allopathic form of medicine is necessary and beneficial when it comes to repairing damaged bodies that have been in accidents, and a few of the medicines developed since the mid-20th century have been life-saving or at least comforting to those who are suffering.

As a larger and larger percentage of the population fails to respond to allopathic approaches, holistic medicine will flourish. More and more souls will return to natural remedies, such as herbs, homeopathy, naturopathy, kinesiology, etc. A large body of previously allopathic physicians will begin exploring the psychological and spiritual causes of illness. Currently, these doctors are still in the minority among the general population.

Your genetics researchers will continue to map out the "immortality gene" and develop new technologies for splicing and combining it with existing "mortal genes." Stem cell research will continue, despite opposition from some religious groups. Cloning and related practices will be extended and refined.

Although these new medical advances will start prolonging the lives of a few human beings, the vast majority will be unresponsive because the cause of their aging and decay will not have been addressed. Keeping a human body alive when the soul has given up interest in living does not work, and eventually the soul will find a way of exiting the body in such cases. Of course, the egoic self will continuously try to prolong itself, mostly out of fear of death or belief in self-importance.

In order for humans to attain physical immortality while in fourth density, they will need to have a great degree of enthusiasm and excitement about being alive. They will need to have a strong sense of purpose and commitment to being on Earth. They will also need to clear their subconscious and unconscious fear of death. If they are ready to move into fifth density ascension, then they will not need modern medicine to attain immortality anyway. For the rest of surviving humanity, the thought of living a robust existence without debilitating diseases will spur on the medical researchers.

In addition to isolating certain genetic material responsible for mortality and illness, and revitalizing the DNA through stem cell implantation and induced mutation of mortal cells through splicing, blending, etc., there will be recognition of the electromagnetic nature of the human being. Etheric healing modalities will be combined with more traditional medicinal approaches. These etheric approaches include aura clearing, chakra balancing, sound and color therapies, the use of crystals, etc.

The application of orbitally rearranged monatomic elements (ORMEs) and other aspects of revitalization previously known as alchemy of metals will be revisited by researchers. Brain research will continue to advance as well. Physicians will begin to understand the relationship between consciousness, the mind and the brain. The brain is like a central computer system that processes signals. It receives its instructions from the mind, which in turn is a product of consciousness.

ET technologies are already playing a vital role in the advances of medicine. The fourth density Pleiadeans have developed ways of prolonging the life of the physical form on their home worlds and have brought elements of those technologies to the Earth over the past 50 years. It may appear, to mainstream scientists, that some researchers suddenly got inspired to investigate a particular aspect of the genome, while in fact, they were telepathically contacted by the Pleiadeans often without their conscious knowledge (but with their soul's consent, of course.)

The fourth density Sirians have also played a part in the development of medical technologies on Earth. Some of their more enlightened members were behind the ancient alchemies, especially in Egypt and Sumeria (along with the Annunaki and others). These groups used radionics and EM field therapies to balance the etheric body and thereby remove the imprints of disease and illness from the physical body. Because the consciousness of the human recipients of those technologies contained a great deal of subconscious denial, most of the advances made were impermanent.

Some of the music currently being produced on Earth originally came from the Lyra/Vega star system, where the human DNA ultimately began. There are specific sequences of chords and melodies that trigger the immortality gene and higher awareness in the DNA molecule. Repeated listening, under the right environmental conditions, to these sequences can result in rapid or even instantaneous healing.

The use of Light, in the form of color therapy, can also trigger DNA activation. The Lyrans, the original root race of the Pleiadeans, have inspired millions of souls on Earth to compose music and light sequences that truly uplift the vibrations of humanity.

In the years to come on Earth, many of the synthetic medicines will be replaced with music, sound and color therapies as well as herbal remedies. The pharmaceutical companies that are not evolving holistically will either convert their facilities to the manufacture and distribution of these natural technologies, or they will cease to exist. In countries where the profit motive drives research, the collapse of the economic system will take away this incentive. In some cases, the fourth density souls will simply take over the pharmaceutical facilities and retool the machinery for more enlightened pursuits.

The medical approach we most encourage is that of the holistic model. This involves having a knowledge of what this channel calls the "six lower bodies" – the physical, emotional, mental, astral, etheric and causal levels – and learning how to balance and bring all these bodies into perfect alignment. When the six lower bodies are in perfect alignment, information flows effortlessly through every level. In essence, all the levels of Self talk to each other, or even commune together. This is likened to a symphony orchestra, where the attunement of the individual musicians to the harmony of the whole determines the quality of the performance.

You will note an important analogy here. You can have a great deal of knowledge about each of the six lower bodies, but if they do not work together, very little will be accomplished. A group of musicians can each be an individual virtuoso, knowing every detail of the instrument, music theory, etc., but if they cannot play together in harmony, the orchestra will sound awful. This can also be analogous to medical specialists who have detailed knowledge of every cell, fiber and tissue related to their specialties. However, they may not be very effective as healers if they do not understand how their element or body part works in harmony with the whole body.

There are techniques for establishing communication between each of the six lower bodies, including this channel's Conference Room Technique, which he will be happy to describe upon request. The simplest way to align the six lower bodies is to listen carefully to each of them, by tuning in quietly and patiently any time you feel some part of self is out of balance. Usually, your physical body will tell you when something is not right. As soon as you begin to feel pain or discomfort, stop and tune in. Ask to have the source of the problem revealed to you. Imagine the part that is out of alignment is like a small child trying to get your attention.

You can think of your lower bodies as inner children, and use an inner child technique to communicate with them. For example, if your emotional body is out of alignment, you can visualize a small child standing in front of you that represents your emotional body. Begin by asking this child what he or she wants from you. Listen carefully. You might feel the answer, or hear it clairaudiently.

The idea here is not to blindly follow what the child says, because sometimes it will not be appropriate to honor the child's request, but the vital part of this exercise involves listening and acknowledging, and the willingness to work with the child to create greater joy and happiness. Often, the part of the self that is out of alignment simply wants to be acknowledged and respected, with love. This part wants to be heard. If there is a specific request, ask the other parts of the self to work together to help fulfill the needs of the inner child.

As we have stated many times, about 80% of all physical illness and disease stems from unresolved emotional issues. Any successful medical system will devote the majority of its efforts and education to understanding the emotional body and how to meet its needs.

Your psychotherapists, psychologists, psychiatrists, mental health counselors, and other therapists will be in great demand in the years to come, as more and more souls realize that the cause of their suffering is within the emotional self. Right now, in most countries, only psychiatrists are able to effectively straddle both allopathic and psychotherapeutic realities without incurring legal repercussions. In other words, if you have a medical condition that has been traced to emotional imbalance, the psychiatrist can recommend a course of treatment that addresses both the emotional needs and the manifestation of physical illness or disease.

We do not recommend that you all become psychiatrists, but we do anticipate major changes in your medical system to expand the role of those who address both the physical and emotional bodies.

In addition to the psychological approach to medicine, we see a resurgence of shamanic healing practices. The shamanic approach involves the ability to build a bridge between the spiritual and physical realms, or the six lower worlds and the higher celestial planes. Included is what this channel calls the study of the intermediate realms (astral, etheric and causal). Oftentimes, the shaman will call upon a nature spirit, elemental, deva, faerie, animal totem, or beings from other time frames and dimensions, for assistance in gaining clarity with a particular issue.

This channel uses the Arcturians as medical specialists (taking care not to violate medical laws). In his case, the Arcturians do not prescribe, diagnose or cure any illness, but they do provide education relevant to the client's needs, and they perform spiritual healing techniques on the astral, etheric and causal levels of the soul.

In the New Earth, spiritual healing will be just as recognized and valued as other forms of healing. The primary purpose of medical care will be to assist in the healing of the soul on all levels. In the old third density model, profit and special interests often dominated the medical profession. Doctors were hesitant to adopt new ways of thinking and to speak out on the importance of spiritual practices because they were often funded by companies earning a profit on the sale of pharmaceuticals and related medical supplies. The third density medical system is based on the premise of treating sick people. In order for this dying system to keep functioning, there must be a ready supply of ailing souls spending a lot of time and money on medications.

In the psychotherapeutic industry, the situation is similar. Third density psychotherapy depends on long-term gradual improvement costing many thousands of dollars per patient, and it would not be profitable to have powerful, effective psychotherapeutic remedies available that would often cure a patient in just a few weeks. In countries with subsidized or government-run health care, the same problems exist but they are not quite as obvious.

You had cures for cancer nearly 100 years ago, but they were suppressed, and many of the doctors who found such cures operated in countries with subsidized health care. In many cases, their laboratories were raided and sometimes they were killed.

We recognize that over the past several paragraphs we have once again repeated ourselves and we hope you will indulge us for our redundancy, especially considering the importance of these ideas.

In the New Earth, all advances in medicine will be greeted with open arms because fourth density consciousness is dedicated to the well-being of all souls, regardless of income or any other factors. Higher principles instruct that when you help one soul, you help all souls. Every time someone is healed, it has a positive effect on everyone else. The selfish ego concept of win-lose will fade away in future medicine.

Medical care is one area where the new technologies will shine. Whether it is sophisticated imaging equipment, air temperature regulators, diagnostic robots, or airtight laboratories, zero-point and other systems will enable the healing profession to focus on what really matters – the well-being of humans – rather than conservation of energy and other cost-cutting measures.

The ability to send blood samples thousands of kilometers away in a matter of minutes to a remote laboratory, or to fly a patient to a specialist on the other side of the planet, will at most be experienced as a minor inconvenience.

Reconstruction of the Third Density World after the Shift

Another area that the new technology will improve upon is in the construction and building industry. While there will be some new building, the majority of work will be in reconstruction.

With the new advances in technology, there will be a lot to do to restore your beloved Earth to its pristine state. That will gradually become one of your highest priorities as you begin moving out of your intentional communities and back into the world at large.

Throughout the cleansing and purification taking place in the third density Earth, you have not been isolating yourselves in your conclaves of Light, but rather, networking and connecting with other communities around the world. Your fourth density Earth will be a thriving place as the Galactic Shift reaches its peak and starts to decrease its intensity.

With the advances of zero-point technology, the energy necessary to reconstruct the old world cities will be available. With your strong immune systems infused with Light from higher dimensions, you will have no difficulty walking among the dead and entering the abandoned buildings and automobiles. Bodies will be properly buried or burned, homes worth salvaging will be refurbished and restocked, and the rest of the infrastructure will be taken apart and rebuilt, or razed and restored to nature.

The population of Earth will likely be around 1.5 billion (perhaps as little as 1.0 or as much as 2.0 billion), probably some time around 2030 to 2035, and will then stabilize a bit, with low birth and death rates. The average life span of fourth density humans will increase as Earth is restored, and by 2050, fourth density humans will be typically living 100 to 150 years. The advances in medicine discussed earlier will likely extend this even further and a few souls will attain a degree of physical immortality prior to going through ascension into fifth density.

The fourth density souls will be counseled and guided by the 15 to 30 million who have moved into fifth density. They will probably still be visible to fourth density souls, but may perhaps be emanating golden light as they walk among the citizens of the New Earth.

Many of the fifth density souls will have developed advanced psychic and intuitive powers and will be able to enter virtually any part of the Earth to render assistance. A few will be able to teleport themselves without the need for a transport device. The great majority will be offering healing modalities, spiritual support and general advice to assist the blossoming communities of the New Earth.

The fifth density souls will assist in bringing forth the technologies necessary to clean up the pollution in the land, air and water. Some of these cleanup methods will be organic and some will rely on synthetic chemicals. Among the organic techniques will be the introduction of beneficial bacteria, molds and fungi that will neutralize or transmute harmful pollutants. Once these neutralizing factors have done their job, the new humans will work with nature to restore her perfect balance.

In the next chapter, we will detail the roles of the Earth Spirits and Elementals in helping restore your beloved planet. By the year 2050, a major portion of the Earth will resemble the mythical Garden of Eden, which actually refers to the pre-separation state of humankind.

CHAPTER 11
The Cosmic Order

The Mission and Purpose of Humanity

We have taken great care not to repeat excessively the advice given in our previous book, "*Earth Changes and 2012*," any more than absolutely necessary. However, some of the following information will be an expansion of the information presented in that earlier work.

The purpose of all souls is to grow and evolve in awareness. From a soul's perspective, everything is a learning opportunity. Lessons are not good or bad, but they do provide contrast. As the soul evolves, painful lessons become less and less desirable. At first, they seem to be an inevitable part of the journey. The younger soul goes back and forth between simply accepting pain as a necessary part of life, and fighting against it. Such a soul will try to do battle with pain in the hopes of finally overcoming it.

Once a soul has learned all about the different forms of pain and the lessons inherent within it, the focus shifts to learning about enlightenment. The first thing the older soul realizes is that the way to enlightenment is through service to others. By focusing on the needs of others (without excluding one's own needs), the soul gets out of his own self-preoccupation and begins to realize that others are just like him, more or less.

The wheel of reincarnation was given to humanity by the Godhead in order to allow souls as much time as they need to learn their lessons. If it were not for the entropic state of the lower worlds resulting in short physical lifetimes, souls would simply stay with a present experience until it is complete. However, the hazards of third density, including illness, disease, accident, and degeneration of bodily tissues, made it necessary for souls to reincarnate into similar situations to those which they left in the previous lifetime.

Reincarnating to complete lessons from past lifetimes is not the same thing as being punished for the sins of the past. The belief that souls must atone, in this lifetime, for karma incurred in a past lifetime, is erroneous. However, souls will often choose to come back in an opposite role in order to learn fully all there is to learn about a particular relationship. The relationship between the oppressor and the oppressed, or the victim and the perpetrator, is a good example.

A soul may be a perpetrator in one lifetime, inflicting injury on others with callous disregard for anyone but self, and in the next lifetime, may choose to incarnate into the role of victim in order to understand what it feels like to be oppressed.

As soon as souls have learned all they desire from these roles, they move on to other lessons and no longer create situations in their lives that keep them locked in these roles.

Some lessons are learned by individuals, and others are more of a group experience. When an ET race comes to Earth and takes over by force, or sabotages the gains of humanity, or otherwise interferes in the affairs of humans, there is a group soul lesson involved. On one level, humanity may be playing the role of victim, while the other race (say, the dark Dracos) may be the aggressor, or perpetrator.

As soon as a sufficient number of souls no longer desire to learn the lesson of group victimization, something will occur to prevent aggression by the invading race. Of course, you do not have to venture into space to see how this works. The invasion of native peoples by the Europeans in the Americas and Australia, for example, is a case in point.

It may be that some of the victims were aggressors in a past lifetime, or may be aggressors in a future lifetime. In some cases, the victims may have agreed to play this role as a way of teaching love and compassion to the invaders (if the souls involved believe the invaders are ready to soften their warrior-like stance). It is important not to judge the victims and aggressors. This is not to say that you should condone the actions of aggressors. It is simply to look for the deeper soul lessons behind such actions.

Souls who are stuck in ego may play these roles over and over, lifetime after lifetime, civilization after civilization, until they are tired of the game and decide to move on. That is the case this time. The Lightworkers are weary of the games of war, poverty, misery, oppression, control, domination, and such. They are ready to create a new Golden Age of peace, prosperity and cooperation.

The Earth herself is now ready to graduate to the next level of being. This means she will no longer support third density consciousness. The beings that incarnate upon her will be here to learn different lessons. They will learn about building intentional communities, taking responsibility for the environment, growing food cooperatively, designing new transport systems, and all the other activities described earlier in this book.

Humanity is not alone on this planet. In addition to the enlightened animals, such as dolphins, whales and a few others, there are many beings on various levels ready to assist in the awakening process. Below, we have given some information on the roles of various entities as humanity awakens.

Chapter 11 – The Cosmic Order

The Earth Spirits and Elementals

Just above the physical plane is an etheric realm that has been depicted in some of your visionary paintings. Perhaps you have visited this version of Earth in your dream state, or have had visions. You might have dismissed these as the activity of an overworked imagination, but they are real. As children, some of you saw faeries and other creatures, but you were told they were not real and soon you abandoned them.

In upper fourth density and lower fifth density, there is still duality, but it is much more refined than in third density. Nevertheless, you have positively and negatively-oriented beings occupying the realms just above the physical Earth plane. If you get quiet and tune in deeply to the natural world, you may be able to communicate with them. As you grow and evolve, you will eventually be able to interact directly with them.

The beings of the inner Earth (gnomes, elves, sprites, etc.) can be called to the surface to interact with you, or you can be transported into the inner Earth to their homes, as you prefer. You have a lot of myths surrounding these entities, some of them accurate and some distorted. We are not going to go into tremendous detail on who is who in the inner Earth, but we will say that your intention to communicate with them will draw them to you. They answer to those Lightworkers who love the Earth and want to protect nature from the ravages of so-called "progress." By this, we mean unrestrained development, indiscriminate clear-cutting of forests and plants, and blatant disregard for the well-being of plants and animals through the discharge of wastewater or pollutants.

If you are kind to the Earth and spend time among the plants and animals, you will not only become telepathic and able to carry on inner conversations with God's creatures, but you will start to see the nature spirits, first in your inner vision and eventually, with your outer eyes.

As you ascend in vibration and your physical eyes begin to change, you might notice sparkles and patterns in the air. Next, you might start to see wiggles and squirms near the periphery of your vision. This is not your eyes going bad; it is the movement of elementals, nature spirits and the like.

The benevolent and loving spirits of a forest, for example, might beckon to you, and you might choose to sit among them and simply feel their presence. Or you might meditate until you are able to see them as clearly as you would other human beings.

Often, these beings want advocates for their way of life. They might, for instance, urge you to stop the tearing down of their living space by giant bulldozers hell-bent on clearing enough forest to put in a new set of chain stores for the consumers of a society out of control. While your highest option may not be to become militant about your opposing of unchecked development, your nature spirit friends might propel you forward toward protecting a piece of the Earth.

The nature spirits and elementals may teach you how to read natural events, such as weather patterns, leaves, streams, etc. You might choose to live a simple life in the forest. Without the help of these beautiful beings, your life there might be fraught with difficulty. Yet working together with them, you may be warned of impending storms, or shown where a stash of food is available, etc. They may even be able to scare away pests from your garden.

Talk to the nature spirits of vegetables and flowers. They will tell you how to take care of your plants. Likewise, the totems (animal spirits) will instruct you on how to get along with your four-legged friends (or six or eight-legged insects, for that matter).

You will quickly find that the entire natural world is your friend, rather than something to be subdued and conquered. With the whole world as your friend, there is nothing you cannot do if it benefits the whole.

The Angels, Archangels and Ascended Masters

There are over one million helpers from the celestial planes available to assist humans at this time. As you know, you must ask for their help and be open and receptive to their guidance. We will use the quicksand analogy once again to illustrate the role of celestial spirit guides.

Planet Earth can be likened to a swamp full of quicksand. The people of Earth, for the most part, are sinking into the swamp and are flailing their arms and legs wildly in a desperate attempt to escape.

Beings from the higher realms are standing on the shore with rope in hand, instructing the humans on how to grab the rope and pull themselves to safety. Not only do they teach the method of pulling oneself out, they send a lot of love, compassion and encouragement. In other words, they are both the coach and the cheerleaders.

Some of the struggling humans are pleading for the angels, archangels and ascended masters to jump in so they can be lifted out instead of having to grab the rope. What they don't realize is that if the celestial beings were to jump in, they too would be caught in the quicksand.

Also, it could very well be that one of the soul lessons for the struggling humans involves learning how to climb up a rope to safety. Even if the celestial

Chapter 11 – The Cosmic Order

beings could safely jump in and rescue the humans, it would deprive them of necessary soul experience.

This brief analogy can be summed up by a popular Zen phrase. "Give a man a fish and he will eat once. Teach him how to fish and he will eat for a lifetime."

Another important aspect of help from the higher realms involves the fact that it might not always appear in the form you think it will. Consider the story of the man who was drowning in a flood. He had "learned" to trust God (according to his image of God) and therefore turned away a rowboat, helicopter and cruise ship when they offered to rescue him. "You go on ahead," he shouted, "God is going to save me." When he drowned, he became furious with God. "How could you let me drown? You said you would save me." God calmly replied, "I sent you a rowboat, a helicopter and a cruise ship. What more do you need?"

Although most of you are familiar with these parables, as well as numerous ones from your scriptures and inspired writings, it is still tempting to fall back into old belief systems about the way you think the higher beings should be helping you.

A favorite we hear all the time is, "I've struggled long enough. Just take this from me." When a soul gets to that point, the healing is almost complete. Just a little more ego surrender may be all that is needed. Stripped to complete emptiness, the struggling soul becomes quiet and receptive. Having exhausted all apparent remedies, the one remedy he did not see before, which is quiet readiness, then descends upon him, finally moving him beyond ego.

The celestial helpers come when the mind is quiet and the heart is receptive. They come gently, reminding you of what you have forgotten – that you are eternally innocent, free and unlimited, and are simply having a dream of separation, fear and loneliness. They remind you that the ego's concept of self is an illusion and that it is futile to spend your whole life seeking the approval of others, or trying to cling on to the little bit of stuff you think you have, lest someone wrestle it away from you.

The angels, archangels and ascended masters teach by demonstration. During the few incarnations when they came to Earth and were able to remember their magnificence while in embodiment, they pass that wisdom forward from generation to generation and even though it often gets distorted along the way, some of it survives. These are the stories of your scriptures, all containing a few kernels of the original experience even though there is much distortion.

They teach that all is One, and that you can remember your Oneness. They teach that if they can do it, you can do it as well. They do not pretend it is easy and feed you airy-fairy fluffy words of no substance. If you encounter a channel who works with beings that are all words and no substance, they are not truly enlightened spirits.

The enlightened ones in the celestial realms not only inspire you, they empower you and encourage you to think for yourselves and if necessary, go against the grain. They teach that it is okay to rebel, as long as it is not coming from unexpressed anger and judgment. With total love and compassion, they practice non-violent resistance (when incarnated on Earth), which is not the same thing as passivity.

The celestial helpers are quick to remind their human students that they are equal to the ascended masters in every way. The angels and archangels are not superior to Earth-bound souls. Ultimately, things are no better in the heavens than they are on Earth, but perhaps it is easier for them to stay centered because they do not have the constant challenges that exist on Earth. They have the utmost respect for human souls. They consider it a courageous act to choose incarnation in this world.

We in the higher realms have never had a physical body in a lower density place, and while we have a great deal of knowledge and wisdom about the Universe and soul evolution, we cannot live your lives for you. Our main function is to give you the bigger picture so that it is easier to free yourselves from the daily illusions of Earthly life.

Through communication with our many channels, we help bring you together with extended soul family members and others with whom you have compatibility. Your soul family on Earth, when they come together, represents a powerful force capable of creating a wonderful new expression of Divinity.

In the years to come on Earth, many of you will find your soul family members who are embodied in human form. Of course, you will still be guided from on high by those members who have chosen not to come to Earth. Eventually, your cosmic family and your Earth family will be seen as One, and you will never, ever experience loneliness again.

Many of you ask, "How do I communicate with my angels, archangels and ascended master guides? How do I know it is really them?"

This channel and others teach various methods for opening the lines of communication, but really it is quite simple to speak to your guides (notice we did not say *easy*, since you are attempting to break through the frequency fence, which is still a bit arduous).

Start with a simple invocation. "*I now call forth the power and presence of [insert name of being]. Come forth, beloved [name]. Reveal your wisdom to me. Thank you, beloved [name].*"

Chapter 11 – The Cosmic Order

Then breathe deeply, relax and clear your mind, becoming open and receptive. At first, you might not notice anything out of the ordinary, but if you keep doing this, eventually you will recognize the form of the reply. It might be clairaudient, meaning that you actually hear voices in your head. Or it may come as energy, with patterns that you know are not just your own higher self. Sometimes, the energy gets downloaded into the higher mind as new ideas suddenly popping into your conscious mind.

The more you practice communicating with spirit guides, the better the chances of succeeding in becoming aware of their presence. They have no trouble being aware of you because they are outside the veil. However, their messages get distorted as they are filtered through the barriers between their dimension and yours.

All channeled messages are filtered through the channel and are colored by that channel's particular education, idiosyncrasies and prejudices.

When we, the Founders, choose a channel, we take into account the likelihood that the message will be distorted in such a way that the basic intent and purpose remains intact. Generally, we choose scientifically oriented souls that have had spiritual experiences and are seeking to integrate the spiritual and scientific realms. The angels, archangels and ascended masters have varying criteria for the souls they select to be their channels. Many of the "chosen ones" choose not to be chosen, and so the call goes unheard to those ones, and other potential channels are selected instead.

There are approximately 10,000 human channels for the celestial realms, along with several thousand more for various ET groups, including the Galactic Confederation. Then there are as many as 100,000 humans who are not actively channeling information from the higher realms, but who have been inspired by angels ("touched by an angel," as your popular media would call it). Then there is the larger group that believe in angels (close to one billion souls) but have not had direct experience.

We, the Founders, have 22 channels currently residing on Earth. Not all of them call us by that name. Some call us Creator Gods, or Watchers, or some other term. The name does not matter, nor does the level of vibration, ultimately. The concept of levels is convenient for your conscious minds, to categorize and to assist you with discernment, but eventually levels will become irrelevant.

The quality of the energy is the most important part of contacting celestial beings. If you do not feel the high quality of love, compassion and service, then rest assured you are not truly communicating with celestial beings. Many fourth density souls from other worlds will claim they are celestial beings in order to get an audience or work with humanity more directly. With enough practice invoking higher beings, you will learn to recognize when imposters are on the prowl.

We do not say this to scare you, but only to help you discern. In our previous book, and this channel's first book, he gives a checklist of criteria for deciding if the being speaking to you is truly of the celestial planes. We recommend you contact the channel for additional information on discernment.

One item on the list is vitally important to us, because it involves our greatest challenge in working with you, and that is the issue of free will. Do the beings wishing to make contact with you understand and respect human free will? Do they seek to empower you to make your own decisions and to think for yourselves, rather than giving you easy answers?"

If you find yourselves becoming dependent on a spirit guide for answers, then something is not right. Sure, we in the higher realms will give wisdom, but we will also encourage you to apply it in your own lives and to investigate everything we say.

Please excuse the brief review of your responsibility to practice discernment.

Communication with ETs

We will not spend a lot of time on this subject because it is explored in detail in this channel's first two books (*Life on the Cutting Edge* and *Earth Changes and 2012.*) We will, however, update you on the latest situation with the ETs currently interacting with Earth.

The number of Zetas has decreased dramatically on the Earth since 1995 because most of them have completed their mission and are moving on to other worlds. Those who remain have been advised that they must move into fourth density or they will no longer be able to be here once Earth goes through the portals and becomes completely fourth density.

The dark Dracos have been allowed to influence a tiny portion of humanity, because those souls being controlled by the Dracos have karmic relationships with them, or are so stuck in fear and anger that they still need appropriate mirrors for their emotions. The Dracos are not allowed to enslave the Lightworkers or any soul who truly desires peace and freedom. Every time they try to take over your world, or introduce a dangerous new technology, the Galactic Confederation intervenes and partially quarantines their operations.

The dark Sirians are decreasing rapidly in number because most of them are awakening, with the help of the light Sirians and other groups.

The dark Orions are still the dominant group on Earth and pose the greatest risk to the well-being of humanity. This is because their warrior-like aggressive mentality is still considered by many to be "human nature." Therefore, most souls do not realize they are being controlled. The dark Orions are shrouded in secrecy at the top of their pyramid and comprise about 80% of the dark Illuminati and about 75% of humanity (meaning the dark Orion DNA is in a plurality in about three-fourths of all humans).

The majority of the dark Orions will be leaving the Earth between 2012 and 2030, along with some of the Pleiadeans and Sirians who are not ready to move into enlightened fourth density.

The remaining ET groups (Venusians, Arcturians, Polarians, Tau Cetians, Essassani (also known as Hathors), Antareans, and of course, the Andromedans, make up less than 10% of humanity. Keep in mind that we are talking about plurality of DNA. For example, if a soul is 5% Pleiadean, 4% Orion and 3% Sirian, he is generally considered to be Pleiadean.

Once again, we caution you about getting too caught up in the composition of your DNA. Most of you reading this are eclectic souls that have been all over the Universe. That means you might have 100 or more DNA configurations from your cosmic journeys throughout the galaxy. Your so-called "junk" DNA contains the ET sequences, which your scientists do not understand. If they were to capture ET souls from those different worlds and examine their DNA, they would make the discovery about the real purpose of the "junk" DNA because the ET sequences would almost exactly match their corresponding human sequences in the "junk" DNA.

ET Involvement in Human Affairs during the Shift

As we have stated previously, there will come a time on Earth (very soon, possibly within the next few years) when certain ET groups will be able to communicate quite openly with humans. A lot of you have asked when this will be, and we have deferred to a standard answer, "Humanity is not ready for mass visitation."

There are three reasons we have given this answer. The first is the free will issue. Most of you still need to make your own decisions without relying on ET intervention. If you believe your friendly extraterrestrial is going to solve all your problems, you might be less motivated to find your own answers and hence, grow as a soul.

In many parts of your world, there is a delicate balance, meaning that certain trigger events could cause a lot of trauma and instability. For example, your major religions are not ready for mass ET visitation and would probably treat us as saviors to be worshipped, or devils to be vanquished.

The second reason, which we have gone into quite deeply in our various dissertations, involves the non-interference policy. This is, of course, closely related to reasons given above. Being worshipped or feared are among the likely scenarios that would occur if we did not have a non-interference program and ignored your free will and soul lessons.

So the non-interference doctrine, along with the fact that most of humanity is not ready to interact with us or the other higher-dimensional groups working with Earth, means that humanity will still need to evolve further before we can walk openly among you.

The third reason is not about you, but about us. As high vibrational beings, it is important that we maintain an environment supportive to our well-being. If we were to come to Earth and interact with you, the nature of the lower worlds is such that even we could become subject to the lower frequencies. This happened to the seventh density Sirians during Egypt and Israel (witness the fall of the god Jehovah who began his time on Earth as a seventh density Sirian and quickly fell to a third density human).

Those higher beings who do come to Earth periodically usually do not stay long and quickly retreat into the higher mountainous regions or hide in caves until their time on Earth is complete. An example is Babaji, the yogi who brought Kriya yoga to the Earth. He has manifested at least ten different bodies and has kept them just long enough to bring through a new teaching or impart wisdom to a few individuals, before leaving again.

As we have said before, those of you waiting for the spaceships to pick you up and take you off the planet so that you do not have to face the difficulties of the Earth changes, may be waiting a long time. While we cannot rule out an occasional evacuation of someone deemed important to your well-being, we will not deprive you of your soul experience by whisking you away at the first sign of trouble.

You chose to come here to learn, grow and help others through the Earth changes. You will be given the strength and wisdom necessary to make it through tough times. It is not easy incarnating on Earth. We understand that and we have compassion for what you are going through. We are asking you to stick it out and know that the portal shifts are upon you, quickening your pace and eventually gladdening your hearts.

Already, major changes are taking place upon your world and although it still looks pretty negative, most of what you are witnessing is a necessary part of the cleansing and purification prior to the new Golden Age.

Becoming Galactic Citizens

For millions of years, Earth has been quarantined from the rest of the galaxy, as described earlier. As detailed in prior books, some of the positive and negative groups in the heavens went to war with each other over the issue of controlling the humans on Earth. The major soul lesson for the positive groups was to learn how to transcend duality. By making the negative groups their enemies, something to be forcefully overcome, they fell in vibration, essentially matching the negative energy of their perceived enemies, thus keeping the drama of duality going.

Most of you have memories in your causal bodies of your participation in the war in the heavens. To the extent that you now recognize the higher truth beyond duality, you are able to detach from the light versus dark drama. By sending love and compassion equally to both light and dark factions, with no judgment whatsoever, you are truly transcending karma and the wheel of reincarnation.

Every day you are tempted, by your media and so-called powers that be, to polarize (take sides) on issues facing your world. If you feel guided from within to speak for a cause, or travel around gaining support for a political candidate, or working to defeat oil drilling in the wilderness, etc., then by all means do so, but do not get caught emotionally in the drama. Do not make the mistake of setting up those with differing views as enemies, even if they hold a very dark energy field.

While you are working to bring about change, send love and compassion to all who seem to oppose you. Always question your motives behind actions designed to counteract dark forces. Why are you doing what you do? Is there a hidden agenda? Are you trying to right a past wrong? For example, it is one thing to care for the Earth and encourage responsible stewardship and quite another to angrily fight against multinational corporate polluters.

In the end, you will be a lot more effective with your cause if it is presented with genuine love and sincerity, rather than revenge or self-righteousness.

As you move beyond duality, you become aware of your place in the cosmic scheme of things. You welcome into your heart your cosmic family, both on Earth and in the stars. At first, your communication will be telepathic with those outside the Earth's frequency barrier, but eventually the barrier will break down and your ET brothers and sisters will once again walk among you.

There are several groups waiting to welcome the Earth back into brotherhood and sisterhood with star alliances. The councils of Pleiades and Lyra/Vega, where humanity began, have been waiting a long time to welcome you home. The councils of Alcyone and Aldebaran continue to send their representatives to

Earth, knowing that some day soon there will be Earth humans among their councils.

As Earth ascends and the new technologies are able to flourish, so too will higher technologies from the stars be given freely to humanity.

Barriers between countries, nationalities, religions, social groups and races will end. Humanity will unite in One holy purpose, to embrace and support life no matter where or what it is. Priority will be given to developing self-awareness and encouraging soul growth, at the expense of nobody.

We in the higher realms are waiting to reunite with our family on Earth and we know the time is coming very soon.

CHAPTER 12
Life On Other Worlds

We have added this chapter in an effort to give you an idea of the civilizations present on other worlds in this section of your galaxy, in the hope that you can find some useful ideas here that will assist you in implementing an enlightened structure for the New Earth.

Although your mainstream scientists have estimated that the likelihood of intelligent life on other planets amounts to about one civilized world per 100,000 star systems, the actual number is about 1 in 1,540.

We have given our account of the civilized worlds pertaining to this part of your galaxy in order from most relevant to least relevant, in order to give you some perspective.

As we have stated in previous writings, the Universe is about 80% benevolent enlightened beings, and about 20% malevolent ego-oriented beings. On Earth, the situation has been reversed, making this one of the darker planets in the galaxy. We also stated earlier that Earth is one of about 12 planets going through a major shift into higher frequencies.

Below, we have listed the star systems and their various planets with advanced civilizations. Keep in mind that there are many more we have not listed. The groupings below represent only about half of the star races that have visited Earth since life began here. Although some of this information duplicates what was given in previous writings, we felt it was important enough to reiterate:

Pleiades

The Pleiadeans are the root race of humanity. The humanoid form began in the Lyra/Vega system and the early souls with humanoid form migrated to the Pleiades where the majority of early soul evolution took place.

The Pleiadean system we are using here probably does not correspond exactly with your star charts or scientific classifications. We have included the following stars as part of the greater Pleiadean system even though not all of them are strictly in the Pleiades star cluster. In some maps, the Seven Sisters are the only stars included. However, from a governing council point of view, there are over 100 stars in the Pleiadean system with over 300 inhabited planets. We are only listing the ones most relevant to Earth (that have influenced or visited Earth in a significant way).

The Sun and Solar System

Your solar system is included within the governing councils of the Pleiades, since you were originally a Pleiadean race (before the invasion of the Orions half a million years ago).

Earth

Your planet is the densest of the inhabited worlds in the Pleiades system. To illustrate this, we are going to digress a bit and review the vibrational model used by this channel.

The composite vibration of your planet is currently 3.48. Once it reaches 3.50, Earth will be considered a fourth density planet. This number represents the average consciousness of the souls on Earth, combined with the natural resonant frequency of the Earth herself (calculated using multiple variable differential equations. The math involved in differentiating and integrating composite frequencies will be discussed at a later time).The souls residing on Earth have individual composite frequencies ranging from 2.50 to 4.99.

Your composite frequency is a complex series of averages integrated over a specified period of time, usually one Earth day. It includes your state of consciousness in the six lower bodies (physical, emotional, mental, astral, etheric and causal levels), as well as influences from your higher celestial selves.

The consciousness of humans can be much higher than 4.99, but the physical form only exists as a mortal human up to that value. Those souls with a composite vibration above 4.99 are already in their ascended crystal light body form.

The lower density animalistic attributes range from 2.50 to 3.00 in vibration, while the so-called "normal" range of human behavior and perception corresponds to 3.00 to 3.50. The higher mind, refined intellect, and basic creative urges are in the 3.50 to 4.00 range, while those who have a highly developed self-awareness and spiritual perspective are above 4.00 in vibration.

Many of the enlightened spiritual teachers have a consciousness in the 5.00 to 12.00 range, but if they are still in mortal human form, their composite vibration is below 5.00.

Below, we will discuss the composite frequency of other worlds in your sector of the galaxy (that are relevant to your evolutionary process) and will attempt to describe some of the qualities and environment of those civilizations.

Chapter 12 – Life on Other Worlds

Venus

Your nearest ET world is a logical place for beings in the etheric realms that are working with humanity to use as a vantage point to observe and interact with Earth. Venus is a hot, gaseous, poisonous planet on the third and fourth density levels, but in fifth and sixth density, great cities of Light with beautiful crystalline architecture and indescribably colorful gardens, fountains and plazas can be found in abundance.

Venus has two levels of vibration, fifth and sixth, and is called a "midway station" by the ascended masters. This is because it contains a "stepping down" portal that allows beings from the ascended realms (seventh density and beyond) to communicate and interact with souls on Earth that have reached a fourth density composite vibration and fifth density consciousness.

It is generally quite difficult for a seventh density ascended being to drop three levels in order to interact with a fourth density soul on Earth. In order to make themselves more accessible, higher beings use the midway station to temporarily step down their frequencies before attempting telepathic communication with their channels. A few souls on Earth have evolved to the point where this is not necessary, but it is still used a lot to make the experience flow more easily.

Those souls who are growing and evolving on Venus reside in fifth density crystal light bodies or sixth density radiant causal bodies. You can visit them in the dream state or in meditation. This channel's primary spirit guide, Leah, resides in sixth density Venus.

The social systems and cultures of Venus are geared toward creativity, art, music, dance, and other various "right-brain" disciplines. Science is important, but not the emphasis. The majority of activities in Venusian society are centered around supporting the mystery schools and temples of Light that are set up all around the planet to teach souls between incarnations on Earth, and to orient souls who have recently ascended spiritually or are ascending physically into their crystal light bodies. The latter function is just coming into focus, since very few humans have accomplished physical ascension prior to the portal shifts on Earth.

There are no wars, poverty, social or economic inequities on Venus. Education is the top priority of all children. Fifth density children are conceived and born a bit differently than third and fourth density children. Sixth density children are "manifested" through an energy merger between sixth density couples, rather than incarnating through the birth canal.

At a later time, we will go into more detail on fifth and sixth density procreation processes.

A large number of Venusians are involved in helping the Earth, using one of three avenues: (1) Assisting telepathically by establishing contact with telepaths on Earth from the comfort of their own world; (2) Visiting the Earth using holographic projection techniques utilized from spacecraft in the upper atmosphere of Earth; or (3) Incarnating on Earth in the usual manner. Approximately 1.4% of humanity on Earth has Venusian DNA as a dominant matrix, meaning these souls have had numerous lifetimes on Venus and consider it their "home" world.

Jupiter

Your largest planet has an upper etheric or lower celestial civilization comprised of a few hundred thousand souls. They are considered "gatekeepers" or portal maintenance technicians, if you want to get specific. Essentially, souls entering the energetic field of the solar system from beyond the planets must pass through a portal overseen by the councils of Jupiter. The souls of Jupiter are responsible for keeping stability and balance within the solar system, and for monitoring planetoids, asteroids, comets and other objects as they make their trajectory through it.

The etheric/celestial civilization of Jupiter exists in the outer layers of the large planet's atmosphere. There are no life forms on the surface of the planet. Jupiter's surface is not easily defined, as it consists of liquid atmosphere intermixed with some solid gases and minerals. Humanoids vibrating below seventh density cannot live under the extreme pressure and volatility (which includes winds in excess of 1000 km/hr and volcanoes the size of Mercury).

The cities in the upper atmosphere of Jupiter are composed of temples of Light and meeting places where the councils of Pleiades hold some of their gatherings. A lot of Earth souls go to Jupiter to be counseled and guided between incarnations. There are extensive counseling facilities there designed to prepare souls for future incarnations. Communication is strictly telepathic or through energy mergers. There is no discord, disharmony, war, poverty, hunger, or any other malady in the Jovian world.

Saturn

Saturn is known by many visionaries and oracles as the place where the councils or lords of karma meet and decide the weighty issues of the day. This is somewhat correct, as there are great halls of learning in the upper atmosphere of Saturn where souls come to work out unresolved issues from their incarnations on Earth. Saturn also exists as an outpost for travelers coming from other regions of the galaxy, and is a home away from home for council meetings typically held on other Pleiadean worlds.

The cities of Light on (or above) Saturn include magnificent structures made of rare metals and crystals that house many of the records of the evolution of the solar system. The beings that live there vibrate at seventh or eighth densities. Most are assigned to work with specific souls or groups of souls on Earth. They have over one thousand channels on Earth and these ascended beings go by various names, which we will not detail here. (Many of the names are energetic vibrations rather than discrete spellings in Earth languages, so the names given by Earthly channels are usually approximations or interpretations, rather than the actual vibratory sounds.)

Alpha Centauri

The closest star to your sun, Alpha Centauri, has five planets, of which one is inhabited by fourth density humanoids. These souls are very scientific and have fairly advanced technology. They are very much dedicated to the non-interference policy and, therefore, have very few channels on Earth. Many of them belong to the various councils of the Pleiades and travel to the Seven Sisters frequently in electromagnetically propelled spacecraft to attend meetings.

Being a fourth density society, they have not transcended conflict and violence, but these are quite minimal overall. There is no hunger. Food is manufactured and distributed by highly efficient technologies utilizing zero-point energy. Schools are a center piece of their cities and are set up to educate children about the workings of the Universe.

Although they are technologically advanced, they have not evolved significantly in terms of spiritual awareness. Most of their attention is on the mechanical nature of things and how to navigate and propagate. They are in trading agreements with certain other worlds within the Pleiadean system. Their humanoid bodies are a bit more perfected than on Earth, but they still procreate in the usual manner. They have strict limits on population, and medical technologies to ensure they only have children if and when they deem it appropriate. Everything is about efficiency, and their world is a well-oiled machine.

Lacking is a lot of emotionality and creativity. There is art, but it is rather "institutional" by your standards. Dance and ballet are highly refined, but still rather mechanical. The Alpha Centaurians, in general, are a law and order society. They have subdued their emotional bodies just enough to keep this order, but not enough to create severe soul fragmentation and atrophy.

Tau Ceti

One of the worlds orbiting the Tau Ceti star system has a highly evolved race of intelligent humanoids that have visited Earth on numerous occasions (including the present time). They are tall, slender Light beings who often come with other ET races to bring advanced technology and spiritual teachings to Earth (as much as permitted under the non-interference policy).

The Tau Cetians tend to vary between fifth and seventh densities. They travel in saucer-shaped vehicles that can move up and down through the dimensional continuum. Their vehicles are rarely seen by humans. They have perfected the art of teleportation, levitation and even bilocation to some degree. They use the latter to holographically project themselves into virtually any place or situation on Earth in order to observe, and in some cases, interact with humans.

They have highly advanced storage technology and were instrumental with the process of installing the crystalline disks used in Earth's Hall of Records (Halls of Amenti) located underneath the Great Pyramid at Giza. They have inspired many of the early spiritual teachers on Earth, including Thoth the Atlantean and Isis in her Egyptian incarnations. (For review, Thoth is a seventh density Pleiadean and Isis an eighth density Sirian.)

The Tau Cetians are very humble beings in service to the One Source, and they prefer to remain quite anonymous most of the time. They have a few channels on Earth who call them by their star of origin, and a few who use individual names of contacts.

Their civilization on Tau Ceti planet number five is etheric and composed of temples, gardens, pathways, and halls of creativity that highlight both their artistic endeavors and their scientific achievements. They settled on this Tau Cetian planet shortly after migrating from the Seven Sisters millions of years ago.

Fomalhaut

This star system boasts four planets with various forms of intelligent life. Not all of the sentient beings are humanoid. Some have an insect-like appearance, while others seem more reptilian. The humanoid race exists at seventh density. They are blue-white, translucent beings who can seem to shape shift into other forms. In actuality they use a form of holographic projection to change their appearance when desired. (True shape-shifting occurs at densities at or above ninth.)

Their primary focus is working with the other species within the Fomalhaut system to help them develop and grow. They have sent a few ambassadors to Earth in times past, and are assembling a group of souls to make a visit to Earth during the portal shifts in order to observe, learn and grow from what they experience. Although they are inquisitive beings, they adhere strictly to the non-interference policy. As far as we can determine, they do not have any Earth channels at this time.

Seven Sisters

The seven large blue-white stars at the center of the Pleiadean system are home to 12 intelligent races and three councils, or governing bodies. The vibrations of the central Pleiadeans range from fourth to seventh densities. Souls who have evolved beyond seventh density have usually gone to other regions of the galaxy. (Beyond seventh density, location in space/time has very little meaning anyway.)

The planetary system that houses the high council, or central governing body, is located near several portals (stargates) that allow ascending souls to access the eighth and ninth density realms.

About two dozen fourth density Pleiadean factions have visited Earth over the course of humanity's evolution. At this time, there are at least four of these groups actively engaged with humans. One of the groups has several channels giving forth information at this time. This fourth density Pleiadean group is well-known to the Lightworkers. They are commanded by a female known as Semjase and a male known as P'tah. They have 12 scout craft and a mothership in the etheric realms of Earth at all times.

They are assisting the Arcturians in helping balance the grid system of Earth, and one of the other factions is responsible for the majority of crop circles.

The fourth density worlds on the Pleiadean planets are mostly scientific in nature. Some are heavily populated and resemble the cities depicted in one of your science fiction shows, Star Wars (without the constant violence, which is more of an Orion trait). There is minimal poverty and violence on the Pleiadean worlds, although they have not completely eliminated it.

Most planets depend heavily on trade with other worlds to supply their physical needs. Some are relatively self-sufficient. They have evolved rather haphazardly in many cases, with over-development and pollution being major concerns. Within the last two thousand years, they have advanced technologically to the point where a lot of the problems have been cleaned up, but they still have a ways to go.

Semjase and P'tah are two of the more spiritually evolved members of the fourth density Pleiadean races. A lot of the people of their worlds are technologically evolved, but have not really developed their inner awareness all that much. This is why a few of the groups have caused problems on Earth in the past even though their intentions were usually peaceful.

High Councils of Pleiades

The governing body of the Pleiades consists mostly of seventh density souls who are original descendants of the Lyra/Vega migration millions of years ago. Many of them are also souls who chose not to incarnate in the lower worlds, but are members of your own soul families.

Representatives from nearly every star system in the Pleiades attend regular meetings in one of the great cities on the 14th planet from the sixth star. Keep in mind, beloveds, that these blue-white stars are massive and have spawned dozens of planets. The planet housing the central government is almost three billion kilometers from its star, yet the star fills the sky with its brilliant blue-white light. Being seventh density, these souls do not mind temperatures in excess of 1,000 degrees Celsius during the long daytime. Despite the over-abundance of starlight, they have achieved great architecture, gardens, and "fantasy adventures" where souls can play and rejoice in the splendor of the Creator's infinite variety.

The beings inhabiting the planets of the Seven Sisters are governed by the high councils. They have put away the childish toys of war, poverty, control, oppression, domination, competition and greed over a million years ago and have dedicated their lives to bringing balance and harmony to this region of the galaxy. They are working with over 10,000 human souls on Earth, telepathically, through channeling, visionary artwork, and even mathematical inspiration to your scientists. The high councils of Pleiades are the elders of your race, and our descendents, and we are quite proud of them (in a non-ego sort of way).

The Orion System

Although Orion has been the source of the majority of conflict and aggressive energy on Earth, the star systems that were originally at war signed a peace treaty about 100,000 years ago and have been living in relative peace ever since. This is not to say that they have no conflict, but it is kept to a minimum. After nearly destroying themselves several times, Divine Intervention and numerous council meetings between the various factions resulted in a major milestone of humanoid evolution in the peace accord.

The seemingly endless battles between various planets in the Betelgeuse and Rigel star systems were imported to Earth during the Luciferian Rebellion, or War in the Heavens, that took place about 500,000 years ago on the Earth timeline. This is when the Orions essentially took over the more peaceful, feminine-like Pleiadean race that had been evolving on Earth up until that time. While the Rigel and Betelgeuse star systems have enjoyed relative peace for millennia, the Orion factions that started reincarnating on Earth have continued to play out the drama of duality through three major civilizations and countless minor ones.

During the "cleaning up" of the conflict in the Orion system, many of the "laggard" souls, those who fomented the most conflict, were sent to Earth (which the Orions at that time considered a penal colony). Needless to say, the warring ways of the laggard souls have influenced humanity on Earth for a great while. Although we in the heavens do not support the actions of the original Orions in sending their troublemakers to Earth, we chose not to intervene, after much deliberation.

The dark Orions make up the largest group of humanity. About 80% of the souls on Earth have Orion DNA as their dominant matrix, meaning that their Orion configuration is more embedded and deeply programmed than any other DNA configuration. About 10% of the Orions on Earth are among the Lightworkers and souls who came here specifically to bring the dark Orions back to the Light so that they can get caught up with their kindred souls now evolving on Betelgeuse and Rigel.

The remaining 20% of humanity is mostly Pleiadean root race, with a sprinkling of Venusian, Sirian, Zeta, Draco and a few others.

Betelgeuse

This star, home of two primary inhabited planets (and a few outposts), originally belonged to the councils of Light for the Orion system. They became the Lords of Light versus the Dark Lords of Rigel. The councils of Betelgeuse became polarized, which means they perceived the Rigelians as an evil force to be overcome through war, rather than seeing them through the eyes of love and compassion.

The fall of the Lords of Light was due partly to the Archangel Lucifer's decision to view the emotional body as undesirable and unworthy of inclusion in the human soul.

Lucifer portrayed the Rigelians as crude, rude, lewd, vicious, undisciplined heathens who were preoccupied with the pleasures of the flesh. He told the Lords of Light on Betelgeuse to eliminate the Rigelians. He told the Lords of Light to deny their own lustful nature. He then extended this Victorian attitude to the shaming of sensitivities in men, including the open expression of emotions.

Lucifer wanted strong soldiers who would not show any signs of weakness while in battle. He wanted "killing machines." He wanted cold, calculated, intellectual armchair strategists who had no feelings for the horrors being perpetrated upon the citizens of Orion.

The councils of Light were conned into going to battle with the Dark Lords, but eventually Lucifer turned on Betelgeuse as well when there were disagreements among their leadership. At that point, the battle became three-pronged, with Lucifer's renegade army battling both major factions of Orion.

Rigel

This star system, home of the Dark Lords, often initiated conflicts among various nearby planets. Your modern entertainment industry has a mascot that correctly exemplifies that deep rage and terror lurking underneath the Rigelian mindset as it existed hundreds of thousands of years ago. His name is Darth Vader, and his masquerade stems from deep wounds received early in life (eventually portrayed in the ongoing series of movies).

This channel had an experience many years ago between several archetypes of his own psyche, which he labeled Lucifer and Pan, the god of the first major civilization on Earth. In a symbolic battle (arising out of the real confrontations in the heavens), Lucifer and Pan are fighting under the following conditions: Pan is enraged at having had his feelings held down and suppressed by Lucifer, and lashes out at the cool, calm, detached presence of the fallen angel. Meanwhile, the Godhead, represented as the neutral backdrop of the drama unfolding on the main stage, simply observes this duality playing itself out in the theatre of life, and is sending love and compassion to each archetype equally.

The major soul lesson for the Lords of Light is to simply send love and compassion to all who wander lost and confused in the worlds of fear, ego, control, domination, and oppression. Do not engage them in battle, lest you be drawn into the drama and sink in the quicksand along with the Dark Lords.

Both the Light and Dark factions eventually evolved to the point where they were able to sign a peace treaty, and miraculously, the treaty held for thousands of years until enough generations had passed that the etheric imprint of the battle no longer made a significant impression on the minds of the Orions.

(Note: At one point, Archangel Michael got caught up in the duality of good versus bad. This soul lesson for him lasted about 1,000 years. Now, Michael has integrated the lesson of duality and is simply sending love, compassion and protection to all souls who invoke his presence.)

Mintaka

This star in the belt of Orion was and still is home of the high councils of Orion and is the place where mediation occurred between the commanders of Rigel and Betelgeuse. There is a large portal (stargate) at Mintaka that allows souls to come and go through many dimensions and wormholes. Your Great Pyramid is exactly aligned with Mintaka because the pyramid served as a mini-portal, among other things.

As the larger portals of Mintaka opened (several times over 100,000 years), the energies emanating from the etheric realms became strong enough to collapse the dualistic mindset that had entrapped the people of Orion for so long. Some of the peaceful energy reached Earth, but it was not enough to turn things around. The dominant Orion strain of warrior-like, aggressive energy was so firmly entrenched on Earth that not much headway was made on your planet until recently.

High Councils of Orion

The modern-day justice system on Earth is a mirror reflection of the justice system employed to handle disputes in the Orion system for hundreds of thousands of years. Like the early Roman times on Earth, for a long time on Orion the "jury" and "judge" amounted to nothing more than a group of souls getting together to arbitrarily decide guilt or innocence, depending upon the personal whim of the court.

In other words, if they liked you, you got dismissed and if they didn't, they had all manner of torture, punishment and death in store for you. Never mind your guilt and innocence.

Of course, both systems have evolved and today, there is probably more true justice in the court system of Orion than on Earth. At least there are far fewer problems on Orion.

The civilizations of Orion today are highly structured and resemble your modern cities, with more buildings and less open space than on Earth. Although times have been peaceful for hundreds of generations, all three of the Rigelian planets and both of the Betelgeusean planets have an elaborate justice system, military, police, and government structure in place.

Slowly, the Orion people have been ascending spiritually, but they have had to clear a lot of negativity and karmic lessons to get where they are today. Nevertheless, creative expressions, including arts, music, etc., have been slow in coming. In recent years, a lot more trade with other star systems has been taking place, and new cultures and attitudes are being integrated into Orion lifestyles.

The Orions had terrible pollution problems for thousands of years, but eventually developed propulsion systems and factory machines that ran on a plant-based fuel (derived from plants local to the planets there).

The Orions are led to believe that they would be defenseless without a huge military even though there have been no significant wars for 100,000 years. This devotion to the military has kept their evolutionary process slow. Some of the more enlightened members of the current high council are watching Earth closely to see if they can participate in some sort of ascension program themselves. Many Orions who are vibrating at fourth density will be allowed to incarnate upon the Earth in the coming years, so they may get to fulfill their desire for ascension. (Despite the problems on Earth, she is evolving much more rapidly than the planets in Orion at the present time.)

As mentioned earlier, the more enlightened Orions have been encouraged to incarnate on Earth to help those stuck on the wheel of reincarnation and duality. Many of the struggling dark Orions on Earth have not been very receptive to the incarnated light Orions. The dark ones have been subjected to many different forms of misinformation. Due to interference from other dark ET groups, progress has been slow indeed. These other dark groups have relished in the deep-seated anger and fear embedded within the laggard souls from Orion.

As the Lightworkers increase their frequencies (light quotients), more and more dark Orions will turn, often in desperation, to the offerings of healers, teachers and therapists.

Despite the constant help being offered to the dark Orions on Earth, about 90% of them will likely be unable to make the shift in time to be part of the New Earth and will cycle off to another world, possibly in the Orion system itself. Already, many Light beings are preparing themselves to be of service on the planets receiving the dark Orions.

Alpha Draconis

The Draco system, home of the reptilians, has been, for a long time, about 90% dark and 10% Light. There is an active program at this time to bring enlightened Draco children to Earth (known as the "dragon children") to help bring more dark Dracos on Earth to the Light.

Dark Dracos

The dark Dracos, like most lower-density life forms, exist in three realms as far as the Earth is concerned. (1) They have incarnated into human form, (2) they are in spaceships in the upper atmosphere of Earth, or (3) they are influencing Earth from the astral realms.

The dark Dracos have attempted to conquer Earth by force on several occasions, and every time they have been pushed back by the Galactic Confederation. They are allowed to interact with humanity to a certain extent, but when they jeopardize the Lightworkers and other star races beyond a certain point, intervention is approved. Only about two percent of humanity has dominant Draco DNA, and most of the abductions and possessions undertaken by Dracos in spaceships are simply beings attempting to communicate and work with their own people who have incarnated on Earth. However, some dark factions have concentrated on abductions and possessions of world leaders. These factions have a strong lust for power and control and believe they can only experience their addiction through humans who are in positions of power and control.

About 60% of the visible world leaders are totally or partially possessed by dark Dracos. Those that have worked through their ego issues and have a minimum of fear and anger are less likely to be infiltrated by the dark beings.

About 30% of the souls who are helping maintain the illusion of power and control on Earth behind the scenes are also possessed by Dracos. This would include non-leadership members of the dark Illuminati, including most of its operatives in London, as well as a significant part of Israel's Mossad, Russia's KGB, America's NSA and to some extent CIA, and many other semi-secret operatives and agencies are also largely under the control of the dark Dracos.

The East has a different possession problem, mainly by dark Andromedans and dark Zetas. We will talk about that in a moment.

Light Dracos

About 10% of the Dracos incarnated on Earth and in the skies above Earth are enlightened. They are here primarily to help their brothers and sisters to the Light. They are in both adult and child bodies. Many of them are fascinated by dragons and absolutely love dragon stories and movies. To review, most dragon myths on Earth arose from periods of brief habitation by early Dracos thousands of years ago. The Dracos in native form did not remain with the Earth very long due to problems with Earth's gravity and atmospheric gas combination. The total time Dracos were on Earth throughout 10 million years of human history amounts to about 3,000 years.

Draco High Council

This channel has visited the Draco High Council while in meditation. The council is chaired by enlightened eighth density ascended Dracos. Most of the regular members are seventh density ascended Dracos. The council has intervened countless times in the wars occurring in or around the various planets in the Alpha Draconis system. There are six main stars, and four main planets, and all have been at war on and off over the past several million years.

The Draco High Council is now being assisted by many other star races and councils from across the galaxy in an effort to finally bring an end to the wars. Nearly 60% of the population of the four planets has been decimated by war. It is hoped that the new Golden Age on Earth will become a haven for newly enlightened Dracos who are tired of the nearly endless bickering inherent within their race.

The Draco Worlds

The architecture of the Draco civilization resembles caves and mud huts where the serpent-like beings interact. Unlike most of the humanoids in this part of the galaxy, early mutations in the DNA caused the Dracos to grow scales and become serpent-like in appearance. Various Draco-human hybrids produced the dragon and also the bird tribe (beings appearing somewhat half-human and half-bird). The entire history of interbreeding programs involving the Dracos is too complex to be included here. The role of the Dracos in Egypt is covered in *"Earth Changes and 2012."*

Chapter 12 – Life on Other Worlds

Zeta Reticulus

In our earlier works, the various sub-species of Zetas were detailed ("whites," "greys," and others). It was also discussed that about 90% of the Zetas left the Earth in the 1990s when they had acquired sufficient levels of human DNA to restore the balance within their own DNA. Only about 10% of the original Zeta members remain on or around the Earth, mostly in clean-up roles, or to monitor their members who have incarnated here. Most of the Zeta abductions were performed on their own race, though not all of the abductees remembered their karmic agreement to incarnate on Earth. Some abductions were done against human free will.

The Essassani and Hathors

The Zetas were desperate to save their race and were therefore allowed more leeway than the Dracos when it came to interbreeding with humans. Two of the hybrid races that came out of the interbreeding program include the Essassani and the Hathors. Actually, the Hathors usually refer to early hybrid leaders who engineered the later programs. You could say that the Hathors are the most enlightened faction of the Essassani.

Both the Hathors and the generic Essassani are tall, slender beings with half-human, half-Zeta facial features. In fact, they are about twice as tall as the whites and greys, standing as much as 2.5 meters high.

The Essassani and their leaders, the Hathors, have about a dozen channels around the Earth at this time.

Zeta Reticulus has two planets, one that is primarily inhabited by the whites and one that primarily houses the greys. There is a rogue planet in the Zeta system where the "type 3 Zetas" dwell. They have been quarantined until such time as they learn to cooperate peacefully with the other Zeta races.

Zeta civilizations look a lot like insect colonies, though there are more differences between their members than you might see at first glance. One of the things they have been trying to save, besides their ability to reproduce, is their individuality. Today's Zetas are more creative and expressive than ever, and their numbers are slowly increasing.

Despite the bad press the Zetas have received on Earth, most Zeta cities are relatively crime-free. Efficiency is paramount, with everything conducted like clockwork. A lot of the futurist spectacles of robots taking over society have been made manifest in the Zeta worlds. The Zetas themselves are actively engaged in many activities, but they have numerous androids and artificially intelligent beings doing the more mundane tasks.

When the Zetas travel to other planets and star systems, they often send fully automated scout craft guided by robots to avoid the hazards of face-to-face contact with other life forms. Some contactees on Earth have described automated or artificial life forms dressed in Zeta costumes.

A considerable amount of DNA experimentation has gone on in the Zeta society, which has produced both beneficial and catastrophic results at different times. Several decades ago, some of this genome modification reached the point where the Zetas could no longer reproduce. From a spiritual standpoint, the Zetas had suppressed their emotional bodies to the point where the soul fragmentation inherent in denial had caused their reproductive organs to atrophy.

The colony-like mental state, coupled with almost total reliance on artificial intelligence, had bred the creative life force out of the Zetas to the point that they were facing extinction if they did not do something quickly. So they realized that the highly emotional DNA of humans could be the answer to their problems.

The interbreeding program with humans lasted about 50 years, from the 1940s to the 1990s. A few programs are still operating, but for the most part, the Zetas have successfully altered their DNA in such a way that they are finally able to reproduce once again and to some extent balance their masculine and feminine energies.

Approximately 0.8% of human DNA has a Zeta configuration. Most of these are Zetas who incarnated on Earth in the normal manner. Despite frequent sightings by humans of Zeta spacecraft and recovery of their humanoid forms through an occasional crash (such as Roswell 1947), very few products of interbreeding have remained with the Earth. Almost all humans impregnated by Zetas have had the fetuses removed to spacecraft once they can be bred independently of their mothers.

As stated in previous writings, several Zeta factions entered into secret agreements with rogue branches of Earth's military and government entities. They traded technology in exchange for being allowed access to certain areas of the Earth without interference from inquisitive humans.

We in the higher realms have taken a neutral stand in the human-Zeta interbreeding program, for the reasons discussed earlier.

Sirius

The Sirians have played a significant role in the history of humankind, as detailed in previous writings. Even some of your mainstream scientists are now concluding that accounts of Sirian intervention in human affairs, as meticulously documented by your anthropologists, has merit.

It is common knowledge that many tribes, such as the Dogon in Africa, had advanced knowledge of the Sirian star system, with detailed drawings on cave walls depicting both major stars in the binary system. (Sirius is actually a tertiary system with a third star, Sirius C, in a rogue orbit about the other two stars. There are no intelligent life forms associated with Sirius C.)

Sirius A

The majority of the humanoids associated with Earth came from the Sirius A star system and its two major planets. One of the planets is more physical and accommodates souls vibrating at levels three through five, while the other planet is more ethereal and hosts fifth through seventh density Sirians.

The high councils of Sirius are in the upper atmosphere of this second planet. They consist of eighth density ascended masters, including Isis, the goddess who incarnated several times on Earth, including Egypt in approximately 7,500 BC and again around 2,500 BC. Isis is now an eighth density ascended master who holds the position of high priestess in the Sirian councils. She is channeled by over 100 souls on Earth. Her primary focus is helping humankind balance the male and female aspects of being. She frequently teaches sacred sexuality and helps humans build a bridge between the physical and spiritual aspects of intimate relationship.

Another Sirian who has had a significant role in the evolution of humanity is Jehovah, the god of the Old Testament of the Christian Bible. Jehovah was a seventh density being who fell in vibration after coming to Earth. He became a "jealous and angry god." There are many accounts of visitations with the Sirians in your scriptures, especially in the book of Exodus, where Sirian electronics are described in great detail. Their ascension device called the "ark of the covenant" is well-known. The purification necessary to prepare oneself to enter the electronic field of the ark is the basis for many of the rituals currently practiced in the Jewish faith.

(Note: There are two origins to Judaism. Jehovah and the Sirians were instrumental in the most recent evolution of the faith. The Pleiadeans and Sirians collaborated thousands of years prior to the time period of the Old Testament. The earlier Sirians were partially responsible for bringing the Kaballah and ancient Hebrew language to Earth. The ancient Hebrew language was derived from the light keys and codes of the DNA molecule. It is literally a sacred language capable of encoding and decoding various energy fields in the human body. A little bit of the science behind the Hebrew language has been given by one of your scientists, James Hurtak, in a channeled book, *"The Keys of Enoch."* Enoch was an ascended master who interacted with both the Pleiadeans and Sirians during various times in Earth's history. There is a book in the Old Testament – suppressed by the early Church but available once again – that details one of Enoch's incarnations on Earth.)

When the Sirians interbred with the evolving Pleiadeans during the first Egyptian period (10,500 to 7,500 BC), the resulting humanoids had large heads with bushy hair resembling a lion's mane, and were henceforth called the "Lion Tribe." The sphinx is a creature found on the Sirian planets and was built as a tribute to the Sirian gods.

There were many hybrid races during the time of Egypt including the Draco and Orion blends, as well as the Sirian Lion Tribe, and this interaction is detailed in *"Earth Changes and 2012."*

If you travel to Sirius A today, you will find highly advanced technologies and a bustling society on the lower density planet. The other planet appears barren to your scientists, but houses the ascended beings we spoke of earlier.

Sirius B

There is one planet in the Sirius B solar system that supports intelligent life. These beings have also visited Earth and have interacted and interbred with humans. They look a lot like the Pleiadean and Orion humans and can walk among you unnoticed, for the most part. They are peaceful beings who have attempted to act as Messiahs on many occasions. Seeing the mess the earlier Sirians made of things on Earth when they fell in vibration, the beings from Sirius B have organized many trips to your planet in the hopes of "rescuing" you from yourselves. Collaborating with the beings from Sirius A, they are still organizing rescue missions and have plans to evacuate large numbers of souls from Earth during the portal shifts.

Many of the Sirians who fell have joined the ranks of the helpers in the hopes of atoning for their perceived "sins." They have fashioned extensive protection devices around their spacecraft to avoid getting caught in the negative vibrations of Earth. This careful preparation for their rescue mission is designed to ensure they never make the mistake of falling into duality again.

They are overlooking one important factor, however. Very few souls on Earth need to be evacuated as part of their soul lessons. Most need to remain with the Earth through the changes to assist those who are having difficulty making the shift. The Galactic Confederation and other groups have intervened in the affairs of the Sirians to prevent them from violating the free will of Earth souls.

Not all Sirians have moved onto the path of atonement. About 20% of the fourth density Sirians are of the dark persuasion and are still heavily caught in their delusions of grandeur. They are the ones usually responsible for impersonating higher beings, often for egotistical purposes. They are advocating for evacuation of the Earth not so much because they care for you, but because they want to be seen as saviors, thus fulfilling their desire for self-aggrandizement.

We have spoken of the Sirian dilemma many times before, so we will not elaborate any further.

Andromeda

You have at least two science fiction shows being aired on your planet that depict wormholes between the Andromedan galaxy and your own Milky Way. Have you ever wondered where this idea came from?

Andromeda is a huge galaxy, at least 1-1/2 times the size of your own. A tiny portion of it resides along a wormhole that links it to a section of your galaxy near the constellation of Sagittarius. Beings from several star systems in Andromeda have been coming through the wormhole and visiting your planet for thousands of years. Most of the recent visitations started when you began exploding nuclear devices.

Some of the Andromedans have joined the Galactic Confederation's program to prevent nuclear disaster on Earth. They have been closely monitoring your nuclear tests and experimentation with the ionosphere to keep you from blowing holes in the protective layers around your planet.

They do have several channels on the Earth, and have appeared in various forms to contactees since 1945. In some cases, they have collaborated with the Zetas. Many contactees have reported tall, thin beings accompanying the short, spindly legged Zetas. Although there are several sub-species of Andromedans associated with Earth, the tall thin beings with the almond eyes are the most prevalent.

The Andromedan worlds have a lot of variety and offer a broad spectrum of levels and densities. The fourth density ones have highly advanced technologies on planets with billions of souls. They are great writers, poets, storytellers and actors, and are in touch with beings from all over the Universe. Although many of them are spiritually evolved and have a loving, compassionate focus, they have also overstepped their authority at times regarding Earth.

One of their councils in the fourth density worlds is responsible for the Urantia material, which attempts to give a cosmology of the Universe from their perspective. While the hierarchical constructs in the early part of the material are basically accurate, a lot of the accounts of Earth's history are inaccurate or are biased toward their early experiences visiting Earth.

These Andromedans are governed by a central planet in one of the star systems mentioned repeatedly in the Urantia material, known as Nebadon in those writings.

Councils of Nebadon

The spiritual overseers of the Andromedans visiting Earth are found in the Nebadon system located near the center of the Andromeda galaxy. These beings are vibrating at levels eight through ten on the density spectrum, which means they are capable of intergalactic travel. Some of the 10th density souls have used pure consciousness to traverse the vast distances between galaxies and have influenced the spiritual evolution of souls on Earth. Several are members of the priesthood of Melchizedek, a 9th density organization with links to the lower realms.

There are black holes near the center of Andromeda that link it to other universes. The more advanced members of Nebadon have navigated their way into these alternate realms and have described the structure of what they call the "Paradise Worlds." The High Councils of Andromeda have had the foresight and wisdom to seek an understanding of human free will and their members have restrained themselves from intervening excessively in human affairs. Mostly, they work through numerous Earthly channels and are focusing on correcting the earlier mistakes made in the Urantia material, as well as downloading the archives and records of Andromedan civilizations, which are too numerous and varied to describe here.

Antares

One of the red giant stars in your region of space, Antares, has spawned numerous inhabited planets, though most of them dwell far outside the immediate aurora of the massive star. The Antareans are not major players on the Earth, but have visited on numerous occasions. They are mostly benevolent.

The Antarean worlds are similar to yours, except everything is much larger, including their bodies. This may be where some of your legends of giants originated. It appears the "red giant" race mentioned in the book of Genesis of your Bible refers to the Antareans. These are beings over ten times your size, resembling humanoids. Their worlds are rocky and barren, with huge mountains rising out of desolate plains. Mostly, they live in large metallic compounds with artificial environments that soften the massive infrared emissions of their star. Nevertheless, they are a very creative race and are actively seeking to develop themselves spiritually.

Nibiru

This rogue planetoid, scheduled to make a pass through the inner solar system in 2030, is home to various levels and dimensions of entities commonly known as the "Annunaki." They have interacted with humanity several times in the past, usually when the planetoid is closest to Earth (approximately every 3,600 years). The majority of them are peaceful and enlightened, but some rebel factions have occasionally caused trouble on Earth. In addition, the enlightened Annunaki have often fallen in vibration during times when they stayed with Earth more than a few days. The Annunaki have several levels of civilizations ranging from fifth to ninth densities. To your scientists, Nibiru will look like a barren world about one-third the size of Earth. It will pass within 25 million miles of Earth at its closest point.

Now, let us take a look at the more highly evolved star systems working with Earth.

Arcturus

We have included Arcturus in the second part of our discussion on other worlds, not because they are unimportant – that is far from the case – but because they have little or no karma with the Earth and have virtually no dark members.

During the early days of the humanoid form, a group of souls migrated from Lyra/Vega to the Arcturus system and took up residence on three of the Arcturian worlds. For various reasons, they were able to avoid many of the pitfalls that befell the other humanoids once they descended in vibration.

Some of the Arcturians have never gone below seventh density, while others have explored realms down to level five. For over a million Earth years, the civilizations and councils of Arcturus have been completely benign, meaning there are no dark Arcturians. Those that did take on the karmic energies of the worlds they explored have long since integrated and healed those experiences.

Being extremely loving and compassionate, the Arcturians have come to Earth to help humanity evolve and awaken. Due to the urgency of the time, they have actively sought out channels in order to share their advanced scientific understandings and technologies, as well as their spiritual enlightenment. While they do not violate human free will, they stretch the limits about as far as they can go, involving themselves in the restoration of Earth's grid system (as described in earlier chapters).

The Arcturians range from fifth to ninth densities. The lower density ones have tall, dark blue bodies, while the upper density ones are translucent and have energetic protrusions similar to angel wings. They come through portals into the Earth plane and traverse the ley lines. They also oversee the popular "Arcturus Midway Station" where a lot of Earth souls travel during the dream state and between incarnations. The Midway Station portal also serves as a stepping down point for beings from the ascended realms so they can acclimate themselves to lower densities.

The Arcturian worlds are varied, but incredibly beautiful, with elaborate architecture, fountains, gardens, and temples. Many galactic council meetings are held in the Arcturian system.

Most of the Arcturians have never known war, poverty, misery, suffering, oppression or control, but rather than insulating themselves against these experiences, they actively seek to learn about them and understand races, such as yours, that have become ensnared in separation and fear. That is the main reason they are taking such an active position in your healing process.

Councils of Aldebaran

The Aldebaran star system is home to many of the higher density beings in this part of the galaxy. They have central councils that oversee the various galactic organizations, including the Galactic Confederation.

Included within the Aldebaran system are many sister star systems, all evolved beyond seventh density. Some are working with Earth and the other evolving planets in the Milky Way. Others are intergalactic travelers exploring neighboring galaxies, while a few have evolved to the point where they have complete access to the entire Universe.

Chapter 12 – Life on Other Worlds

Councils of Alcyone

This star system is home to what has been called the "Great White Brotherhood," a name given by souls on Earth that simply did not know how else to describe the magnificent beings they were in contact with.

The Councils of Alcyone, along with the Polaris High Council, are considered the supreme governing bodies of this region of the Milky Way galaxy. The 9th and 10th density beings at the highest positions of leadership are in communication with the Great Central Sun of the Galaxy and the various 11th and 12th density beings who govern this Universe.

Galactic Confederation (aka Galactic Federation)

This organization, which has been detailed many times in previous writings, is comprised of over one thousand star systems in this part of the galaxy. Some members have access to the entire galaxy and a few have intergalactic capabilities. There are various sub-groups of the Confederation that are well known on Earth, including Ashtar Command, Solar Cross and others. You have what some channels have called the "ground crew," human beings (star seeds) who have incarnated specifically to assist the Confederation in achieving their goals.

The primary goal of the Galactic Confederation is to assist humanity in awakening. Because they are so well known, some of the darker souls of fourth density Orion and Sirius have impersonated members of the Confederation.

We, the Founders, do not openly criticize or evaluate the various channelings coming into the Earth, but we do lay some guidelines.

Specifically, if anyone is channeling information that suggests blatant intervention and interference, use extreme caution and discernment. Members of the Galactic Confederation do not beam themselves into the corporate boardrooms of organizations to intimidate and coerce members to vote in a certain way. They do not interfere with your political decisions except in the case of nuclear war or development of technologies that can destroy the entire planet.

Members of the Confederation do not prophesy doom and gloom, or the idea that your entire world will become uninhabitable. They do not give you financial fantasies, such as the idea that you will inherit quadrillions of dollars (or pounds or yen). They will not attempt to mislead you by denying the tenacity of the dark Illuminati and convincing you that the dark ones will gladly give up the reins of power in the coming years.

On the other extreme, they will not over-emphasize global war and focus on the few extremists who are attempting to poison the general populace. While we do not deny that these things exist on Earth, we also recognize that those who are embracing their own God Presence within have nothing to fear from the misguided souls who are hell-bent on destroying humanity.

Beware of any channel or entity that suggests you are powerless in the face of dark alliances or dark ET groups. Imposters will often instill fear in you. They will focus on the move to create concentration camps, or reptilians that want to harvest you for food, or electronic devices designed to explode your brains, etc. The less you focus on these things, the better. We are not suggesting you should go into denial. Be aware of the antics of the dark ones and then shine your brilliant Light of Truth directly into their darkest places. Simply shine your Light, that's all. Do not judge what you are bringing to the Light. Simply send love and compassion to all misguided souls who would act as imposters. Forgive and release those entities that give false information. Have compassion for those channels that have not done their homework and have allowed their own fears to cloud their ability to discern. Review the information given previously on how to discern the nature of the entities that are coming through.

True members of the Galactic Confederation are loving and compassionate. They do not "talk down" or "patronize" human beings. They have great respect for each and every one of you. They admire your courage and fortitude. They understand how difficult it is to remain clear, calm and centered on Earth, especially during this time of turmoil. We are grateful for their dedication to your well-being.

Polaris

The highest vibrational star system in this region of the galaxy resides in the celestial realms of the star system Polaris. It is no coincidence that this star resides directly above your north pole, making it a navigational beacon for ships in the northern hemisphere.

The councils of Polaris represent the stability and enlightenment necessary when undertaking projects as varied and massive as those of the Galactic Confederation.

The Polarians consist primarily of counselors and guides for beings from the other organizations. They are the supremely enlightened and compassionate elders, offering advice and support for commanders of various fleets. They range from 7th to 12th density.

Lyra/Vega

The Lyra/Vega star system is where it all began, as far as the humanoid form is concerned. We, the Founders, operate through the portals of Lyra/Vega, stepping down our vibration from level 12 to level 7 in order to communicate with our channels. The portal that allows us to do this resides in the Lyra/Vega system. We helped engineer the human DNA over 100 million years ago in this system. Then about 10 million years ago, the early humanoids migrated to the Pleiades. The first humans on Earth were seventh density Pleiadeans who dropped to fourth density first, and third density later.

As stated in this channel's two prior books, the Lyra/Vega worlds are highly creative and artistic. Music as you know it originated in this system. In fact, the word "Lyra" comes from "lyre" which is a musical instrument similar to a harp. Civilizations today on the Lyran worlds are beyond your ability to comprehend, since they have all evolved beyond seventh density. However, you can visit the Lyrans any time in your meditations and the dream state.

Table 10 – Vibratory Levels of Worlds/Races Relevant to Earth		
Star System	Races	Vibration
Lyra/Vega	The Founders	Level 12
Polaris	Wise/Ancient Ones	Levels 10-12
Alcyone	Councils of Alcyone	Levels 9-10
	Great White Brotherhood	Levels 6-8
Aldebaran	Councils of Aldebaran	Levels 8-10
	Galactic Confederation	Levels 6-8
Nebadon	Andromedan Councils	Levels 7-10
Arcturus	Several groups	Levels 5-9
Andromeda	Various races	Levels 4-7
Pleiades	Various races	Levels 4-7
Nibiru	Annunaki	Levels 5-9
Antares	Red giant race	Level 5
Alpha Centauri	One race	Level 4
Tau Ceti	Various races	Levels 3-5
Fomalhaut	One race	Levels 4
Sirius A	Councils of Light	Levels 7-8
	Various races	Levels 4-7
Sirius B	Various races	Levels 4-5
Orion	Betelgeuse, Rigel, Mintaka	Levels 4-5
	Lords of Light, Dark Lords	Level 4
Zeta Reticulus	Essassani, Hathors	Levels 5-7
	Whites, greys, hybrids	Levels 3-4
Alpha Draconis	High Council of Draco	Levels 7-8
	Light Dracos	Level 4
	Dark Dracos	Level 3

CHAPTER 13
Life in the Ascended State

The ultimate goal of humanity is to ascend into the crystalline Light body, a state of true immortality. Evolution does not stop there, but continues beyond fifth density into sixth and finally, seventh, the original level of the soul.

At some point, your soul's journey through the lower worlds will be complete and you will return to the seventh plane where you will reunite with your soul family. Whether this happens in 100 years or a million does not matter, for what is in front of you now is what matters.

This is the most exciting time in the history of your soul's journey. Even though most of you have had numerous incarnations in fourth and fifth density worlds before, never have you moved directly into the higher dimensions in the manner set before you now.

Planets evolve through the lower densities, taking approximately 108 million years to complete one density level. In the case of your Earth, which is approximately 4.5 billion years old, it took most of that time to get established on the path of ascension. Now that Earth is moving into fourth density, we anticipate that she will remain a fourth density world for the next 108 million years, although souls will be able to reside upon her that are fifth density.

In your fifth density state, you will not be subject to the same laws and principles as fourth density humans. You will be walking in two worlds, or rather, two different levels of Gaia, the conscious being you call Earth.

A Further Summary of the Parallel Earths

For some of you, we may not have given an adequate explanation of the three Earths that will emerge during the portal shifts. For the rest of you, the following will summarize the main points of this book, including what it means for a planet and her people to awaken.

From a nonlinear perspective, the Earth exists simultaneously in seven different dimensions. Human beings have access to three of these dimensions: third, fourth and fifth. Here, we are using the term "dimension" rather than "density" because we are referring to a realm rather than a specific state of vibration.

It is ultimately possible for a human soul to experience all seven levels of Earth, or Gaia. Gaia is actually the name of the "higher self" of Earth, or the seventh dimensional Earth. However, for our purposes, we will concentrate on the third, fourth and fifth levels only.

To fully explain what is taking place during the portal shifts, let us use an analogy from Einstein's physics – the black hole. As an observer to a spaceship who is positioned outside the ship at a "neutral" point of observation (but within the realm of Einsteinian space) it is as though the ship disappears over the event horizon of the black hole. In other words, the ship simply vanishes while normal linear time continues along its merry way.

To a traveler on the spaceship, time will seem to slow down until it stops completely at the event horizon. To the traveler, it will seem as though he gets stuck forever in a timeless place (eternity). In actuality, the traveler will enter a higher state of consciousness and move on into other experiences, all within the eternal now moment.

To an observer completely outside Einsteinian space, the ship will appear to emerge on the other side of the black hole in a sister universe, coming through a white hole into this alternate time/space continuum, but where time and space are "reversed" or mirrored.

All three points are valid and true, depending on the perception of the observer, just as in quantum physics, an object can be a wave or a particle depending upon how it is perceived. Now let us use this analogy to explain the three parallel Earths:

From the point of view of a soul stuck in Earth's third density, Earth will seem normal, although the world will also seem to be going to hell in a handbasket, to quote one of your favorite phrases. In other worlds, life will seem to get worse and worse until eventually the third density soul loses his body and reincarnates on another world to continue his soul lessons.

Those souls moving into fourth and fifth densities will disappear out of his life. He will not see them vanish right before his eyes, because this process starts with psychological invisibility. Having almost nothing in common with higher density souls, there will be nothing to attract higher and lower level beings to one another because each will have learned all there is to learn from the other, as far as the Earth plane is concerned.

From the point of view of a soul entering fourth density, the world will appear to get better and better, as souls become enlightened and form intentional spiritual communities around the world. The third density world will appear to diverge, or become farther and farther away from the day to day reality of fourth density. It will eventually seem completely unreal, like a bad dream.

When the third density souls exit third density, their buildings and architecture will remain and will be rebuilt by fourth density souls.

Chapter 13 – Life in the Ascended State

From a fifth density perspective, the world will have become a shimmering, sparkling place of great beauty. The ascended soul becomes aware of the nature spirits and elementals and now a whole new world of beings comes into view. The more ordinary world is still available, but it seems less real than the bright, vibrant, sparkling, faerie-like realm now visible.

The fifth density soul is able to come and go from the fourth density world, and may be able to still perceive the remnants of the third density world, but it will be as though he is looking at the lower worlds from on high – which is indeed the case.

The fifth density soul will have access to the worlds beyond Earth. At first, the contacts with other worlds will be telepathic, but as the soul continues to evolve, he will visit other worlds in his mental and astral bodies, and eventually, his crystal Light body (etheric body). As he continues to vibrate faster and faster, he will become invisible to third density souls (if any still exist on Earth). Third density ETs in their spacecraft will not be aware of his presence, but he will be aware of them if he so chooses to be.

Although the fifth density souls will assist the fourth density souls in rebuilding their world, there will appear to be a divergence between fourth and fifth densities. As the portals close after 2030, the simultaneous realities will seem a little less permeable, meaning they will solidify and become more independent of one another (even though they are all One from the highest point of view).

The overriding spiritual principle during the Earth changes is that of the vantage point of the perceiver. "What you focus on, you become," is the supreme law of the lower dimensions. An ascended soul will see an ascended Earth. A third density soul will see a deteriorating Earth. Because Earth is moving beyond third density, the life force will be withdrawn from that realm. Eventually, the third density Earth will seem to be devoid of all life, but that will take a while. Once human souls have completely left third density, then for all practical purposes, the third density Earth will no longer exist. The surviving plants and animals will be transformed into fourth density. Their DNA structures will change to accommodate the higher frequencies.

The lower worlds are ultimately an illusion. That means their reality depends on the viewpoint of the perceiver. The realms that have nobody to perceive them essentially cease to exist, although there might be new first, second and third density life forms entering into them to grow and evolve. Such life forms will give a degree of reality to the first three realms. This is a bit hard to explain because your minds are third and fourth density creations and do not easily perceive dimensions above or below these levels.

For those of you reading this book, the most important thing to remember is that you have chosen either the fourth density Golden Age or the fifth density realm of ascension. Our purpose in working with this channel is to help prepare you for the journey into these worlds. They are bright, shining and ready to welcome you as you extend your awareness into them. Do not concern yourselves with other realms beyond fourth and fifth densities, as such higher realms will be a distraction to your soul's path until you are ready for them. The main focus of your higher awareness is as follows: Stay focused on the Light. Stay committed to bringing all dark places within yourselves to the Light. Embrace all aspects of your One Holy Self that is beyond all space and time.

We, the Founders, salute and congratulate you on your willingness to be the pioneers of humanity and to move beyond limitation into your natural state of perfection.

CONCLUSION

By reading this book, you are a part of the consciousness being described here. In other words, you are weaving a new timeline for planet Earth that includes co-creating, with us and this channel, a new reality, one that goes beyond the limitations of so-called normal human reality. The material herein is drawn from our wisdom, plus the experiences of the channel through many lifetimes on Earth and other worlds. It also depends on the wisdom and insight of many teachers, both human and otherwise, who have come before, or who are currently teaching from their own perceptions.

The higher self of the channel has formulated a viewpoint of reality that includes all of the partial perceptions of the lower self, plus the viewpoints of the collective soul of humanity (the collective unconscious and collective conscious selves). This "macro" self is then partially merged with our consciousness, or you could say he has downloaded a tiny part of our reference point into his, to complete the picture.

The result is that the picture of reality that has been presented here includes a larger perspective than the average ego-centered viewpoint. If you resonate with this book and want to see these realities come forth, make the decision to focus on those aspects you wish to create. Be the change you want to see in the world.

This channel, along with hundreds of other seers and visionaries, are co-creating, along with us and many groups in the higher realms, the realities being described herein. Your consciousness is what activates the levels and dimensions of this vast Universe. Your self-awareness brings dreams to life and achieves miracles. You are the miracle of Creation.

We, the Founders, are privileged to be a part of your growth process and look forward to continuing a relationship with you as Earth moves into the portals of change and rebirth.

INDEX

INDEX

INDEX

INDEX